UNITY LIBRARY & ARCHIVES
English monasteries and their p
BX 2592 W85e

0 0051 0032854 3

OXFORD HISTORICAL SERIES

Editors

V. H. GALBRAITH J. S. WATSON R. B. WERNHAM

BRITISH SERIES

NOTE

This Series comprises carefully selected studies which have been submitted, or are based upon theses submitted, for higher degrees in this University. In 1948 a new General Series was added to a British Series. The British Series is a collection of works which advance the knowledge of the structural development, whether political, ecclesiastical, or economic, of British Society. The General Series comprises works on any aspect of non-British history, and also works on British history which lie outside the scope of the British Series.

The works listed below are those still in print.

BRITISH SERIES

Bishops and Reform, 1215–1272. By M. GIBBS and J. LANG. 1934.

The Medieval Administration of the Channel Islands, 1199–1399.
By J. H. LE PATOUREL. 1937.

Public Order and Popular Disturbances, 1660–1714.
By M. BELOFF. 1938.

The Corporation of Leicester. By R. W. GREAVES. 1939.

Northamptonshire County Elections and Electioneering, 1695–1832.
By ERIC G. FORRESTER. 1941.

The English Lands of the Abbey of Bec. By M. MORGAN. 1946.

The Economic Development of some Leicestershire Estates.
By R. H. HILTON. 1947.

The Oxfordshire Election of 1754. By R. J. ROBSON. 1949.

Durham Jurisdictional Peculiars. By FRANK BARLOW. 1950.

Medieval Ecclesiastical Courts in the Diocese of Canterbury.
By BRIAN L. WOODCOCK. 1952.

The English Land Tax in the Eighteenth Century.
By W. R. WARD. 1953.

GENERAL SERIES

Canonization and Authority in the Western Church.
By E. W. KEMP. 1948.

Indians Overseas in British Territories, 1834–1854.
By J. M. CUMPSTON. 1953.

The Viceroyalty of Lord Ripon, 1880–1884.
By S. GOPAL. 1953.

ENGLISH MONASTERIES AND THEIR PATRONS
IN THE
THIRTEENTH CENTURY

By

SUSAN WOOD

FELLOW OF ST. HUGH'S COLLEGE

OXFORD UNIVERSITY PRESS
LONDON: GEOFFREY CUMBERLEGE
1955

UNITY SCHOOL LIBRARY
Unity Village
Lee's Summit, Missouri 64063

Oxford University Press, Amen House, London E.C.4

GLASGOW NEW YORK TORONTO MELBOURNE WELLINGTON

BOMBAY CALCUTTA MADRAS KARACHI CAPE TOWN IBADAN

Geoffrey Cumberlege, Publisher to the University

PRINTED IN GREAT BRITAIN

PREFACE

My thanks are due first of all to Sir Maurice Powicke, who suggested the subject of this book, supervised my first year of work on it, and has given me the kindest encouragement and help ever since. Mr. W. A. Pantin later supervised my work most helpfully; and more recently in preparing the book for the press I have had much kind criticism and advice from Professor V. H. Galbraith. I should also like to thank those who have helped me with information or by reading parts of my manuscript at various stages, especially Mr. H. M. Colvin, Miss Kathleen Major, Dr. Rose Graham, Professor C. R. Cheney, Miss May McKisack, and Professor D. Knowles. Finally I am grateful to Somerville College, to the Trustees of the Gilchrist Studentship, and to the British Federation of University Women, for grants enabling me to begin research.

I have not gone much beyond the printed sources: the subject could be taken much further by the study of unprinted charters, cartularies, and plea rolls.

S. M. W.

CONTENTS

PRINCIPAL ABBREVIATIONS

C. and Y. Soc.	Canterbury and York Society.
E.H.R.	*English Historical Review.*
Knowles, *M.O.*	D. Knowles, *The Monastic Order in England.*
,, *R.O.*	,, *The Religious Orders in England.*
Mon.	Dugdale, *Monasticon Anglicanum*, ed. Paley, &c.
Powicke	F. M. Powicke, *King Henry III and the Lord Edward.*
R.S.	The Rolls Series.
V.C.H.	*Victoria County History.*

I

INTRODUCTION

IN most of Europe in the early Middle Ages, while fighting
kings and nobles were building up wealth in land and
men, monasteries sprang up and survived as more or less
unarmed communities in a violent and acquisitive world; and
this, of course, was through the enterprise and the forbearance
of these kings and nobles. The foundation of a monastery
might be haphazard at first, or elaborately planned from the
start; it might begin with a landlord sending supplies to
wandering monks who turned up in his woods, or more probably with business-like negotiations for a nucleus of monks
to be sent from an existing house. But it involved at some
stage the solemn setting aside of lands and men.

It might be at once an act of penance, an investment in
lordship, and a great man's conventional act. Its value as an
investment varied. The monastery was likely to be treated
much like a proprietary parish church.[1] The lord might exploit the estate himself, or use it as a *beneficium* or a fief to
provide for a dependant or reward a vassal, perhaps as a lay
abbot;[2] but only part of the crops and rents would go to the
lord or his abbot—the rest would be supporting the community of monks, as long as there was one. Against this
would be set special revenues such as tithes and offerings,
and perhaps freedom from public burdens. But it would turn
largely on how else the land could have been used: its degree
of cultivation, its possibilities as an estate for the lord himself,
and his current need or opportunity to endow fighting men.
Probably the scale was always tipped by his assumptions
about prayer and purgatory, and by the social prestige of
owning a great church (this prestige, like the privileged position of a monastic estate, itself depending on other laymen's
assumptions).

The monastery's survival with some degree of regular life

---

[1] See especially U. Stutz, 'Eigenkirche, Eigenkloster', in *Realencyklopädie für
protestantische Theologie und Kirche*, 3rd ed., vol. xxiii (Leipzig, 1913), esp. pp. 371–4.
[2] See Lesne, *Histoire de la propriété ecclésiastique en France*, II. i. 124–31, 197–202;
ii. 70–81, 133–5, 140–3, 157–64; iii. 2–20, 33–34.

depended on much the same conditions as its foundation. It would be in the hands either of the founder's descendant or, if that family had lost its hold or been submerged, of the king or some other great man who had acquired it by commendation or by royal grant.[1] These later lords would regard it as a piece of property, exploit it, sell it, or bestow it on kinsmen and followers. But as long as it remained a genuine monastery it was likely to be something less or something more than simple property: something whose very existence was resented by its lord and therefore precarious, or a matter of family pride and piety. The stronger were these modifications of the crude proprietary attitude, the more likely was a king or noble to forward the reforming movement—to turn out a lay abbot, for instance, and replace him by a picked man from some famous reformed abbey. But in some ways this is still the proprietary attitude on a different level: the monastery is amongst other things an investment for his and his ancestors' souls.

The proprietary claim was to some extent refined and limited in both feudal and canon law, as these developed out of the tensions between violence and the need for security and between principles and the facts of power. In England in particular, with its comparatively stable and consistent feudal society, the patronage of a monastery was treated as a kind of feudal lordship with standardized characteristics. And canon law had come to recognize not the lay owner but the lay patron, and to allow him strictly limited rights; this by the thirteenth century had real influence on English practice. Meanwhile on the continent the lord's power might depend less on being the founder's heir than on having become hereditary advocate—defender and agent in secular affairs, originally chosen by the monastery or appointed by the king. A monastery ostensibly given up to the Holy See, for instance, might be in the hands of its former owners under the title of advocate. But the patron in post-Conquest England was primarily the founder's heir and the acknowledged feudal lord.

So in thirteenth-century England the same forces of rapacity and piety were at work, but broadly within a framework of

---

[1] Lesne, I. 132–9; II. i. 15–19; ii. 22–26, 140–3; iii. 9–27.

routine—of partially effective canon and common law. This is the situation I am concerned with in this book; I have tried to describe English patronage more or less in working order in the comparative daylight of the thirteenth century.

For England the subject as a whole has been somewhat neglected.[1] Yet the relationship between religious houses and their patrons is of some importance as one factor in the relations of Church and State, or of church and lay interests. At its fullest, patronage could involve custody of the property in vacancies, and formal rights in elections with some degree of informal influence; feudal dues and services, such as the knight service owed by many royal abbeys; hospitality for the patron and his household, corrodies and benefices for his dependants; a burial place, and masses and prayers for his and his family's souls; the giving and receiving of help and counsel; an interest in protecting the house against impoverishment. But the relationship varies widely: the king's dealings with his ancient and famous abbeys would differ from his dealings with a remote and obscure priory whose advowson had escheated to him, and both would differ from a country knight's relations with a small priory occupying a corner of his manor. It varies, too, from order to order. Benedictines, Austin canons, and most nuns had normally a close and well-defined bond with their patron; he had the rights which in common law were the criteria of patronage, and which canon law recognized with limitations: custody in vacancies, and licence and assent in elections. But houses of the exempt orders—Cistercians, Carthusians, and Pre-

---

[1] See Powicke, *King Henry III and the Lord Edward*, esp. ii. 718–24, for illuminating passages on the social and personal relationship and on the effect of papal claims; and Colvin, *The White Canons in England*, pp. 38, 291–306, for a discussion of the Premonstratensians' relations with their patrons, stressing the importance of the subject in general. Cf. Morgan, *English Lands of the Abbey of Bec*, pp. 28–32. Baskerville, *English Monks and the Suppression of the Monasteries* (London, 1937), pp. 45–58, ranges briefly over the claims of English patrons throughout the Middle Ages but mostly on the eve of the Dissolution. Knowles, *The Monastic Order in England*, traces the development of the king's relations with religious houses especially in the twelfth century (pp. 395–401, 561–615), but hardly touches on other patrons apart from the actual founders. Reich, *The Parliamentary Abbots to 1470*, pp. 293–334, deals in detail with some of the king's claims on royal abbeys. Coulton, *Five Centuries of Religion*, iii, chs. 3–5, provides a background for Europe generally in chapters on the reasons for founding monasteries and on burials, confraternity, and masses.

monstratensians—seem invariably to have been free of these
specific powers,[1] a freedom which went with their normal
tenure in frankalmoin; though they nevertheless had lords
and patrons, whose tenure of the advowson was often recorded (not always correctly) in their inquisitions post mortem, however little profit it brought.

The twelfth-century founders of houses of the new orders
had evidently accepted from the first their lack of those rights
in vacancies which were normal for other houses. Professor
Knowles points out the comparative cheapness of founding a
Cistercian house, on undeveloped land worth little or nothing
to its lord at the time;[2] this meant that he lost nothing by
giving the house the frankalmoin tenure required by the
order, and had no great interest in the choice of abbot.
Besides, some of these moorland settlements were founded
in an enthusiastic fit which possibly precluded much fore-
thought for the abbot's future position as feudal tenant of
developed land.

Then the coherence of these orders held their members
fast, and their temper was in general jealous of influence by
'princes and magnates'. Yet there was sometimes a close personal relation. Cistercian houses often wrote genealogies or
histories of their patrons;[3] the patron might be more to them
as founder's descendant than he was as landlord, and even
in the latter capacity he had some control over the disposi-
tion of property,[4] and might make unwarranted claims to
services.[5]

The Gilbertine order was even more centralized and at
least as independent, and it is possible that the order did not
recognize any patrons at all. It is probably significant that,
while canon law allowed patrons to be met in procession,[6] the
Gilbertine rule laid down a list of those who might be so
honoured which included the king but no other layman.[7]
The whole order had been taken by Henry II into his protection as his 'free and special alms', with privileges that in Dr.
Graham's words 'made it independent in temporal matters

---

[1] See Knowles, *M.O.*, p. 633; Colvin, pp. 292–3.
[2] Knowles, *M.O.*, pp. 246–7.
[3] See p. 124, n. 6.   [4] See p. 155, n. 3.
[5] See pp. 161–2, 163–4.   [6] See p. 127, n. 6.
[7] Dugdale, *Monasticon Anglicanum*, vi, p. lviii,* c. xxxvi.

of all save the king'.[1] The master of the order appointed
priors and had custody in vacancies;[2] his consent was needed
for sales and purchases above the value of 3 marks; he appointed obedientiaries, sealed charters, and was necessary to
any lawsuit.[3] However, the Gilbertine priories were separate
landowning bodies, with landlords whom they could vouch
to warranty; and even though they normally held in frankalmoin, their landlords might make feudal claims on them, as
Agnes de Vescy distrained Malton Priory (founded by her
late husband's ancestor Eustace fitz John) for suit of court,
contrary to its charters;[4] or they might claim a patron's rights
such as hospitality, as the same Agnes probably did when she
stayed too long and with too large a train at Watton, also of
Eustace fitz John's foundation.[5]

A few express claims to be the patron of a Gilbertine house
are found in the later Middle Ages. According to the Lincoln Cathedral statutes the bishop spent the night before his
installation at St. Catherine's Priory, 'which is of the foundation of the church of Lincoln and of the bishop's patronage';[6]
in 1387 German Hay was called 'advocate' of Ellerton Priory
in Yorkshire.[7] The advowsons of Gilbertine priories are very
occasionally included as property in inquisitions post mortem;[8] though this might be due to the jurors' assumption that
the founder's descendant or the largest present lord must
have the patronage. Very often, Gilbertine priories had no
one obvious founder, but began with lands in small amounts
from many benefactors.[9]

Dependent houses, and alien priories especially, had very
variable relations with their patrons, complicated by the
powers of the mother-house. A dependency had its mother-
house, its patron, and the local bishop to reckon with; any
two of these might ally against the other, and the house itself

---

[1] R. Graham, *St. Gilbert of Sempringham and the Gilbertines*, pp. 78, 87.

[2] Ibid., p. 82. [3] Ibid., p. 53. [4] Ibid., p. 84.

[5] Ibid., p. 83; Bodleian MS. Laud 642 (Alvingham cartulary), f. 36. Shouldham
evidently had patrons; see pp. 98, n. 2, 130, 169.

[6] *Lincoln Cathedral Statutes*, ed. H. Bradshaw and C. Wordsworth (Cambridge,
1897), ii. 273, 553.

[7] *Mon.* vi. 2. 977; *Victoria County History of Yorkshire*, iii. 252.

[8] Shouldham, 1297, 1360, 1369 (*Calendar of Inquisitions Post Mortem*, iii, p. 284).
Sempringham, 1340 (ibid. viii, p. 195). Poulton, 1358 (ibid. x, p. 346).

[9] R. Graham in *V.C.H. Lincs.* ii. 181.

might play off one against another.¹ The mother-house's powers were sometimes like those of a patron—a part in the choice of prior, perhaps custody in vacancies, and some control over property; consequently the patron himself might have little power left him. In fact the mother-house might have the technical patronage.² On the other hand if the mother-house were remote, the cell might be thrown into the patron's hands; a small alien priory might be peculiarly dependent on its patron for protection.³

Cathedral priories were in a special position, being in a sense obviously of royal patronage (except Rochester), but in the thirteenth century in some cases beginning to treat the bishop as technically patron instead of or as well as titular abbot.⁴

So for houses of all orders, possibly excepting most Gilbertine priories, the patron was in some degree someone to be reckoned with; and for many of the nobility, patronage of religious houses was an important interest. The king was of course the greatest single patron. Almost all the pre-Conquest foundations were of his advowson, and many new houses, by foundation or escheat or forfeiture. Out of 425 monastic houses⁵ (excluding the cathedral priories) whose patrons have been found for a substantial part of the thirteenth century,⁶ 106 were of royal patronage, including most of the greatest. Then most bishops had one or more monasteries of their advowson, normally their own or their predecessors' founda-

---

¹ See pp. 55–57 ; also Morgan, *English Lands of the Abbey of Bec*, pp. 32, 34.

² e.g. St. Albans and Hatfield Peverel (*Gesta Abbatum Monasterii Sancti Albani*, ed. Riley, i. 471); and after 1266 (see p. 82, n. 2) probably St. Mary York, and Wetheral Priory (*V.C.H. Cumberland*, ii. 185: papal provision). The mother-house would probably have the advowson when the original endowment for a cell consisted of a parish church: when King John tried to present to the 'rectory' of Bamburgh, the canons of Nostell objected not that it was a conventual church but that it was of their advowson (*A History of Northumberland*, ed. E. Bateson, &c., Newcastle, 1893–, i. 76–82). See Colvin, pp. 329–30, 333, on Premonstratensian dependent nunneries.   ³ Morgan, p. 28.

⁴ See pp. 48–52.

⁵ i.e. of monks, regular canons, and nuns.

⁶ The figures which follow are of course liable to error, and it is impossible in the space of this book to supply the evidence for them: but it consists mostly of printed cartularies, chronicles, accounts of founders, bishops' registers, inquisitions post mortem, patent and close rolls (for vacancies of houses in the patronage of the king or of a baron's minor heir), occasional final concords, &c.—often from references in the *Victoria County Histories*, the *Complete Peerage*, or Dugdale's *Baronage*.

tions, within or without their own dioceses: at least 27 houses had bishops as patrons.

Amongst laymen other than the king these advowsons were very widely held. Although the distribution naturally varied in the course of the century, with escheats, marriages, and divisions amongst coheiresses, approximate numbers may be given. It seems that no earl was without one or more such advowsons,[1] and between them the earls or their widows or heirs were patrons of at least 89 religious houses; and at least 203 houses were in the advowson of about 148[2] barons and country gentlemen, of whom about a third were only sub-tenants or minor tenants-in-chief. The 300 or so houses un-accounted for cannot be assumed to fall into even roughly the same proportions, for most of them are dependencies whose mother-houses probably had the advowson; but some would certainly be added to each of these classes of patrons.

This patronage was an interest in which the baronage felt some solidarity;[3] so that the monks of Lewes, excusing themselves to Cluny in 1201 for submission to their patron's claims, said that the king, earls, barons, and all the magnates were of one opinion in supporting the Earl Warenne, and would take anything done against him as done against the whole realm.[4]

---

[1] Hubert de Burgh bought one (see p. 22, n. 6).
[2] Excluding earls' coheiresses (e.g. Balliol).
[3] See pp. 64, 75, 98, 151-2, 153.
[4] Duckett, *Charters and Records of Cluny*, i. 99-101. See p. 57.

II

PATRONAGE AS PROPERTY

i. The English patron of a monastery was normally the founder's heir or assign, and therefore the sole or chief feudal lord of the house or its head. The founder who endowed a monastery was enfeoffing a tenant, even if only for unspecified spiritual services. He or his heir was commonly called 'our lord and patron', almost as commonly 'advocate'; and *dominium et patronatus*, *dominium et advocatio*, are standard phrases.

Lordship and patronage are dealt with together in King John's charters by which in 1215 he gave the advowson of Glastonbury to the bishop of Bath and Wells,[1] and that of Thorney to the bishop of Ely.[2] In each case, the bishop was to have the ordination of the abbot and custody in vacancies; the abbot was to receive the temporalities, 'hitherto called the regalia', from the bishop as lord and patron. The bishop was to have some of the usual feudal dues and liberties, and to do the knight service hitherto done by the abbey.

Later, when an abbot of Glastonbury tried to pay his service directly to the king, the bishop obtained letters saying he was the mesne between the king and the abbey, and ordering the abbot to accept the bishop 'as his lord and patron'.[3] Finally in 1275 the bishop gave up to King Edward the 'dominium temporalium cum patronatu abbaciae', and the abbots were to answer to the king as lord and patron as the bishops had done.[4]

This normal identity of lordship and patronage was taken for granted in the dispute about the advowson of St. Swithun's cathedral priory, in the 1270's and 80's. The monks argued that the king and not the bishop was their patron on the

[1] Adam de Domerham, *Hist. de rebus gestis Glastoniensibus*, ed. Hearne, p. 447. *The Great Chartulary of Glastonbury Abbey*, ed. Watkins, i. 89–90.

[2] *Mon.* ii. 605–6.

[3] Domerham, p. 536.

[4] Ibid., pp. 551–5. *Glastonbury Cart.* i. 105–7. When King Edward gave up the custody of Wintney Priory it was for the two concurrent reasons that the priory was not founded by his predecessors, and held nothing in chief, although they did suit of court to the hundred of Odiham Castle for the founders; that is, presumably, this suit was forinsec service and so did not prove royal patronage as intrinsec might have done (*Registrum Johannis de Pontissara*, ed. Deedes, ii. 509).

grounds that in the time of the Britons, before there were any bishops of Winchester, there were monks there 'enfeoffed' with many possessions and 'holding in chief' only of the king; and, more soberly, that their refoundation was due to King Edgar, while they had no endowments from any bishop; that the property divided between bishop and convent constituted two parts both held in chief of the king, and therefore the king was as much patron of one as of the other unless he had given away the advowson of the priory by charter; that the prior and convent owed no service or rent to the bishop; and that the prior owed knight service to the king as a tenant-in-chief, although nowadays this happened to be performed through the bishop who held some of their land (not, it seems to be implied, as mesne between them and the king). Combined with these are arguments from the rights of the patron as such, in election and custody.[1]

Conversely for the bishop it was argued that he did service to the king for himself and for the priory as a single barony, and therefore he was patron; the wardship of the vacant priory, falling to the king only when the bishopric was also vacant, was compared to the wardship of a baron's vassal, falling to the king only when the barony was itself in wardship. Furthermore, the bishop had scutage and the incidents from knights' fees on the monks' manors, and suit of court and a variety of services from them and their tenants. Any bishop was lord of his chapter or convent. The king's foundation of the church of Winchester made him patron only of the bishopric, not of the monks separately; these merely had goods set aside for them by the bishop. As for the monks in the time of the Britons, nothing was known of them, and the present church was not the same church.[2] Finally in his appeal to Rome, Bishop John de Pontissara said he had always been the true patron and recognized as lord, with 'many services and feudal recognitions belonging to the chief lord of a fief by the custom of the realm of England'.[3]

Yet the statements joining lordship and patronage show that the two aspects were distinguished; and they might just

---

[1] *Reg. Pontissara,* ii. 609–15. See pp. 49–50, 52, 79.
[2] Ibid., pp. 676–85.
[3] Ibid., p. 688.

possibly exist apart. Geoffrey fitz Piers succeeded in Richard I's reign to the Mandeville lands, apparently including the lordship of Walden Abbey, and the Walden chronicler refers to him naturally as 'advocate'; yet only after some years was he actually granted the right to institute the abbot so far as belonged to a layman, that is the patronage, which the king had kept for himself. However, this was regarded as anomalous.[1]

The patron might possibly not be the lord if the founder gave land to the house to be held not of him but of his own lord.[2] One might expect this to be the general rule for those few houses founded after *Quia Emptores*, since all alienation was to be by substitution; and it is commonly held (following Lyttleton) that this statute made grants in frankalmoin impossible. But Coke said that *Quia Emptores* might be dispensed with by consent of the Crown and mesne lords;[3] and in fact the licences to alienate or acquire in mortmain, for new foundations, sometimes allow the grantee to hold in free, pure and perpetual alms of the grantor and his heirs. Haltemprice Priory, founded in 1314, was to hold 'of Thomas (Wake) and his heirs';[4] and he and his heirs were credited with the advowson later.[5]

On the other hand a foundation by a tenant-in-chief was sometimes specifically to hold of the king, and yet the advowson stayed with the founder and his heirs. For example, Flansford Priory, founded in 1347 by Richard Talbot, was to hold in chief;[6] but the advowson stayed with the Talbots,[7] and in this case it carried concrete powers, for they presented the priors[8] till the eve of the Dissolution.

[1] *Mon.* iv. 148 (chronicle); Duchy of Lancaster 25/8, 27/5 (charters of archbishop and bishop). See pp. 98–99, 169, n. 6.

[2] See p. 12, Jervaulx.

[3] See H. W. Challis, *Real Property*, ed. C. Sweet (London, 1911), p. 21.

[4] *Mon.* vi. 1. 522. Cf. Badlesmere (ibid., p. 522) and Axholm (ibid., p. 25).

[5] *Cal. Inqu. P.M.* ix, p. 207; x, p. 50; *Calendar of Close Rolls, Henry IV*, iv. 157.

[6] *Mon.* vi. 1. 534.

[7] *Calendar of the Patent Rolls 1467–77*, p. 414, and see next note. Cf. Denney (*Mon.* vi. 3. 1550–1; *Cal. Pat. R. 1361–4*, p. 134; *Cal. Close R. 1360–4*, p. 404) and Mountgrace (*Mon.* vi. 1. 23; *Cal. Close R. Henry IV*, iv. 147).

[8] *Cal. Pat. R. 1399–1401*, p. 340. *Registrum Johannis Trefnant*, ed. W. W. Capes, C. and Y. Soc. xx (1916), pp. 184, 186. *Reg. Thome Spofford, Reg. Ricardi Mayew, Reg. Caroli Bothe*, ed. A. T. Bannister, C. and Y. Soc. xxiii (1919), p. 365; xxvii (1921), p. 281; xxviii (1921), p. 345.

In some of these cases, and others where the situation is obscure, neither the lordship nor the advowson would mean very much in material interest, since they were Carthusian and should have been free both of feudal services and of the criteria of patronage;[1] though sometimes a money value is given to the patronage in an assignment of dower.[2] But on the whole where the patron's rights were firm, the lord's were likely to be non-existent, and vice versa.

For any such distinction must have been very hard to maintain in practice. The chief rights by which the patron made his existence felt, and the main criteria of a patron, were custody in vacancies and the grant of licence and assent in elections. But custody was a feudal right, analogous to wardship on a layman's fief; and assent, too, was closely bound up with acceptance of the new tenant's fealty. Once a vacancy had arisen, lordship would naturally absorb this technical patronage, or vice versa—that is to say, tenure of the chief lord after *Quia Emptores* might be meaningless, merely words to accord with the statute.

The breakdown of an attempt to distinguish lordship from patronage may be shown in the case between the archbishop of Canterbury and the bishop of Rochester in the Exchequer in 1253, when the bishop denied his liability to pay aids and scutages to the archbishop. He claimed that the archbishop, though his patron, was not his lord, because no bishop had consented to the transference of his homage and service from the king to the archbishop, and thus 'no bishop has held or claimed to hold . . . any tenement or fief from the church of Canterbury . . . although after the grant of the patronage' (i.e. of the bishopric, by King John to the archbishop) 'the bishops had received the temporalities from the hands of the archbishops'. But this defence was only a second string; both before and after adopting it he admitted by implication that the lordship had been transferred, and based his case on frankalmoin tenure originally of the king and now of the archbishop.[3]

At a later stage he refused either to admit or deny that he

---

[1] See pp. 3–4.

[2] e.g. Mountgrace and Haltemprice (*Cal. Close R. Henry IV*, iv. 147, 157).

[3] *Registrum Roffense*, ed. Thorpe, pp. 73–75.

held of the archbishop. The latter had a royal writ which
made the normal assumption that lordship and patronage
went together: the bishop 'ought to do services . . . to the
archbishop as lord and patron'; as indeed was stated in John's
charter.[1] The bishop's defence was again on mixed grounds:
that King John could not alienate the patronage, that even
if he could services were not owed 'for patronage of its own
nature', and that anyhow no services had been owed to the
king originally. He won his case, but apparently solely on
the last argument.[2]

The patron in the common law sense could, then, hardly
be other than the lord at least of the site.[3] In the mid-twelfth
century Hervey, son of the founder of Jervaulx Abbey,
allowed the monks to move from his fief into that of his lord,
the earl of Richmond, provided that he kept his spiritual
benefits and 'lost nothing of the advowson'; yet soon the
earls called themselves patrons as well as lords.[4] Similarly
a monastery apparently founded to hold of the founder's lord
might be regarded as a joint foundation of lord and tenant,
and in this way the lord would be a patron and perhaps later
the sole patron.[5]

A 'patron' who was not lord was probably limited to the
spiritual benefits of a founder's descendant; a distinction between the technical patron and lord exercising the standard
rights in vacancies, and the family for whom the convent
prayed and towards whom they felt *pietas*, was far more
plausible than one between lord and patron which left to the
latter the patron's standard rights. Descendants of the founder
of Jervaulx were buried there;[6] the spiritual benefits were

---

[1] *Reg. Roffense*, p. 73.   [2] Ibid., pp. 77–80.

[3] As the monks of Durham were told by the bishop's clerks in 1272, 'if he [the
bishop] were not your patron and lord of the place, you would have no need to ask
licence of him' (see p. 51). Of course there could be other lords for other lands,
heirs of various donors besides the founder.

[4] *Mon.* v. 572, 575.

[5] Probable examples are St. Thomas's Stafford, founded *c.* 1174 by the bishop of
Coventry and Gerard de Stafford (*Chartulary of St. Thomas's Stafford*, ed. F.
Parker, William Salt Soc. viii, 1887, pp. 132–4), and Alcester Abbey, founded 1140
by Robert earl of Leicester and Ralph le Butler (*Mon.* iv. 175–6). In the latter case
each seems to regard himself, in his charter, as founder; and in 1300 a Butler descendant tried to claim the advowson; but this had long been in the king's hands along
with the advowsons of other Leicester foundations.

[6] Bodl. MS. Dugdale 39, f. 136v.

probably all that Hervey was able to keep from, or more likely share with, the earls of Richmond. In 1299, when the patronage of Whitby had passed from the Percys to the Crown more than a century ago,[1] Henry Percy, endowing an anniversary there 'pur plus solempnement a aver le alme de nous en memoyre', spoke of 'our monks there serving God'.[2] And when Bernard de St. Walery gave Henry II the lordship and advowson of Godstow Abbey, he reserved to himself and his heirs their prayers and alms.[3] Yet even these spiritual benefits perhaps needed either fresh endowment or explicit reservation; for they were regarded as services, and would naturally belong to the lord along with any other services.[4]

Sometimes these benefits were almost all that the lord and patron had in any case. If the house held in unqualified frankalmoin the lord would not have custody nor any feudal service. For though houses holding in free pure and perpetual alms might in fact pay fixed temporal services,[5] it seems that these could be challenged unless specified in the charter. The early fourteenth-century judges' opinion that frankalmoin tenure gave exemption from all temporal service[6] was not mere theory, for religious houses in the thirteenth century could get exemption from custody[7] by proving frankalmoin tenure; it had been successfully pleaded to excuse from knight service or scutage;[8] and in the fourteenth century it was sometimes accepted as excusing from attendance at parliament,[9] and certain other services,[10] in contrast to tenure by barony.

Frankalmoin tenure was in principle universal for houses

<hr/>

[1] See p. 99, n. 6.
[2] *Mon.* i. 415–16.　　　[3] *Mon.* iv. 364.
[4] See case about Hartland, p. 25.
[5] Bracton, *De Legibus Anglie*, ed. Woodbine, ii. 93. E. G. Kimball, 'Tenure in Frankalmoin and Freedom from Secular Services', *E.H.R.* xliii. 347–9. But one can hardly put in this category the administrative or diplomatic services of individual abbots, as Sister Reich does (*Parl. Abbots*, p. 297).
[6] Kimball, *E.H.R.* xliii. 343.　　　[7] See p. 83.
[8] Though this did not prevent repeated summons (Kimball, *E.H.R.* xliii. 348–9).
[9] Ibid., p. 351; H. Chew, *English Ecclesiastical Tenants-in-chief*, ch. v.
[10] Corrodies, &c. (see pp. 114–15). Hospitality to steward (p. 103). Homage and other services (Godstow cartulary; Exch., King's Remembrancer Misc. Books 20, facing f. 1). These are surely the 'practical applications' that Miss Kimball misses, by which to test the theory (*E.H.R.* xliii. 344).

of the exempt orders.[1] Inquisitions post mortem sometimes say of one of these houses that its advowson carries no earthly profits.[2] Many examples could probably be found of their paying rents for some of their lands. But when in 1302 Nicholas de Crioil quitclaimed to the Premonstratensian abbey of Langdon lands in two vills given by the founder in frankalmoin, with the homage, relief, scutage, suits, and services which he might claim or had claimed, reserving to himself the name of advocate and a share in their spiritual benefits, he was probably restoring the more normal and proper relation (though he still kept a rent of 40*d*. in one vill).[3]

In any case, their freedom from custody and from licence or assent to elections was invariable;[4] and the former at least was an essential part of full frankalmoin tenure, though it might be regarded as specially characteristic of these orders as such.[5] An inquest in 1325 found that the earls of Pembroke had at the Premonstratensian house of West Dereham no custody or profit in a vacancy, and did not give licence or have the elect presented to them; but at a patron's death he had masses and alms as for the death of an abbot.[6]

The patron's existence was usually remembered even if he had very few rights. But obviously the absence or lapse of concrete rights made confusion easier about who was patron. In a lawsuit in 1258 about the advowson of Shelford Priory, where the best seisin that either party could claim was the presentation of an earlier prior, the present prior said he did not know who was patron.[7] Occasionally (even apart from the Gilbertines) it is not clear that there is a patron at all.

---

[1] See p. 4, n. 1.

[2] e.g. Shouldham and Richard fitz John, 1297–8 (Chancery inquisitions, Edw. I, File 80/6/18): 'That advowson is worth nothing except in the prayers and alms which are done in that house.' Dore and lords of Ewyas, 1300 (*Cal. Inqu. P.M.* iii, p. 455).

[3] Langdon cartulary; Exch., King's Remembrancer Misc. Books 29, ff. 11*v*–14**v*. See Colvin, p. 296.

[4] Though the escheator might in error inquire into the value of the temporalities in a vacancy, as at Cockersand in 1376 (see Colvin, p. 293) or even take seisin, as at Netley (see p. 84).

[5] Cf. the bishop of Winchester's reference to the Cistercians in argument with the monks of St. Swithun's (*Reg. Pontissara*, ii. 677).

[6] *Cal. Close R. 1323–7*, pp. 287–8.

[7] *Mon.* vi. 1. 578.

Rights of patronage might be quitclaimed or simply fall into abeyance. In 1244 Robert de Valognes claimed to be patron of Campsey Abbey in Norfolk and though there seems to have been no rival claimant the nuns themselves resisted his claim at first.[1] In 1287 the Austin canons of Caldwell perhaps for the time being recognized no patron: at Bishop Sutton's visitation they hurried through in a single day the resignation of one prior and the election, confirmation, and installation of his successor, 'because of some who unjustly claimed the advowson of that monastery'.[2] William de Aubervil, descendant of the founder of Butley Priory, had the advowson 'restored to him at the gates' by the canons, as if they had had no active patron for some time; and later quitclaimed the advowson, which seems to be identified with giving up custody.[3] It seems doubtful whether in these cases the feudal lordship was also unknown or denied; but it might be if even fealty had lapsed.[4]

Very rarely, there might be confusion as a relic of the old connexion between jurisdiction and ownership. A monastery's exemption from the diocesan might have been originally bound up with its being owned by someone else: king, pope, or mother-house.[5] The exemption of black monk houses had often begun with their 'commendation' to the pope, sometimes combined with royal ownership and its attendant privileges; a matter of ownership rather than of jurisdiction, with the pope as with the king.[6] As canon law developed, however, papal ownership was turned into a reserved jurisdiction, though the exemption of some great English abbeys was uncanonically connected with royal ownership as late as Henry II's reign.[7] But the rationalizing of the pope's claim was not quite complete, and exemption might, very exceptionally, be taken to imply papal patronage. Early in the thirteenth century there was some confusion about whether

---

[1] *Mon.* vi. 1. 587 (bishop's composition).

[2] *Annales Monastici*, ed. Luard, iii (Dunstable), p. 340.

[3] *Mon.* vi. 1. 381 (account of founders). Myres, 'Notes on the History of Butley Priory', in *Oxford Essays ... presented to H. E. Salter*, pp. 191-2.

[4] See pp. 24-25 for a motive for dropping lordship.

[5] Lesne, II. ii. 18; iii. 89-100.

[6] Knowles, *M.O.*, pp. 570-2, 575-85, 591; Lunt, *Financial Relations*, pp. 86-87.

[7] Knowles, *M.O.*, pp. 588-90; J. F. Lemarignier, *Les privilèges d'exemption des abbayes normandes* (Paris, 1937), p. 155.

king or pope were patron of the exempt abbey of Evesham. Marlberge maintained, perhaps hardly seriously, that the pope should have custody in vacancies because the abbey was founded on soil given to him. Yet he admits farther on that the king must give licence to elect; and soon it was quite unquestioned that the king was patron.[1]

ii. The English patron, who was the founder's heir and the feudal lord, was more or less acceptable to thirteenth-century canon law. The patron, as distinct from the 'pure advocate'—the defender or agent turned master—was defined as the founder;[2] and whatever tendency there may have been, in turning lay ownership into the *ius patronatus*, to regard it as in theory a privilege, a concession made by the Church to the founder and his family,[3] it was in effect the feudal relation, not denied but limited and charged with obligations of defence.[4] Where English law was concerned to safeguard a valuable kind of property without flouting the Church, canon law was concerned to secure the Church's freedom without excessively offending her sons in their secular interests; and for all the elaboration of thirteenth-century canon law it was still a great consideration to prevent plain barbarian abuse of the relationship by robbery and violence.[5] In the thirteenth century the Church only tried to stop the artificial creation of relations giving a layman a hold on the property: the Second Council of Lyons forbade putting the goods and rights of a church under a layman by name of 'avoher' without papal consent; where such a contract existed already the layman must respect its terms.[6] It further de-

---

[1] *Chronicon abbatie de Evesham*, ed. Macray, pp. 258–9. Cf. Tonbridge Priory, founded by Richard de Clare shortly before 1192 and apparently given to the pope (*Reg. Roffense*, pp. 666–8), but counted as a Clare advowson by 1262 (*Cal. Inqu. P.M.* i, p. 155; cf. ibid. v, p. 344).

[2] Friedberg, *Corpus Iuris Canonici*, ii. 617: III. 38. xxv. Innocentii IV, *Commentaria*, pp. 180v–1v. Hostiensis, *Commentaria*, pp. 146v–7v. Cf. Bernard of Pavia, quoted by Thomas, *Droit de propriété des laïques*, p. 155, n. 3: 'patronus dicitur qui aedificavit vel solum praestitit vel dotavit . . . pure autem advocatus dicitur, qui nullum horum fecit, sed est solummodo ad defensionem vocatus.'

[3] Thomas, op. cit., pp. 115–20. But Innocent IV distinguishes the patron from the advocate in this respect: 'patronatus est quasi ex debito, sed advocatio de gracia tantum' (*Commentaria*, p. 287).

[4] e.g. Friedberg, i. 614: 10, q. 1, c. 6; 616–17: III. 38. xxiii. Hostiensis, pp. 146v–7v.

[5] 4th Lateran Council c. 45 (Hefele and Leclerq, *Conciles*, v. 1367).

[6] c. 22 (ibid. vi. 199–200).

clared excommunicate anyone usurping the custody of vacant
monasteries by name of advocacy or defence, while those who
claimed the right as founders or by ancient custom must not
abuse it.[1] So the Church admitted the established rights of
the founder and landlord more readily than the accumulated
or newly acquired powers of the continental 'advocate'.

The question then arises whether there were in England
any such advocates: in principle chosen officials paid with
privileges or a fief, in practice hereditary masters with numerous rights, who were not necessarily either the founder's heir
or the present landlord.[2] Could there, in fact, be a distinction
in thirteenth-century England between the technical patron
of the canon and common law, and the advocate?

If so, it was almost as exceptional as the other distinction,
between technical patron and feudal lord. *Patronus, fundator,*
and *advocatus,* or *patronatus, fundacio,* and *advocacio,* were
normally interchangeable. The legal use of 'advowson' would
have been impossible if advocates had often been distinct
from patrons.

Occasionally a religious house of royal patronage seems
to have had something like a chosen advocate, but not apparently under that name.[3] In John's reign Earl Roger Bigod,
who was the chief tenant and the standard-bearer of the abbot
of Bury St. Edmunds, claimed that 'it belongs to us to keep
all the liberties of the Blessed Martyr unharmed . . . and to
advise his flock in difficulties';[4] possibly he was enfeoffed as
a kind of advocate.[5] Or a great neighbour might be more or
less vaguely recognized as a protector; in Henry I's time
Robert de Ferrars, as a powerful neighbour to Burton Abbey,

---

[1] c. 12 (ibid. vi. 192).

[2] F. Senn, *L'institution des avoueries ecclésiastiques en France,* esp. pp. 88–91,
103–14, 133–51. R. Laprat, 'Avoué, avouerie', in *Dictionnaire d'histoire et de géographie
ecclésiastiques,* v. 1222–35. German advocacy, centred on the exercise of higher jurisdiction in the house's lands, is not in question here.

[3] A possible exception is Earl Roger of Hereford, called *advocatus* of Gloucester
in 1144; in the Anarchy the abbey may have resorted to him for defence, or he may
have usurped the advocacy. The context, however, was an exchange of lands of which
he was lord (*Hist. et cartularium monasterii S. Petri Gloucestriae,* ed. Hunt, i. 311–14).

[4] *Memorials of St. Edmund's Abbey,* ed. Arnold, ii. 77.

[5] Cf. Athelney Abbey c. 1150, giving land and confraternity to Robert de
Beauchamp (probably one of the neighbouring Beauchamps of Hatch) for 'going on
the pleas and business of the church' (*Two Cartularies of Muchelney and Athelney,*
ed. Bates, p. 152).

constituted himself its friend and protector;[1] and much later, Edmund of Cornwall was 'a kind of bounteous defender and protector' to Abingdon, where he founded a chapel.[2] But as a rule the natural protector was the lord.[3]

On the other hand the word 'advocate' is sometimes used in a loose sense for any considerable benefactor, probably meaning the person who can be vouched to warranty for the particular lands held of him. Fountains Abbey was in the archbishop of York's patronage,[4] but Alice de Rumely (lady of Allerdale) was referred to as 'advocatrix de Fontibus, de Crostweyt et de Watendelangre';[5] this must mean advocate of Fountains for those two vills, which she did in fact give the abbey.[6] There is no evidence of a special arrangement for protection.[7]

The Cluniac priory of Thetford, however, may in the late thirteenth century have had a specially appointed advocate under that name. This is suggested by the combined facts that a brother—probably John Bigod—of the patron the Earl Marshal was living there in 1279 and was referred to by the Cluniac visitors as *advocatus*:[8] and that in 1301, when the priory made a bid for greater independence of Cluny, it was said to be relying on the power of the bishop of Norwich, of John Bigod, clerk, and of his brother Earl Roger the patron, in that order.[9] But this was evidently not an hereditary position, and was within the patron's family.

But Mr. Colvin has given one clear and some possible examples for Premonstratensian houses of an advocate as a deliberately appointed and afterwards hereditary protector

---

[1] Shaw, *History of Staffordshire*, i. 3.

[2] *V.C.H. Berks.* ii. 54, from obedientiaries' accounts. But in 1247 the monks bought land to stop Earl Richard getting it, considering what an oppressive and dangerous neighbour he would be (R. Hill, *Ecclesiastical Letter-books of the 13th Century*, pp. 73, 268).

[3] At least till the development of bastard feudalism: cf. Colvin, p. 301 and n. 4.

[4] *Memorials of the Abbey of Fountains*, ed. Walbran, i. 179, 187.

[5] In a genealogy in their register (*Mon.* v. 394).

[6] *Memorials*, ii. 29, 32.

[7] This possible use of 'advocate' for the donor who can be avouched may explain why Robert Bardolf was called 'advocate of Barlings' though the founder's heirs had the patronage (Colvin, pp. 291, 305); unless, as Colvin suggests, he really had the 'advowson' of the extra canons he endowed.

[8] Duckett, ii. 142–3.

[9] *Calendar of Papal Registers: Papal Letters*, i. 595.

distinct from the founder's heir or successor. The case of Dale Abbey[1] seems doubtful; William de Grendon, called advocate in the thirteenth-century chronicle, might reasonably be regarded as a founder in the complicated early history of the abbey.[2] And at Newhouse in the mid-twelfth century, where Ranulf de Bayeux had the title of advocate and his tenant Peter de Goxhill that of founder,[3] Ranulf was really a joint founder; he gave some land and relieved the house of some forinsec service, wishing to share in the foundation.[4] In 1296 the Crown took both lord and tenant into account as potentially having patronal rights; the escheator inquired into what might fall to the Crown through the minority of Ralph de Goxhill, whose ancestors founded the house, coinciding with the wardship of the barony of Bayeux, *que est tanquam advocata eiusdem.*[5] The formula is anomalous and suggests doubt about where the real patronage lay[6]— doubt which need not be resolved on this occasion because there were no rights in vacancies. But in this case it is clear that even if the foundation was in fact joint, by lord and tenant, it was chiefly attributed to the tenant, and there was some definite reason for distinguishing the lord as 'advocate'.

The clear case is Titchfield where, after the death of the founder Bishop Peter des Roches, the canons definitely appointed Sir William de Cantilupe and his heirs as 'advocates and patrons',[7] with the new bishop's consent but with no implication that his lordship or technical patronage was transferred. The bishops of Winchester continued to regard them-

---

[1] Colvin, p. 302.

[2] He made the third attempt at a foundation at Depedale; and his uncle William fitz Ralph approached him before he began the successful foundation at Stanley Park, near 'that ancient place of Depedale of which you are patron, where have flowered successively congregations of various religious men', and asked him to give that place to the new foundation provided a chapel were maintained there for his soul ('Chronicle of Thomas de Musca', ed. Hope, in *Derbyshire Archaeol. Journal,* v. 12–14).

[3] Stenton, *Documents illustrative of . . . History of the Danelaw,* No. 239. Colvin, pp. 43, 302.

[4] Ibid., pp. 42–43. *Danelaw Documents,* Nos. 235, 238, 240, 244, 255.

[5] Harl. Charter 44 H. 13.

[6] But in Harl. Charter 44 H. 12 (referred to by Colvin, p. 293) only Peter de Goxhill's descendants are mentioned.

[7] Colvin, pp. 302–3. The operative word is 'advocate': 'patron' seems to be used non-technically.

selves as patrons[1] and were occasionally referred to as patrons by the abbey;[2] but the advowson in the fourteenth century was in the hands of the Cantilupes.[3]

Similarly West Dereham was founded by an archbishop of Canterbury, and in 1478 the then archbishop was recognized as founder; but it was in the advowson of Aymer de Valence in 1325, by inheritance from his Munchensy ancestors; possibly a Munchensy had been chosen as advocate.[4]

Again, St. Radegund's was probably founded by its own first abbot perhaps out of several small grants, and in 1478 the abbot was called *fundator in se*;[5] but from the fourteenth to the sixteenth centuries the Poynings family claimed the patronage, perhaps by a grant of the advocacy to their thirteenth-century ancestors the Criols.[6]

But it is important that in these three cases the advocate's position by the fourteenth century seems to be the ordinary, technical, common law advowson, recorded as property by escheators, assigned as widow's dower, and so on.[7] For these houses there would be few or no firm criteria of the patron, since there were no rights in vacancies; but if the situation was defined at all, it seems likely that the founder's feudal rights were retrospectively regarded as having been transferred along with the name of advocate. Indeed, at West Dereham and St. Radegund's the original transaction may really have been a straightforward grant of the whole advowson.[8] The patronage of the archbishop at West Dereham or of the bishop at Titchfield perhaps became something rather vague, the social and religious position of the founder rather than any property right which the common law would recognize; while at St. Radegund's, however firmly the order regarded the abbot as sole founder, the Poynings family took a different view. For when Thomas Lord Poynings referred

---

[1] See p. 103; *Reg. Pontissara*, ii. 431–3, 797; Colvin, p. 296, n. 4.
[2] In seeking to be excused from corrodians imposed by Edward II and Edward III (ibid., p. 313).
[3] Ibid., p. 303.   [4] Ibid., p. 303.
[5] Ibid., pp. 146, 303.   [6] Ibid., p. 304.
[7] See Colvin's references, ibid., pp. 303–4; and above, p. 14.
[8] See p. 23. Even at Titchfield some initial confusion is suggested by the phrase 'advocates and patrons': see p. 19, n. 7.

to the abbey as *de ma fundacion*, he was clearly assuming that his advowson was the ordinary kind implying foundation by a predecessor and lordship of the site.

iii. Besides involving overlordship of the monastery's land, an advowson was of course a natural adjunct of a wider lordship, particularly of the manor where the site was. It was thus that canon law regarded the *ius patronatus* when it changed hands.[1] It was normally supposed to pass *cum universitate*, with land to which it was an appurtenance; it could then be not only given away but sold, and its inheritance was thus not restricted to heirs by blood (as some canonists had once tried to establish).[2] By itself, however, while it could not be sold, it could according to the later Innocent IV be given without restriction; according to Hostiensis, to a church or with the bishop's consent to a layman. It could also be kept back from a grant of land. In practice in England, when patronage changed hands, it was usually in the first way, passing with the lordship of lands. When Henry III granted Kenilworth Castle to his son Edmund, he had to except expressly the advowsons of Kenilworth Priory and Stoneleigh Abbey, which would otherwise have gone as appurtenances.[3] And when Earl Ranulf of Chester in 1232 gave to Dieulacres Abbey the manor of Leek, this carried with it, perhaps unintentionally, the advowson of Rocester Abbey founded in that manor, and it had to be quitclaimed next year by the abbot of Dieulacres to the new earl.[4] So there were advowsons 'in gross',[5] but these had to be deliberately and expressly separated from the manor (and they would still carry lordship of the house).

The normal way for patrons to succeed was of course by inheritance; a founder's heirs inherited his relationship with the house together with his lands; and his heirs were normally his descendants, for whose souls' salvation, with his ancestors' and his own, he intended his alms. Yet they were often not

[1] Hostiensis, pp. 142, 144v–6v; on III. 38. vi, xvi, xxiii. Innocent IV, p. 180v. And see Thomas, *Droit de propriété des laïques*, pp. 155–8.

[2] Ibid., pp. 152–3.

[3] *Calendar of Charter Rolls*, ii. 66. Cf. Alberbury (Eyton, *Antiquities of Shropshire*, vii. 83).

[4] *Close R. 1231–4*, p. 220; Farrer, *Honours and Knight's Fees*, ii. 256.

[5] Pollock and Maitland, *History of English Law*, ii. 136.

in the direct male line of descent. The Clares, for example, inheriting the honour of Gloucester from Robert fitz Hamon through two marriages, inherited with it the patronage of Tewkesbury; and there seems as close a relationship between the abbey and the family as if their own male ancestors had founded it.[1]

The patronage might be divided amongst coheirs.[2] The important Austin priory in Yorkshire, Gisburn, passed in 1272 from the family of Brus of Skelton to the joint patronage of the Twenge and Fauconberge families, who gave assent in turn.[3] But it was more usual for an advowson to pass intact to one coheir; as two other Brus advowsons went each to one of the other coheirs,[4] and as each of Earl Hugh de Albini's advowsons of priories and parish churches in the eastern counties went to one of his four daughters.[5]

Then the patronage might be granted right out of the family, together with land,[6] as when the lord of Edington, patron of the little Austin priory of Burtle Moor, granted it away in 1286 as an appendage to an acre of land.[7] The difficulty about this is that the essence of the advowson even from a business-like point of view—the masses and prayers owed in exchange for the endowment—could not easily be sold into a strange family; yet this advowson was alienated apparently as lightly as a mill or a right of pasture.

That this bond was not lightly broken seems to have been felt by Oliver de Dinham, who in 1260–1 gave up his rights in the advowson of Tywardreth Priory to Richard of Corn-

---

[1] *Ann. Mon.* i (Tewkesbury) *passim*. But cf. Geoffrey fitz Piers's enmity to Walden Abbey when he succeeded: pp. 167–70.

[2] Then either all could present together, or they could take turns (Bracton, *De Legibus*, iii. 235–6).

[3] *Cartularius Prioratus de Gyseburn*, ed. W. Brown, p. 98. *Cal. Inqu. P.M.* i, p. 267.

[4] Conishead (or Cockersand ?) to Ros of Wark, Nunmonkton to de Bellewe.

[5] *Gesta Abb. S. Albani*, ii. 65. Cf. Tewkesbury (*Cal. Inqu. P.M.* ix, pp. 336, 341; *Mon.* ii. 61), Cumbwell (*Archaeologia Cantiana*, v. 212–16, 218–19), Dunkeswell (Bodl. MS. Top. Devon d. 5 (Newenham cartulary), ff. 16–17).

[6] Cf. grant of Benhall manor 'with the advowsons of the priories of Butley and Leiston and all its other appurtenances' (Harl. Charter 49 A 6; see Colvin, p. 292); and Hubert de Burgh's acquisition of Hornby Castle, with the advowson of Hornby Priory, from the Montbegon heir (*Lancs. Final Concords*, ed. W. Farrer, Lancs. and Chesh. Rec. Soc. xxxix, 1899, i. 56–58 and n. 3).

[7] *Glastonbury Cart.* i. 119.

wall, but reserved his chantry that the Tywardreth monks had to provide at St. Mary du Val.[1] Yet he was hard-bitten enough, to judge by his relations with Hartland Abbey and with Bishop Bronscombe.[2] Earlier, Bernard de St. Walery, giving Henry II the advowson of Godstow Abbey, reserved the benefits of the nuns' prayers and alms.[3]

In these two instances the patronage and lordship constituted the whole grant, complete in itself, not an appendage to wider lands. This sort of transfer might be made as a friendly arrangement for the good of the house, perhaps by a patron who had no heirs. Bishop Richard le Poer before his death put Tarrant Keynes nunnery under the queen;[4] and Henry de Newburgh in 1272 allowed the monks of Bindon to choose their own patron, whereupon they chose King Henry and Queen Eleanor and the future kings of England[5] (this might be not unlike the choice of an advocate, except that there was no question of the patronage staying with the founder even at first). Early in the century the widow Alice de Nerford gave the king the patronage of her foundation Creake Abbey; this was by the advice of men of experience and standing, because she feared that her heirs, being ill provided for, might do the abbey some harm.[6]

On the other hand, the patronage might be transferred solely as a piece of property[7]—as a business transaction or a royal grant. King John granted the patronage of three abbeys to the local bishops—Glastonbury, Thorney, and St. Osyth's.[8] Glastonbury returned to the Crown in 1275 by open barter: the city of Bath, except the barton, was literally 'to be had in exchange for the patronage of the abbey of Glastonbury'.[9] There were misgivings about the legality of this. The ex-

---

1 Oliver, *Monasticon Diocesis Exoniensis*, Add. Supp., p. 5.
2 Ibid., p. 208. See p. 165.
3 *Mon.* iv. 364. See p. 13 and cf. Jervaulx, pp. 12–13.
4 Matthew Paris, *Chronica Majora*, ed. Luard, iii. 392, 479.
5 *Cal. Pat. R. 1272–81*, p. 337.
6 *Mon.* vi. 1. 487 (account in cartulary).
7 It is not always easy to distinguish: in John's reign, Richard de Percy granted the advowson of Handale Priory to his nephew Richard Malebisse for his homage and service of 1 lb. of incense—but the incense was to be paid to the nunnery itself (*Mon.* iv. 75).
8 St. Osyth's in 1206 (*Mon.* vi. 1. 310), and see p. 8.
9 *Mon.* ii. 269, and *Cal. Pat. R. 1272–81*, p. 96.

change the other way[1] in the time of Richard I had been called simoniacal by Innocent III; and at this final settlement the dean and chapter of Wells, advising their bishop, thought it a delicate point.[2]

The little house of Bicknacre came under royal patronage in payment of a sheriff's debts; this was Maurice fitz Geoffrey, who late in the twelfth century founded it out of money that he owed the Crown; when he was pardoned most of this, his priory was counted as having been founded by the king.[3]

When the patronage went out of the family in this way the new patron could hardly have the same feeling about it: could not easily appropriate to himself the founder's anxiety for the souls of his ancestors and heirs, nor feel pride and affection for the entries in the martyrology of successive generations of the same family; nor could this feeling have been strong in whoever parted with the patronage. And to be put into royal patronage, though it might be intended for the house's good, would have the disadvantage of substituting red tape for informal discussion. The prior of Barnwell, when his house with other Pecche property was given to the king, foresaw that his successor would not be able to talk business on equal terms with the king as with the former patrons.[4]

The tension between the natural feeling that blood kinship was essential and the feudal principle that masses and prayers were transferable services like any others is shown in a case of 1310;[5] though it also shows the importance of kinship being exploited and heightened for an immediate material motive, the avoidance of expense. The abbot of Hartland sued Robert Beaupel to acquit him, as mesne lord, of the forinsec services on a tenement which had been given to the abbey in pure alms by Diana, lady of Hole (not actually the patron), who had later enfeoffed Beaupel with all her lands. Beaupel had confirmed the gift to the abbot, reserving nothing to himself but prayers and spiritual benefits; but now, to

---

[1] i.e. the grant of the abbey for a see to Bishop Savary.

[2] Hist. MSS. Comm., *Report on the MSS. of the Dean and Chapter of Wells*, p. 111.

[3] *V.C.H. Essex*, ii. 144.

[4] *Liber Memorandorum ecclesie de Bernewell*, ed. Clark, pp. 51–52.

[5] *Year Book Series* (Selden Soc.), iii. 164–74.

avoid paying the services on it, he denied being its lord at all, arguing that the abbot had never attorned to him for the services and could never do so, because prayers done for the soul of a donor and his heirs could not pass to another; frankalmoin was of such a nature that it could never pass from[1] the feoffor or his heirs, and the lordship ought to continue in the blood of Diana. But for the abbot it was successfully[2] maintained that Beaupel had admitted his lordship by charter; and that he was actually prayed for at the abbey, in fact was seised of the services of 'paternosters and avemaries'; as Justice Stanton put it, 'you have the benefits of the house, and I do not see how a man can be better attorned than by seisin of the services'.

In fact, a new lord could if he chose build up almost the proper patronal relation, though it would at first be thin compared with that inherited from ancestors by blood. The correct attitude was clearly that attributed to Payn Peverel, who in the twelfth century acquired the escheated lands of the founder of Barnwell: 'As I have succeeded Picot in place of his heir in possessing his heritage, so I will succeed him in endowing and cherishing this house.'[3]

But alienations were not common. The Glastonbury monks evidently felt it was unfitting that King John should hand them over to the patronage of Bishop Jocelyn; they wrote to him to remember how venerable their church had been to all kings, even pagans, and especially 'dulcissimo patrono nostro, et patri vestro', who rebuilt it; it was a 'shining jewel of your Crown', not to be so lightly thrown aside.[4] Probably this was the normal attitude, and a baron or knight would set some store by the place where his ancestors' bones lay, or even feel, with the patron of Ford Abbey, that it was 'the finest feather in his tail'.[5]

---

[1] Ibid., p. 167 has 'to', but see ibid., pp. 169–70.
[2] See *Year Bk. Ser.* xix. 106–8.
[3] *Liber Mem.*, p. 41.
[4] Domerham, p. 446. Knowles, *R.O.*, p. 277, implies that the 1218 arrangement (dividing Glastonbury from Bath but leaving the patronage to the bishop) was final and satisfactory to the monks, 'the monastery recovering its independence and leaving the bishop with some churches and the bare title of patron'. This is to underestimate the importance of patronage; the monks were not content until in 1272 their monastery was once more in royal patronage (Domerham, pp. 514–15, 523–5, 536–55).   [5] *Mon.* v. 379.

iv. Just as a change of patron might affect the house, so a change in the house's status might affect the value of the patronage as property. If an existing house were newly subjected to another, by action within the order or by exchange with the house on which it formerly depended, the patron's rights might be seriously affected; for the mother-house sometimes exercised over a dependency some of the patron's functions.[1] Probably the patron's consent was customary in such a subjection or exchange. In 1267 the alien priory of Tregony, whose patrons were the Pomerays, was exchanged by its mother-house, St. Mary du Val, and put under Merton Priory. This exchange stopped conventual life for eleven years, and it is surprising at first that the deed of exchange only mentions the consent of the patrons of Merton and St. Mary du Val.[2] But in fact the Pomerays did give their assent in a separate charter, provided that three priests were still kept at Tregony.[3] So the silence of the principal deed is not conclusive.

The patron's consent might be needed for reducing an abbey to a priory even without subjection to another house. When this was done for economy's sake at Cumbwell about 1219, Mabel de Gatton consented saving the canons' and her own rights in elections,[4] though it is not clear how these were endangered.

Walter and Margaret de Lacy had serious trouble in the 1230's over their new nunnery at Acornbury, through putting it under the wrong order by mistake. Margaret put the nuns under the Hospitallers without consulting her husband or the bishop, and apparently not knowing the difference between that order and the Austin rule; she then found that by their rule the nuns might be ordered to travel about, and managed to obtain papal letters that they were under the Austin rule, as 'in her simplicity' she really thought. The Hospitallers produced their privileges, and there was a long struggle to free the house from them; the election of a prioress was held up for six years, the Hospitallers imposed a bad

---

[1] See pp. 54, 81–82.

[2] *Register of Walter Bronscombe*, ed. Hingeston-Randolph, p. 275.

[3] *Reg. Collegii Exoniensis*, ed. C. W. Boase, p. 321; see E. B. Powley, *The House of de la Pomerai* (Liverpool, 1944), pp. 34–35.

[4] *Archaeol. Cant.* v. 213–15.

chaplain, took away rents, and undermined the sub-prioress's authority. In 1237 the legate Otto cut the knot, released the nuns from the Hospitallers, and made them Austin canon-esses according to the founders' intentions.[1]

Another problem might arise if a house were refounded: perhaps put under a different order, re-endowed, and re-formed, by someone other than the original patron. Canons-leigh, founded by Walter de Clavill in the fee of the Honour of Gloucester,[2] was refounded in 1284 by Countess Matilda de Clare; only three of the seven canons were resident, and she wished to give £200 a year for the support of forty canonesses.[3] It seems that she was interested in her own scheme rather than in the particular monastery, for she had had the same idea ten years earlier for Sandelford in Berk-shire.[4] This evidently came to nothing, and she transferred her attentions to Canonsleigh. What part her tenants the Clavills were allowed does not appear. John de Clavill had made an agreement with the canons only two years before;[5] but in 1308 he confirmed to the canonesses all his ancestors' gifts to the canons.[6] Meanwhile it is possible that the dis-possessed canons, deserted by their real patron, were pretend-ing to be of royal patronage.[7]

The gift of a new site by a new benefactor would drasti-cally affect the founder's rights, for since the new site was in someone else's fief, the founder would be the monks' lord for a part of their lands now outlying instead of central, and would probably lose the effective patronage. His consent to such a move was almost certainly necessary; there are examples from the twelfth century, as when Jervaulx moved out of the founder's fief into the demesne of his lord, with the founder's son's consent.[8] In similar terms the patron of Kingswood, Robert de Berkeley, allowed the move out of his fief to a site at Tetbury given by Reginald de St. Walery.[9]

---

[1] *Cal. Papal L.* i. 134, 136, 141, 152, 153.
[2] *Mon.* vi. 1. 334.   [3] *Cal. Papal L.* i. 478.
[4] Ibid., p. 448.   [5] See p. 83, n. 2.
[6] Oliver, p. 227.
[7] The archbishop, supporting the canons in 1287, said the house was 'of royal patronage, as is said' (*Reg. Epistolarum Johannis Peckham*, ed. Martin, iii. 938–9).
[8] See p. 12, and *Mon.* v. 572–5.
[9] *Mon.* v. 426.

Trouble followed this transaction, by which Kingswood became a mere grange to Tetbury; and later the monks moved
back to land near Kingswood given by Roger de Berkeley to
Bernard de St. Walery for the purpose.[1] It is not clear who
was patron after all; Bernard de St. Walery speaks of 'my
abbey', but by 1415 the Berkeleys were patrons.[2]

So arrangements made by ecclesiastical authority, by the
monks themselves, or by later benefactors, might affect the
value of the patronage as somebody's property, just as a
change of hands of the property might affect the peace of the
house.

[1] *Mon.* v. 425–6.
[2] *Documents relating to the Monastery of Kingswood*, ed. Perkins, p. 255. Bernard
de St. Walery had a similarly doubtful claim to the patronage of Osney, inherited
from Roger d'Ivri. The d'Oillys (later the king) were the accepted patrons, but the
canons had a charter from Bernard implying his joint patronage, which they
evidently found disconcerting: for it was three times endorsed *non ostendatur, nullo
modo ostendatur*, &c. (*Cartulary of Oseney Abbey*, ed. Salter, iv. 31).

III

LAWSUITS AND LEGISLATION

SINCE the patronage of religious houses was property, there were disputes about it as property; and most of these, as matters of advowson, came before the lay courts. Certain assumptions and generalizations would underly the judgements made, setting up standards in the common law of the kingdom alongside those of canon law. Added to these, towards the end of the century, were certain explicit enactments: part of Edward I's legislation was concerned, directly or indirectly, with the patronage of monasteries, showing some of the problems that had arisen for the king or his barons as patrons and landlords. Just as the Church was concerned with the relation between patron and monastery for the sake of its own freedom and discipline, looking on the patron rather as an extra factor, a problem on the outskirts; so the secular power was concerned with it from its own point of view, for the protection of rights and property, looking on the monastery as one amongst several kinds of tenant.

Lawsuits about the patronage of religious houses were either over the advowson itself, between rival claimants, or over the rights attached to it, between the patron and the house itself or its mother-house. The advowson of Eynsham, for instance, was sued for in the Curia Regis twice. In 1196 King Richard's ministers and Bishop Hugh of Lincoln both claimed it in a vacancy, after an abbacy of about forty-four years during which the facts had probably been nearly forgotten; the patronage was adjudged to the bishop in the king's court.[1] In 1285 King Edward renewed the claim, taking custody on the abbot's death, and sued Bishop Sutton for the advowson 'of which he had unjustly despoiled the king'; maintaining that Henry II had had seisin in vacancies and had presented an abbot.[2] Apart from evidence of foundation, these were always the criteria[3]—custody, and rights in the

---

[1] *Magna Vita S. Hugonis*, ed. Dimock, pp. 188–91.

[2] *Cartulary of Eynsham Abbey*, ed. Salter, i. 309.

[3] Cf. case in 1258 between William Bardolf and Adam de Everingham (tenants of moieties of Shelford barony) for advowson of Shelford Priory; the grounds taken

election. Again, a grand assize returned that the bishop had the greater right.[1]

Similarly the advowson of Glastonbury was claimed by the king against the bishop of Bath and Wells; the struggle was long drawn out and intermittent, and proceeded mostly by settlements out of court, or by papal judgements; but about 1250 the king sued the bishop in the lay courts by a writ *quo warranto* he had taken possession of the advowson.[2]

Then there were cases about the advowson of a dependency, in which the parties were the abbot of the mother-house and the founder's heir or assign. In 1285 the abbot of St. Albans was sued before the itinerant justices by Humphrey de Bohun for the advowson of Hatfield Peverel, on the basis of a charter from a Peverel; but he had never had seisin, and he quitclaimed in return for 50 marks and confraternity at St. Albans.[3] In 1293 the next abbot was sued by the king for the advowson of Tynemouth Priory. This case turned chiefly on the priory's degree of dependence.[4] The king claimed that in the time of Henry II a prior had been elected by the king's leave and admitted by his consent —the usual test—and in no way subject to the abbot of St. Albans. The abbot showed charters proving that the priory was a cell. The king's representative produced a writ of Henry II taking the house of Tynemouth under his protection, forbidding interference by the abbot, and allowing the monks to elect their prior. The case then came before the king in parliament, and he, 'on account of the generosity and affection that he and his predecessors had always had to St. Alban the protomartyr of his realm of England', allowed the abbot to have the advowson, and to appoint and remove priors at his will, as in time past.[5]

There are similar cases between patron and mother-house,

on both sides were foundation by an ancestor, and presentation of a prior to himself or an ancestor (*Mon.* vi. 1. 577–8).

[1] *Eynsham Cart.* i. 310.

[2] Domerham, pp. 514–15. Cf. Thorney; advowson granted by John to bishop of Ely; Bishop Hugh de Northwold sued Henry III for it in 1237 (*V.C.H. Cambridge*, ii. 214).

[3] *Gesta Abb.* i. 471; Duchy of Lanc. 25/25 (the fine, which does not mention the money).

[4] See pp. 61–62.

[5] *Gesta Abb.* ii. 19–20. *Select Cases in King's Bench*, ii. 137.

not about the advowson itself but about particular rights. Robert fitz Walter in 1210 sued the abbot of St. Albans about another of its cells, Binham; charging him with oppressing it and removing a prior put in with his, the patron's, will and consent.[1] For these rights in the choice of prelate the patron might sue the house itself: in 1200 Thomas d'Arcy sued the convent of Nocton for electing a prior and presenting him to the bishop of Lincoln, contrary to his assent and liberty; for the house was sited on his lands, his predecessors founded it, and chose and presented its priors. This was called a plea *quare elegit priorem*.[2]

Later in the century when free election had become general a patron could not thus sue for the right actually to choose the abbot or prior; the lay courts recognized the canon law of free election in principle, and the First Statute of Westminster affirmed it.[3] But the rights of licence and assent remained subject to litigation or conveyance in lay courts. In 1248 Roger Corbet sued the prior of Wombridge for letting himself be presented to the bishop before being presented to him as patron. A fine was made settling the wider question of all the patron's rights in a vacancy, leaving him the presentation for which he had sued, but little else.[4] The other criterion, custody in vacancies, might also be sued for, as Bishop Bronscombe claimed that of Hartland against Oliver de Dinham, getting a commission of oyer and terminer issued.[5]

There seems to have been some variety and extemporization in initiating suits about the patronage of religious houses,

[1] *Curia Regis Rolls*, vi. 55–56; cf. *Gesta Abb.* i. 226–8.

[2] *Cur. Reg. R.* i. 307. Cf. Robert de Badelee and St. Peter's, Ipswich, 1205 (*Rotuli de Oblatis et Finibus*, p. 324).

[3] *Statutes of the Realm*, i. 28 (c.v.).

[4] No licence, and no custody except to take simple seisin by a sergeant (Eyton, *Shropshire*, vii. 367). Cf. fine between Cartmel and earl of Pembroke, 1250 (*V.C.H. Lancs.* ii. 145). Cf. also what was perhaps a genuine suit by the prior of Thornholm against Geoffrey and Margaret de Neville, 1271–2, for distraining the prior for having been presented to Hugh de Neville of Cadney as patron (instead of to them). This ended with not only concessions (like Corbet's) to the convent but a quit-claim of the advowson to Hugh de Neville, in return for the grant of a rent, both at the instance of the prior (*Final Concords*, ii, Lincs. Rec. Soc. xvii, p. 266). And cf. suit between Andrew de Saukevil and William de Anemere for presentation (i.e. assent to elections) at Flitcham (Blomefield, *History of Norfolk*; London, 1805; viii. 418).   [5] Oliver, p. 209.

until by the Second Statute of Westminster the writs of *quare
impedit* and darrein presentment were to be granted for
chapels, prebends, vicarages, hospitals, abbeys, priories, and
other houses.[1] This must have answered a need for standardized procedure, in putting monasteries on the same basis as
parish churches.[2]

Cases about elections or presentations, as distinct from
actual advowson, might be taken before ecclesiastical judges;[3]
and in the prevailing rivalry of church and lay courts it was
possible for a case to be bandied about from one to the other,
not so much by the force of the claims of the two authorities,
as by the ingenuity of the parties and their lawyers in making
use of these claims to twist and delay, and in arguing with
whatever principles came to hand. When Nicholas of Ely,
bishop of Winchester, was sued by Edward I for the advowson of the cathedral priory, he first excepted against the composition of the assize, and then appealed to the pope on the
grounds that the case involved the dividing of a church which
was a spiritual matter.[4] And his successor John de Pontissara's arguments why he need not answer the king included
the commission of the church to him by the pope, to whom
he might therefore be driven to resort; the point that though
the king had cognizance of cases about patronage, this did
not apply to cathedral churches, which could not be separated
from the bishops whose brides they were; and the flat statement that cases about patronage could not under canon law
be tried by a secular judge, whatever was the custom or
rather corruption to the contrary.[5]

Similarly in the 1240's and 50's the Glastonbury monks'
attempt to recover property from the bishop of Bath and
Wells, and to escape from his patronage into the king's, was
revived in the church courts. Bishop Roger, shortly before
his death, got a writ of prohibition[6] which took the case into

---

[1] *Statutes*, i. 77, c. v.
[2] Though I have not in fact met a case about a monastery initiated by either of
these writs t. Edward I.   [3] See pp. 54–55, 57, 60, 62–63.
[4] *Reg. Pontissara*, ii. 691–3.   [5] Ibid., pp. 681–2.
[6] Domerham, p. 512. This is an exception to Father Flahiff's generalization that
only the lower clergy or religious used writs of prohibition against church courts,
not 'prelates of the Church' ('The Use of Prohibitions by Clerics . . .', in *Medieval
Studies*, iii. 104).

the Curia Regis; but when the king began to be interested, the new bishop got papal letters forbidding the abbot to sue in a secular court.[1]

But behind such games of dodge lay a real problem, the overlapping spheres of the spiritual and temporal powers; and part of this problem was the nature of endowments of monasteries and other churches: land which the patron regarded as a fief held of him, over which he kept a hold, and which in some circumstances he might recover, but which the Church regarded as a gift to God, inalienable and sacrosanct. Rather, these were the classical extremes of feeling which individual laymen and churchmen would mix in varying proportions. For canon law was not wholehearted in asserting that patronage was only a tolerated privilege,[2] and Grosseteste was exceptional even amongst principled churchmen in taking this line.[3] Becket at his most extreme had said of his lands 'it is not an inheritance that I hold, nor of the king, but of God, to whom the things which I possess were given in alms',[4] but he admitted in other contexts that he was the king's vassal as well as his spiritual father.[5]

The distinction in the assize *utrum* between lay fee, to be sued for in the lay courts, and alms, left to the courts christian, was an attempted solution in regard to jurisdiction for this divergence of principle: each set of assumptions was allowed to hold for some church land. But the 'alms' immune from the lay court was of course narrowed to cover sometimes only consecrated soil, sometimes a parish church's original endowment (in so far as the assize became 'the parson's writ of right');[6] while lay fee, originally meaning the prelate's 'barony', or land for which feudal services were owed, or a clerk's personal inheritance,[7] was steadily widened to cover even land given in free, pure, and perpetual alms.[8] But it is

---

[1] Domerham, p. 516; *Cal. Papal L.* i. 249.

[2] See p. 16.   [3] See Powicke, i. 261, 285.

[4] *Materials for the History of Thomas Becket*, ed. J. C. Robertson (R.S. lxvii, 1875–83), ii. 398. Cf. i. 39.

[5] Ibid. v. 279 (the letter *desiderio desideravi*).

[6] Bracton, *De Legibus*, iii. 329–31. Flahiff, 'The Writ of Prohibition . . .', in *Med. Studies*, vi. 273–4.

[7] Flower, *Introduction to Curia Regis Rolls*, pp. 106, 366; *Cur. Reg. R.* iv. 291; vii. 63.

[8] Pollock and Maitland, i. 246, 250.

not always made clear that the frankalmoin land which was counted as lay fee in this context did not thereby cease to be frankalmoin: 'alms' in the assize was no longer the same as in general feudal contexts. Bracton distinguishes clearly between sacred land or buildings, belonging to the church court, and frankalmoin, belonging to the lay court.[1] The narrowed definition in the assize went with its narrowed use: heads of religious houses were being debarred from using the assize since even frankalmoin land was given not only to the church but also to the prelate, who could therefore use any remedy that a layman could use.[2] And since the assize was used to define lay fee in a plea about a writ of prohibition, such a writ could withdraw from the church courts suits about most church property.[3]

Papal pronouncements also made a distinction, allowing the lay courts jurisdiction over lay fees or temporalities, not over spiritualities; but it is not clear how these were defined for this purpose.[4] Certainly the English clergy objected to the widening definition of lay fee in writs of prohibition. The bishops in their articles of 1257,[5] and Robert Marsh in his 'Privileges of the clergy' drawn up for Grosseteste,[6] made the counterclaim that all land given in frankalmoin was consecrated to God and should be accounted res sacra; while spoliation of any church property, even if held in fee, was sacrilege and so belonged to the church courts.

Other problems besides jurisdiction were involved in the nature of church property; the 1257 articles and those of Merton next year include complaints that the king and other magnates had forced churchmen to do suit to their lay courts, and to pay toll and other secular burdens, for land held in free, pure, and perpetual alms.[7] Robert Marsh says it is sacrilege to exact new services from frankalmoin land.[8] But the Merton articles make the significant qualification that these

---

[1] Bracton, *De Legibus*, iv. 265–6.
[2] Ibid. iii. 329–31; Pollock and Maitland, i. 250–1.
[3] Flahiff, 'Writ of Prohibition . . .', in *Med. Studies*, vi. 274; vii. 259.
[4] Kimball, 'Judicial Aspects of Frankalmoin Tenure', in *E.H.R.* xlvii. 7–10.
[5] *Chron. Maj.* vi. 361–2.
[6] *Ann. Mon.* i. (Burton), p. 427.
[7] Ibid., pp. 420–1; *Chron. Maj.* vi. 361.
[8] *Ann. Mon.* i. 425.

claims were being enforced unless the original charter could
be proved; this suggests that although lay courts and landlords were both stretching the law to its limit in pressing
their claims on church land, tenure by free, pure, and perpetual alms could be maintained, if with trouble and expense.[1]
We know that this tenure was sometimes successfully pleaded
to evade various burdens.[2] Jurisdiction was a more serious
question than suit and service; writs of prohibition were still
used for frankalmoin against all protests.

Later, parts of Edward I's legislation tended to tighten
the hold of the lord, and to widen the scope of the lay court;
and it roused similar objections. In making the statute *De
Religiosis*, though its timing was provoked by Pecham's stand
for clerical jurisdiction, the king and magnates were thinking
first as landlords concerned about the incidents.[3] This does
not of course mean that they were no longer interested in endowing religious houses, despite lamentations by the monks
that it was the end of all liberality of kings and nobles;[4] much
land was alienated in mortmain by licence. But it does show,
like the attacks on frankalmoin, that the monasteries were
regarded rather as overmighty landlords, engrossing the
profits of their endowers' lords and playing on the same
ground, than as institutions reverend and apart, to have
riches piled on them and forgotten. It was an old problem;
the statute had been anticipated in the Provisions of Westminster[5] and, in a limited context, in Magna Carta.[6] As early
as 1227 Henry III had ordered all sheriffs not to let tenants-
in-chief alienate anything to a religious house or ecclesiastical
person without his licence,[7] and more than once he gave
orders to prevent religious men acquiring land of particular

---

[1] Ibid., p. 421. The articles also complained that secular judges had deprived
churches of their possessions and liberties if these were not expressly named in the
charter, or because they had not been used. Cf. 1314 case where a tenant's charter in
frankalmoin was not enough unless the lord's immemorial seisin of homage and
service were disproved as well (Plucknett, *Legislation of Edward I*, p. 64, n. 3).

[2] See pp. 13, 83–84.

[3] Plucknett, pp. 94–102, 109.

[4] William Thorne, *De rebus abbatum Cantuarie*, col. 1961.

[5] *Statutes*, i. 10. Stubbs, *Select Charters* (9th ed.), p. 393, c. 14 and (for Barons'
Petition) p. 375, c. 10.

[6] 1217; c. 43 (ibid., p. 343). Cf. c. 39, later taken to mean 'in alms' (Plucknett,
p. 95).

[7] Wilkins, *Concilia*, i. 561.

fiefs in his hand.[1] About 1244 Richard of Cornwall got
Osney Abbey to promise not to accept lands given from his
fief without his leave.[2] It had long been the practice when
granting land to undertake to warrant it to heirs and assigns
'except religious men and Jews',[3] and conversely a founder
or later patron (or his lord) might in his charter expressly
allow a house to accept lands given or sold by his tenants[4]
(this might even be done in general terms after Mortmain).[5]
Together with this went an occasional desire of the donor
himself or his heir, not only his landlord, to recover lands
granted away; there were several cases of the patron suing
the house for land,[6] and one disappointed heir tried but failed
to recover land under the Statute of Mortmain.[7]

There was, on the other hand, legislation to protect monasteries and check their alienation of lands that they already
held; partly in the house's interest, but partly in the patron's.
For the patron would not want his monastery impoverished
by anyone but himself, nor would he want the lands to fall
still further out of his hands by subinfeudation.[8]

By the Statute of Marlborough an abbot could sue for
anything lost in his predecessor's time, or in vacancy;[9] and
already there was a procedure, by the writ *sine assensu capituli*,
for recovering what had been alienated by a predecessor without the chapter's consent.[10] More obviously in the patron's
interest are clauses in the Second Statute of Westminster and
the Statute of Carlisle, 1285 and 1306–7. The former was
intended either to prevent monasteries alienating or mis-
applying property, or to give patrons a chance to recover it;
probably both. Lands given by the king or his progenitors
to a house of royal foundation, and alienated by the abbot or
prior, were to be taken into the king's hands.[11] Other founders

---

[1] Bartholomew Crek's (*Close R. 1247–5*, p. 401); Dursley barony (ibid., p. 556).
[2] *Oseney Cart.* iii. 80.　　　　[3] Plucknett, p. 98.
[4] e.g. Isabel de Forz to Quarr (*Mon.* v. 319), Earl Conan to Jervaulx (*Mon.* v.
572), Walkelin de Maminot to Cumbwell (*Archaeol. Cant.* v. 196–7).
[5] 1284, Humphrey de Bohun to Walden; Harl. 3697 (Walden cartulary), f. 23.
[6] See pp. 166–7.　　　　[7] Plucknett, p. 102.
[8] See pp. 154–6, and Powicke, ii. 720.
[9] *Statutes*, i. 25 (c. xxviii).
[10] Bracton, *De Legibus*, iv. 35. For an example in 1221 see *Rolls of Justices in Eyre...
1221–2* (Selden Soc. lix), pp. 60–61.
[11] *Statutes*, i. 91 (c. xli). For an example, 1286, see *Calendar of Fine Rolls*, i. 228.

could have a writ, *praecipe tali abbati*, to recover the land alienated. By another writ, *cessavit*, the donor could recover lands given for a special spiritual service, such as a chantry, a light or alms, if it were stopped for two years—just as this writ was used for lands held in fee-farm when the rent was not paid.[1]

The Statute of Carlisle tried to stop the flow of money from English houses to their mother-houses abroad. It complained that religious houses built for the maintenance of a number of monks, for alms to the poor, and for the good of the founders' souls, were taxed and charged by aliens, their superiors, so reducing their alms and good works, and disinheriting the founders—'salutes vivorum, et anime mortuorum miserabiliter defrauduntur'. In future nothing was to be paid or conveyed out of the country; but this was not meant to stop visitation by aliens.[2] The chief point here, as in 1285, was to protect patrons against being defrauded or disinherited, either by loss of their spiritual services or by reduction in value of the property of the house that was held of them.

Much of this legislation involved attacks on the church courts[3] and at the same time ran counter to the clergy's desire to uphold the permanence and sanctity of grants to the Church; articles complaining about the 1285 statutes include the objection that it is the province of prelates to compel performance of chantries and such spiritual services, the grant standing; no lay power can compel the reversion of the grant if the services are withheld.[4] Similarly they object to the reversion of land once given in frankalmoin if it is alienated.[5]

---

[1] *Statutes*, i. 48 (Gloucester, c. iv). I have not found these remedies used against monastic houses, but Coulton quotes two cases of Dominican convents thus sued, 1306 and 1307 (*Five Centuries*, iii. 76).

[2] *Statutes*, i. 150–2. Cf. the 1305 petition which produced the statute: chiefly concerned with Cistercians, 'in serfage to the abbot of Cîteaux . . . because of the tallage which the abbots take' (*Memoranda de Parliamento, 1305*, ed. Maitland, R.S. 1893. See Reich, p. 336).

[3] D. L. Douie, *Archbishop Pecham* (Oxford, 1952), pp. 309–10. But these attacks were hardly 'under the pretence of removing anomalies in the law'; if the remedies were not likely to be used, no competition would have been involved.

[4] By 1300, however, they had accepted the idea of a lay action, though not of forfeiture (*Registrum Roberti Winchelsey*, ed. Graham, p. 1026).

[5] *Concilia*, ii. 119.

Yet it was all part of the general land legislation, adapted to monasteries but not treating them in any peculiar way. The problems of alienation, whether to or by monasteries, were general feudal problems; just as Mortmain must be seen with *Quia Emptores*, so, long before, King John had inquired about fees alienated as alms along with maritagia 'or any other way whereby they are not held of us in chief'.[1] Henry III's ordinance of 1256 forbidding tenants-in-chief to alienate without his licence stated that if they did the king lost his incidents, and his tenants might be too impoverished to render their due services.[2] The former objection would apply especially to alienation in mortmain, to a monastery; the latter, to alienation by a monastery of the king's advowson. This ordinance gives the context for the legislation about monastic property, reconciling any apparent contradiction. There is not a desire to stop monasteries acquiring property contradicting a desire to stop them losing it,[3] but a general desire of all lords to keep a hold on the lands and services of their tenants, lay or monastic.

So the statutes treat the position of patron as a kind of property—naturally, since only in that aspect does it come within the scope of secular law. His feudal lordship of the lands he has given is stressed; and the whole complex of spiritual benefits that his position carries is interpreted on its simplest level, as a kind of feudal service, a heritable and litigable right. The topical problem was to guard against loss or diminution of this property and service. The legislation, and the common law procedure which it supplemented, breathe the spirit of lay ownership, however limited, which the Church's rules were intended to suppress; protests were made; and yet there was no open clash with canon law. For canon law had had to recognize patronage as a right provided that it was not treated as merchandise, that elections and

---

[1] *Book of Fees* (Record Publications; London, 1920), i. 52; see S. Painter, *Reign of King John* (Baltimore, 1949), p. 211.

[2] *Close R. 1254–6*, p. 429.

[3] Though the St. Albans chronicle makes it sound rather like that, writing of the Second Statute of Westminster: the king, 'because he had formerly laid down that religious persons should not increase in secular possessions, now he laid down that what they already had they should not diminish' (*Rishanger . . . Chronica et Annales*, ed. Riley, p. 110).

discipline were not meddled with, and that crude oppression was avoided: things that were either ignored or actually condemned[1] in written English law. And churchmen themselves in varying degrees shared the interests of or felt their obligations to lay patrons; a St. Albans chronicler took the Statute of Mortmain as a natural punishment of the Benedictines' 'sloth and ingratitude' in cutting off prayers for benefactors.[2]

[1] Westminster I, cc. i and v, on hospitality and elections; see pp. 69, 102.
[2] Knowles, *R.O.*, p. 23. *Gesta Abb.* i. 464.

IV

ELECTIONS

AMONGST the rights of patronage which made it valuable
property, the patron's part in the choice of a head was
one of the most important. The patron would see the
abbot or prior as one of his tenants, and also as a servant and
dependant, incumbent of one of his churches, a superior kind
of parson. In each aspect, who held the position was of some
moment to the patron: either negatively, to avoid a treacherous
or dilapidating tenant, or positively, to pay a servant or provide for a dependant; though in the second respect it was in
general neither so useful nor so available as a prebend or a
parish church.

The patron's part in choosing a head had roots in the
Saxon kings' customary powers and the Conqueror's bene-
ficent control,[1] and in the old unreformed disposal of abbacies
by and to laymen. From this it was rationalized into the
enfeoffing of a new tenant, as well as presenting to a vacant
benefice. Thus it was formed to feudal ideas as these grew
up; but it had still, like the disposal of bishoprics, to be reconciled to canon law which was growing up simultaneously.

Beyond the 'common law' of election by the convent and
confirmation by the bishop,[2] thirteenth-century canon law
turned mostly on a ruling of Clement III allowing the
patron only to consent afterwards, unless his jurisdiction
gave him some other claim;[3] and one of Celestine III forbidding the custom of electing two candidates and letting
king or patriarch[4] choose between them or break the election
—though the asking of consent was expressly allowed.[5]
Clement III's qualification was explained by Hostiensis as
meaning that an ecclesiastic who was patron might by special
custom have some advisory part, or a layman by papal privi-

[1] See Knowles, *M.O.*, pp. 396–7.
[2] Friedberg, i. 812; Decretum, 16, q. 7, c. 43; 829: 18, q. 2, c. 2, 4. The last
associates the *dominus possessionis* with the convent.
[3] Ibid. ii. 617: III. 38. xxv.
[4] The decretal was originally concerned with Jerusalem.
[5] Ibid. ii. 54: I. 6. xiv.

lege;[1] while Innocent IV was clear that no custom could allow any patron an actual vote.[2]

In England during most of the twelfth century the king appointed abbots, like bishops, with sometimes some appearance of an election; religious houses that had free election had it as a favour.[3] In the thirteenth century formal free election became normal, under the continued pressure of the reforming movement. King John's promise in 1214 of free election to all churches[4] marked a real change. The wording of the 1214 grant does not show clearly whether it referred only to houses of royal patronage, or to religious houses in general with the agreement of the barons as patrons. The wider interpretation seems plausible now, and probably was so then; certainly in practice other patrons followed the king. The patron's rights became stereotyped: they were usually the right to be informed of the vacancy, and to give licence to elect; to have the elect presented to him, to assent to the election, and to present him to the bishop for confirmation. Licence beforehand, and assent afterwards, were the key points. As has been said, however, the exempt orders were free from these forms of control, which apply only to black monks, Austin canons, and nuns.[5]

Assent at least was quite accordant with canon law. Hostiensis insists that care should be taken to secure the patron's assent, lest he should object to the elect, as was his right if the elect were his enemy, dishonourable, or a maladministrator. If his objection were just it could break the election, as in the privileges of the kings of England. As for giving licence, this seems to have been neither expressly allowed nor forbidden in the Decretals, and Hostiensis raises the point inconclusively.[6] In practice it was certainly accepted by the Church for English churches, as necessary not, presumably, to a canonical election but to a stable one. Inquiries made before papal confirmation of a St. Albans election, in 1290, include the question whether licence had been asked

---

[1] Hostiensis, pp. 146v–7v. [2] Innocent IV, p. 182v.
[3] Knowles, *M.O.*, pp. 397–400.
[4] Stubbs, *Charters*, pp. 283–4.
[5] Including Cistercian nuns, subject to patronal rights as to episcopal jurisdiction; e.g. Greenfield Priory (*Register of Bishop Oliver Sutton*, ed. Hill, i. 124, 199).
[6] Hostiensis, pp. 44r–v, 146v.

of the king;[1] the 1274 election at Glastonbury was quashed by the archbishop partly on the ground that licence had not been asked of the right person.[2] During the Minority the pope even ordered the legate to compel prelates and chapters in England not to elect pastors without royal licence, contrary to right and custom.[3]

For houses of royal patronage the king's part in creating a prelate was primarily the enfeoffing of a new tenant-in-chief, often a rich and important one. Up to 1214 it was still more or less an appointment; usually a deputation went to court, theoretically to elect; but there were some struggles for canonical election.[4] Ramsey Abbey had a seven years' vacancy because the monks would not accept the king's nominee.[5] Bury had a celebrated struggle,[6] an epitome of the whole issue: in 1213—after King John's submission and absolution, and his general order for elections in vacant sees and abbeys—the monks elected Abbot Hugh at home in full chapter, instead of by a few monks at court.[7] For two years the abbot's party tried to win the king's consent, backed by Stephen Langton, and opposed by a party who wished to give up Hugh and please the king by following the old custom. The almoner was reported as saying: 'One thing I will maintain, and that is that Hugh the elect will not get in to this house without the king's consent—not for the legate, nor the archbishop, nor yet the pope himself.'[8] But he misjudged the times. The election was confirmed by papal judges, and the abbot installed; the king gave way and accepted his new vassal's fealty.[9]

Meanwhile in November 1213 the king granted free election to specific houses, including St. Albans, Battle, Selby, Barking, and Elstow, all of which held formally canonical elections soon afterwards.[10] But he named four candidates to the Barking nuns, and one whom they must on no account elect; they chose one of the four, the prioress, but she resigned

---

1 *Gesta Abb.* ii. 9.
2 i.e. the bishop of Bath and Wells as patron. Domerham, p. 540.
3 *Cal. Papal L.* i. 65.   4 Knowles, *M.O.*, pp. 399–400.
5 *Chronicon abbatiae Rameseiensis*, ed. Macray, p. 342.
6 *Bury Memorials*, ii. 29–319.   7 Ibid., p. 31.
8 Ibid., p. 64.   9 Ibid., pp. 128–9.
10 *Ann. Mon.* iii (Dunstable), p. 42.

soon afterwards.[1] And the monks of St. Albans, out of caution, elected a monk who had an active kinsman at court; but when the choice at first seemed a bad one, they considered themselves punished for fearing *plus regem quam legem*.[2]

At this time several bishops besides Langton were opposing the 'customs of the realm' and insisting on canonical elections in which the king should 'intrude no-one, name no-one, but only confer the regalia as a sign of consent'.[3] But they were soon let down by the legate, who 'seemed to favour the king more than was just, and to pursue church interests with too little rigour':[4] he intervened in the king's interest in elections of bishops and abbots, following papal instructions to promote the election of persons 'not only outstanding in life and learning, but also useful to the realm and faithful to the king'. The legate's choice was not always unacceptable to the monks; but his general practice caused scandal, and provoked the archbishop to protest. The outcome was John's general promise, 21 November 1214, of free elections in all collegiate churches, reserving the rights of licence and assent, neither of which was to be refused.[5]

After this the king's overt part in elections to royal houses quickly settled down to routine,[6] and a formalized procedure can be reconstructed from the patent and close rolls, the bishops' registers, and sometimes the monastery's own record.[7]

After the abbot's death or resignation, the convent sent two or three monks to the king, wherever he was, to inform him of the vacancy and obtain licence to elect; then the election was held, canonically, in chapter. The elect then went to the king to be presented for his assent; this was granted, and both the king and the convent wrote to the bishop, or to the pope for exempt houses, for his confirmation, stating that

---

[1] *V.C.H. Essex*, ii. 116.

[2] *Gesta Abb.* i. 250, 254.

[3] *Memoriale Walteri de Coventria*, ed. Stubbs, ii. 213 (Barnwell chronicle).

[4] Ibid., p. 216.

[5] The happenings of 1213–14 are covered in Knowles, 'Abbatial Elections', in *Downside Review*, xlix; Gibbs and Lang, *Bishops and Reform*, pp. 60–61; Powicke, *Stephen Langton* (Oxford, 1928), pp. 105–6.

[6] Though in the Minority the situation was confused by the legate's double position; at St. Augustine's, Canterbury, 1220, fealty and delivery of temporalities came *before* papal confirmation by the legate (Thorne, cols. 1872–3).

[7] See Reich, pp. 319–26, and sample documents, pp. 366–71.

the royal assent had been given;[1] this was the equivalent of presentation of a rector. The bishop, if satisfied with the course of the election, told the king he had confirmed it, and asked him to restore the temporalities; the king ordered his escheator to do so, received the new abbot's homage, and wrote to the tenants to be intendant; the bishop had the new head inducted, enjoined obedience on the monks, and gave benediction.

The need for licence and assent was consciously accepted by the religious as a national custom; at Mottisfont in 1293, when the king had the patronage in the heir's minority, licence was asked of him 'according to the custom of the kingdom hitherto observed and approved';[2] and in a long account of the 1301 election at Bury, it is remarked that 'by right and custom of the kingdom of England' licence to elect was always asked, 'especially[3] for churches which are endowed by baronies'.[4] Then, after telling how the monks sent to ask licence had to find the king at Linlithgow, a sixteen days' journey apart from delays by flood and storm, the account continues: '. . . by the custom of the kingdom not only does licence to elect, as related, have to be asked from the lord king, but after the election it is necessary to require his consent', and to go in person.[5]

But licence and assent were so much taken for granted that the monks' records rarely go beyond the bare mention of them. Where elaborate details are recorded, it is to have a record of relations with pope or bishop rather than with the king;[6] the canon law about free elections was originally largely directed and sometimes invoked against the diocesan rather than the patron.[7] Even when the monastic account omits all

---

[1] There might be a ceremonial presentation to the bishop: e.g. Tewkesbury, 1232 (*Mon.* ii. 81).

[2] *Reg. Pontissara*, i. 367: sub-prior's report.

[3] Some houses were exempt (see p. 46) but these were not likely to be holding by barony.

[4] *Bury Memorials*, ii. 299.

[5] Ibid., p. 307.

[6] e.g. St. Albans, 1235: the first election since the ruling that exempt abbots must be confirmed by the pope, which had involved some discussion about procedure (*Gesta Abb.* i. 307, 509–21. Hill, *Letter-books*, p. 82).

[7] As in the twelfth-century case of Alcester and the bishop of Worcester, where the patron, Earl Robert of Leicester, supported the monks' claim to free election against the bishop (*Mon.* iv. 176).

mention of royal licence or assent, this is not significant; in the account of Abbot Simon's election at Bury in 1257, assent is not mentioned, and the editor of the *Memorials* considered that this 'must probably be regarded as evidence of the weakness and unpopularity of Henry III';[1] but in fact assent was given, as the patent rolls show;[2] the procedure was far too well established for 'weakness and unpopularity' to affect it, or for omissions to mention it to matter.[3]

Something like this formal procedure was normal for patrons other than the king. In the twelfth century they too had uncanonical powers, and an express grant was necessary to ensure free election.[4] Roger de Lacy claimed to be present at[5] elections at Nostell Priory, until an agreement of 1201 allowed free election in chapter followed by the patron's assent.[6] Then their rights like the king's became defined and usually canonical, and were recognized as 'the custom of the realm'.[7] An explicit grant of free election as late as the Breuses' to Yeddingham Priory, about 1270,[8] seems exceptional. In 1427 Sir John Dinham claimed at Hartland Abbey to assign a day for the election and to have two votes in it,[9] but this may have been a recent abuse. One apparently isolated[10] anomaly surviving after John's reign was at Cartmel, where the canons elected two candidates of whom the patron, the Earl Marshal, chose one. This was condemned by Gregory IX in 1233,[11] and a settlement in 1250 gave the patron the normal limited rights.[12]

---

[1] *Bury Memorials*, ii. 259.   [2] *Cal. Pat. R. 1247–58*, p. 538.

[3] Cf. St. Peter's, Gloucester, 1284—assent given (*Cal. Pat. R. 1281–92*, p. 135) but not mentioned in the monks' account (*Gloucester Cart.* iii. 23–27).

[4] e.g. William de Mohun to Bruton (*Two Cartularies of . . . Bruton and . . . Montacute*, p. 2); Thomas de St. Walery to Studley, Oxon. (*Mon.* iv. 252).

[5] Or take part in ? *interesse*.   [6] Duchy of Lanc. 25/1223.

[7] Agreement between Glastonbury and the bishop of Bath and Wells, 1266 (*Glastonbury Cart.* i. 95–100) and between Missenden and Joan de Sanford (*Cartulary of Missenden Abbey*, ed. Jenkins, p. 38). Cf. Roger Bigod's grant to the collegiate church of Weybridge, t. Henry III, that if it ever became regular with an abbot or prior it should have free election with presentation to the earl and by him to the bishop, instead of giving the earl a choice of wardens (*V.C.H. Norfolk*, ii. 406).

[8] *V.C.H. Yorks., North Riding*, ii. 490.

[9] R. Pearse Chope, 'Hartland Abbey and the Dinhams', in *Trans. of Devonshire Assoc.* lviii. 79.

[10] Though there were similar arrangements for appointments by the motherhouse in some dependencies; see pp. 58–59.

[11] *Register of Walter Gray*, ed. Raine, p. 167.

[12] *V.C.H. Lancs.* ii. 145.

How normal these were may be seen partly from the king's exercise of them during the wardship of the patron's heir: as with the right of custody, which he exercised or not according to the result of inquisitions on whether the patrons had done so, so with licence and assent, though exceptions here were rarer. Licence was more often excused than consent.[1] John Mansel, for instance, founding Bilsington Priory in 1253, allowed the canons to elect without licence from anyone;[2] and Edward I, to whom the patronage passed,[3] confirmed this exemption provided that they presented to him for his assent.[4]

The whole procedure might be rather less troublesome when some lesser patron gave licence and assent than for a royal foundation. The king had to be sought at a distance, and every stage involved a letter patent and fees for it; whereas for an ordinary patron, short of the greatest magnates, it might only involve two visits[5] to him or his steward[6] at a nearby manor, a journey with his letters of presentation to the bishop,[7] another visit to him with the bishop's letters of institution,[8] the performance of homage, and a word or a letter from him to his bailiff about the temporalities: the same in essentials as in the case of the king.[9]

For Barnwell the whole procedure in a vacancy was laid down in 1256 by the patron Gilbert Pecche, 'ad dilucidationem iuris patronatus quod habeo'. One or two canons were

---

1 See *Reg. Sutton*, i. 124, 151, 169, 207; ii. 43, 81.

2 *The Cartulary . . . of the Priory of Bilsington*, ed. Neilson, pp. 65–66.

3 Ibid., pp. 67–68.

4 *Cal. Pat. R. 1272–81*, pp. 145–6. Cf. Gisburn and Wombridge, exempt from licence but not from assent (*Gisburn Cart.*, p. 98; Eyton, vii. 367). The Clintons claimed 'no custody or lordship' at Kenilworth except presentation of the elect (Harl. 3650, cartulary, f. 65). An example of release from seeking consent is Richard Engayne's to Fineshed (*Cal. Papal L.* i. 92).

5 Examples of convent's letters asking licence or presenting for consent: Farley and Walden to Humphrey de Bohun, 1304 and 1305 (Duchy of Lanc. 34/1/7 and 9).

6 In 1276 the prior-elect of Nostell could have gone to the steward of Pontefract in the earl of Lincoln's absence abroad, though he chose to go to the earl himself (*V.C.H. Yorks.* iii. 234, from cartulary).

7 e.g. Mabel de Gatton to archbishop of Canterbury for Cumbwell, c. 1219 (*Archaeol. Cant.* v. 212–13).

8 Or asking for restoration of temporalities, e.g. to John Biset and John de Rivers about Maiden Bradley (*Registrum Simonis de Gandavo*, ed. Flower and Dawes, p. 681).

9 There might be an arrangement like alternate presentation to a parish church, when the advowson was divided: the priors-elect of Gisburn had to seek assent on alternate occasions from Twenge or Fauconberge, at Skelton or Daneby (*Gisburn Cart.*, p. 98).

to be sent to him, or to his steward if he were abroad, to tell him of the vacancy, saying, 'Sir, we come to you as our patron and announce to you a vacancy in our house, and with your goodwill we shall proceed to our election.' Then 'petita licencia, licet non obtenta, possunt redire libere ad eligendum'. Then they were to present to him and ask his consent.[1] Occasionally the patron might be on the spot: at this same house, about ten years later, both Gilbert Pecche and the bishop of Ely turned up when the prior was ill; the bishop accepted his resignation and went away, but the patron stayed on, gave his licence, and had the elect presented to him in church, after the ceremony that followed the election.[2]

But the normality of these rights has to be gathered mostly from entries in episcopal registers, recording the confirmations and inductions of abbots and priors like the institutions of parish rectors and vicars.[3] The patron is often named as having presented, or given licence or assent. Whether licence or assent is mentioned seems often merely a matter of the registering clerk's method; at Lincoln, Hugh of Wells's rolls almost always have 'assent' where Grosseteste's have 'licence'. The point was to have a record that the patron had been duly consulted. So it may, on the other hand, be important when the patron is not mentioned at all, as happens quite often. It may be simply a slip, or it may be a regular practice: Bishop Giffard's Worcester register consistently omits to name the patron for religious houses. But it may sometimes show that the rights were not exercised, or that no one had them. At Lincoln again, Sutton's register is more thorough and explicit on these points than those of earlier bishops. Miss Hill has pointed out that he watched presentations by ecclesiastics particularly carefully,[4] but he was not careless about lay patrons: the register almost always mentions licence or assent or both, or records that no licence was asked because it was not the custom,[5] or in one case that it was asked contrary to

[1] *Liber Mem.*, p. 49.
[2] Ibid., p. 128.
[3] In some of the Lincoln registers they are distinguished by being written on the dorse.
[4] R. Hill, 'Bishop Sutton and the Institution of Heads of Religious Houses', in *E.H.R.* lviii.
[5] *Reg. Sutton*, i. 124, 151, 169, 207; ii. 43, 81.

custom.[1] There were discrepancies, however, as with New-stead-by-Stamford, for which the register records in 1287 the licence of the patron Isabel de Ros, and in 1292 the canons' assertion that no licence but only consent had to be asked.[2] There was room for doubt about the patron's rights, and then the bishop might confirm without waiting to hear from the patron; in 1261 Bishop Bronscombe confirmed the election of an abbot of Hartland, 'saving the right of Lord Oliver de Dinham, if he has any, to be declared within a month after he comes to England'.[3] But in this case the bishop himself laid some claim to the patronage.[4]

When a bishop was patron of a house in his own diocese, his assent as patron could conveniently be given together with his confirmation as bishop, as in Bishop Pontissara's confirmation of a prior of St. Swithun's in 1295.[5] But the two capacities were by now clearly distinguished. Adam de Domerham tells how in 1218 Bishop Jocelyn admitted the elect of Glastonbury 'as patron' and blessed him 'as diocesan';[6] and Grosseteste in 1240 gave licence to Eynsham Abbey to elect, and assent afterwards 'so far as belonged to the patronage'; but as diocesan he broke the election as uncanonical in form, and appointed the elect by his own authority.[7]

St. Swithun's is a special case, as a cathedral priory; and Domerham's precision about Glastonbury is probably due to the monks' suspicion, having only just escaped from the position of a cathedral priory. With these there is great variety of practice in elections of priors, complicated by the bishop's position as quasi-abbot. The king was patron of the bishopric;[8] but the status of the priory as distinct from the bishopric varied.[9]

[1] *Reg. Sutton*, i. 65; Elsham and Sir John Dyve. Perhaps this was one reason for his quashing the election as irregular.

[2] Ibid., pp. 99, 169; in 1285 (ibid., pp. 70–71) the patron was not mentioned at all. Cf. Kyme, 1291, no licence because the canons claim that they never ask it; but 1293, Philip de Kyme's licence asked and given (ibid., pp. 151, 179).

[3] *Reg. Bronscombe*, p. 100.   [4] See p. 77, n. 4, p. 165.

[5] *Reg. Pontissara*, i. 77. Cf. form of request for licence sent by Bishop Simon de Ghent to Kington St. Michael for future use, describing the monastery as 'of your patronage and of your diocese of Salisbury' (*Reg. Gandavo*, p. 582).

[6] Domerham, pp. 475–6.   [7] *Rotuli Roberti Grosseteste*, ed. Davis, p. 468.

[8] Except Rochester.

[9] For parallel but different problems in secular cathedrals, see Kathleen Edwards, *English Secular Cathedrals in the Middle Ages* (Manchester, 1949), ch. II.

As a simplification, one might say that the priory could logically either be incapable of having a patron of its own, being under the bishop as abbot and not a distinct church by itself, or else have the bishop as its patron and be a distinct church with the prior as its true head. Most cathedral priories seem to have moved towards the latter situation, while the former seems a fair description of their primitive status.

But in the groping and defining of the thirteenth century, neither bishops nor monks admitted these bare alternatives. Nicholas of Ely and John de Pontissara, successive bishops of Winchester, when sued by Edward I for the advowson of the cathedral priory and pressed by the monks for a revision of their status, both claimed at first to be both patron and abbot.[1] Feudal dues and services made the bishop patron,[2] the right to profess the monks made him abbot,[3] and appointing priors and obedientiaries and hearing their accounts made him both.[4] The arguments against a bishop's patronage of his cathedral priory being challenged in a lay court turn largely, by implication, on his being abbot: that if the prior were prelate, the cathedral church would be a monster with two heads, and that to answer about the advowson would be to the prejudice not only of other bishops but 'of all abbots of the realm of England, who are not bound to answer about their priories'.[5] The concessions proposed to the monks by Bishop Nicholas would have given the prior more power and security of tenure within the framework of the bishop's abbatial powers.[6]

The monks on the other hand denied that the bishop was either patron or abbot, and claimed the king as their patron and the prior as their prelate;[7] which would have left the bishop with merely the jurisdiction as ordinary that he had in

[1] The relation of St. Oswald's, Gloucester, to the archbishop of York seems rather like that of a cathedral priory in this respect: in 1281 the archbishop had the 'collation' or 'provision' to the priory as 'patron and prelate' (*Register of William Wickwane*, ed. W. Brown, p. 234).

[2] *Reg. Pontissara* (which includes documents from Bishop Nicholas's episcopacy), ii. 676–81, 685–8. See p. 9.

[3] Ibid., pp. 678–9.

[4] Ibid., pp. 676, 678–9. These were of course much stronger arguments for being abbot than for being patron.

[5] Ibid., pp. 681, 692–3.   [6] Ibid., p. 664.

[7] Ibid., pp. 609–15.

any non-exempt monastery of his diocese, and justifies his
complaints that he would be a bishop without a church, like a
'fish without water, or a monk without a cloister'.[1]

Such claims by the monks would involve the king acting
as patron of the priory in a vacancy, whether the bishopric
were vacant or not: the Winchester monks argued that despite
repeated intrusions of priors by bishops the proper procedure
was free election with royal licence.[2] In practice such action
by the king was probably rare, though in 1235 Henry III
gave licence and assent for the election of a prior at Coventry
though the bishopric was not vacant.[3]

Normally, however, the bishop exercised the rights of abbot
or patron or both in making a prior. At first it was general, and
later not unusual, for him to appoint the prior, perhaps with
some such arrangement as that at Worcester whereby the
bishop chose one out of seven presented by the convent;[4] then
the bishop was evidently head of the monastery, and the king
still patron of the whole church. This is not incompatible even
with free election: one cannot assume that wherever free election obtained, there the bishop was recognized as patron and
not as abbot. At Durham there was free election from John's
reign,[5] long before the patronage question was settled. Sometimes there was an election in the bishop's presence, with
powers of supervision or scrutiny resting with him,[6] or even
nomination with the monks' votes as a guide: 'not relying
much on his examination but rather on his own conscience and
the advantage of the house', as a witness said about the 1244
election at Canterbury.[7] At Rochester as late as 1329, on the
basis of a judgement of Pecham's,[8] the bishop claimed dis-
cretion about which was the *sanior pars* of the convent.[9] That

[1] *Reg. Pontissara*, ii. 681, 687, 692–3.

[2] Ibid., pp. 613–14.

[3] *Cal. Pat. R. 1232–47*, p. 118.

[4] *Register of Godfrey Giffard*, ed. Willis-Bund, i. 50–51. *Acta Stephani Langton*,
ed. K. Major, pp. 160–2. See Knowles, *M.O.*, p. 626; *R.O.*, p. 255.

[5] Ibid., p. 255. Cf. Winchester, 1258 onwards (*Winchester Cathedral Cart.*, ed.
Goodman, pp. 10–11; *Ann. Mon.* iv. 122).

[6] Cf. Edmund Rich and Christchurch, Canterbury (Knowles, *R.O.*, p. 255.
Chronicle in *Gervase of Canterbury*, ed. Stubbs, ii. 136, 140–3, 145–7).

[7] H. Wharton, *Anglia Sacra* (London, 1691), i. 174.

[8] *Reg. Roffense*, pp. 102–4.

[9] Ibid., p. 131; *Reg. of Hamo Hethe*, pt. v, ed. C. Johnson, C. and Y. Soc. 1934,
pp. 430–1.

this sort of election is compatible with the bishop being abbot is clear from the election of a prior at Bury in 1252, the abbot and convent each choosing a monk to count the votes.[1]

On the other hand the survival of some degree of supervision does not by itself prove that the bishop was acting entirely as abbot and not as patron, since canon law tolerated customs whereby ecclesiastical patrons had some part in elections.[2] The arrangement at Rochester was compared with the confirmation of elections at Malling nunnery, where the bishop was simply patron and ordinary.[3]

But the general movement was towards rule of the cathedral priory by a freely elected and perpetual prior, in full charge of a completely separate establishment: and this was certainly often accompanied by a tendency to rationalize the bishop's position as that of patron, giving licence and assent[4] and probably having custody in vacancies,[5] and almost to eliminate his powers as abbot[6] (though this did not affect the monks' position as the cathedral chapter electing the bishop). At an inquiry about Norwich Priory in 1257 it was asked whether the monks elected a prior freely or whether the bishop created him at will: it was answered that he only gave licence to elect and admitted the prior presented to him, with no power to refuse;[7] here the bishop seems more of a patron than a titular abbot. But it is particularly clear at Durham, where as early as 1231 the 'Convenit' established free election with licence from and presentation to the bishop expressly as patron and as ordinary; the prior was to have 'all the dignity and honour of an abbot'; the bishop was to visit 'as ordinary, not as abbot'; though he kept a share in the profession of new monks.[8] In 1272 the monks asking for licence to elect failed to address the bishop as 'patron and lord', and the bishop's clerks pointed out that 'if he were not your patron and lord of the site you would have no need to ask licence of him'. The monks

[1] Tayster, in *Florencii Wigorniensis Chron.*, ed. B. Thorpe, Eng. Hist. Soc. 1849, ii. 184.

[2] See p. 40.   [3] *Reg. Roffense*, p. 131.

[4] Bishop's licence to elect at Ely, 1271, 1273, 1288: J. Bentham, *History and Antiquities of the Church of Ely*, p. 218. Bishop's grant to Bath, 1261: *Wells MSS.* i. 143.   [5] See p. 79.

[6] Knowles, *R.O.*, pp. 254–6.

[7] *Close R. 1256–9*, pp. 66, 137–8.

[8] *Feodarium Prioratus Dunelmensis*, ed. Greenwell, pp. 212–17.

accepted this, and recorded the new prior's receipt from the
bishop of 'a double cure, of temporalities and spiritualities'[1]—
thus they accepted him as their patron and ordinary, about the
same time as they were trying to challenge his part in the pro-
fessions, all that remained of his position as abbot.[2]

Similarly at Winchester, the solution found in 1284 was
for the king to allow the bishop the advowson and for the
monks to admit the bishop as their patron in return for his
giving up his claims as abbot.[3] When at the bishop's request
the monks formulated their considered demands,[4] these no
longer involved the original claim to be of royal patronage;
they may have been partly convinced by the bishop's arguments that royal custody in vacancies would be ruinous, and
that royal patronage would not necessarily destroy the bishop's
powers of appointing a prior.[5] The bishop's charter of 1284[6]
closely follows the monks' final proposals;[7] it gave free election while reserving the bishop's licence 'as patron', limited
powers of custody 'in the name of advocate or patron', and confirmation of the election presumably as patron and ordinary;
while the bishop gave up to the prior full control of the convent's property, the appointment of obedientiaries, and the
reception of monks, but kept, as the last relic of his powers as
abbot, the profession of monks.

This variety in cathedral priories turns partly on the distinction between the prior in an abbey and the prior at the
head of an independent priory, sometimes called respectively
'claustral' and 'conventual'.[8] The former has his own abbot
by whom he is appointed and removed; the latter is in full
charge of the monastery, receives and professes monks, can
sue and be sued under the common law, and above all is 'per-

---

[1] *Annales Dunelmenses*, ed. Barlow, pp. 32–34, 45. Cf. Robert de Graystanes, in *Hist. Dunelm. Scriptores Tres*, ed. Raine, p. 54.

[2] *Ann. Dunelm.*, pp. 20–27.

[3] The prior and convent were also to help the bishop pay the king £2,000 (*Reg. Pontissara*, ii. 716).   [4] Ibid., p. 693.

[5] Ibid., p. 683 (by comparison with the appointment of Cluniac priors by the abbot of Cluny).   [6] *Cal. Charter R.* ii. 287–8.

[7] These were only less explicit about the bishop giving licence, &c., *as patron*, and more explicit about the prior being 'true and perpetual prelate'; while they reserve the bishop's powers of visitation, i.e. as ordinary; and demand not to have to render accounts (this was separately conceded: ibid., pp. 288–9).

[8] Du Cange, *Glossarium*, v. 450. Alteserra, *Asceticon* (Paris, 1674), pp. 101–4. Friedberg, ii. 1134: Clem. 1. 2. ii.

petual'—elected by his convent and removable only for the recognized canonical causes.[1] The prior of a cathedral priory seems to be somewhere between the two: he has a titular abbot, yet his monastery is called a priory, and he may be made perpetual without entirely destroying the bishop's abbatial powers.[2] Even in an ordinary abbey the prior might have some characteristics of a perpetual prior.[3]

But the most important application of the distinction was to priories of different degrees of dependence;[4] and here it often led to doubt and contention about the patron's rights of licence and assent. For the prior of a true cell was like a claustral prior or other obedientiary, wholly under his abbot, although he was not actually within the walls of his motherhouse. He was appointed and removed by the abbot and therefore often called 'momentary' or 'dative';[5] and since his priory did not count as a benefice he did not need to be presented to the bishop nor owe him canonical obedience, except for his parochial cures as rector of appropriated churches. This can be seen from agreements made between St. Albans and the bishops of Lincoln, Norwich, and Durham,[6] about the abbey's cells in those dioceses: by these the abbot was to appoint and remove the priors, and visit and correct them, but he was to present them to the bishop, and they were to promise obedience, for their parish churches.[7]

A dispute in 1280–1 between the bishop of Hereford and the abbot of Reading, about the status of Leominster Priory,[8]

---

[1] Ibid., 596–7: III. 35. ii. Hostiensis, pp. 131r–v.

[2] See Bishop Nicholas's proposals that the prior of Winchester should be made perpetual like those of Canterbury and (?) Worcester (*Reg. Pontissara*, ii. 664).

[3] e.g. election (though this was against the Rule), as at Bury, 1252 (see p. 51, n. 1); or capacity of suing for prior and convent's goods, as perhaps at Stanley (Flower, *Introd. to C.R.R.*, p. 368).

[4] e.g. *Chapters of the Eng. Black Monks*, ed. Pantin, i. 121: prior 'having' or 'not having his own abbot'. Bracton, *De Legibus*, ii. 53, on removable priors. *Mon.* iii. 449: prior of Malvern claims to be a perpetual prior who 'impleads others and answers to others'. See Alteserra, *Asceticon*, p. 492; Morgan, pp. 33–33.

[5] Flower, p. 368. *Chronicon Iohannis abbatis . . . Burgensis*, ed. Sparke, p. 111. Du Cange, v. 450.

[6] *Gesta Abb.* i. 275–7, 278–9, 390 (1219, 1228, and 1247).

[7] Cf. agreement between bishop of Worcester and abbot of St. Denis for Deerhurst (*Reg. G. Giffard*, p. 37); and between bishop of Carlisle and abbot and convent of York for Wetheral (*Reg. of Wetheral Priory*, ed. Prescott, pp. 73–77).

[8] *Reg. Thome de Cantilupo* (ed. Griffiths) and *Reg. Ricardi de Swinfield* (ed. Capes), *passim*; Knowles, *R.O.*, pp. 99–100.

shows the issues involved. The abbot maintained that it was a pure cell, or a mere manor with a monk in charge; the bishop, that it was a priory, which he visited and whose prior he ought to confirm and admit.[1] The king (patron of both houses) supported the abbot, forbidding the bishop to molest the monk sent to take charge of the 'manor' of Leominster, given to Reading by royal gift;[2] he was taking the line of patron of the mother-house protecting its property, not of patron of the cell upholding its status.[3]

But often the patron of a cell, like the diocesan, lost rights as the mother-house gained them and had an interest in maintaining or raising its status: episcopal registers show that presentations to cells, if made at all, were frequently made by the abbot of the mother-house, who thus exercised one distinguishing function of the patron and might absorb the patronage itself.[4] In 1199 the lord of Richmond's steward ordered the bailiff of Wisset to hold an inquisition about whether the abbots of St. Mary's, York, at pleasure appointed and removed the priors of Rumburgh, not consulting the earl or lord, or whether on the other hand they used to present the priors to the earl for his assent and for seisin of the cell. If, as turned out to be the case, there was no presentation to the patron, the newly-appointed prior (himself the bearer of this order) was to do fealty and be admitted at once.[5]

The patron would then often be inclined to raise the house's status to that of a daughter-house not wholly dependent, whose prior held the priory as a benefice, was elected by his own convent with the patron's licence and assent, and could be removed only solemnly and with serious cause. This position, besides giving dignity to his own foundation, made it more worth while and probably easier to get his own candidates in as priors, and made it less likely that the priors would waste the property[6] or submit to excessive exactions by the mother-house.[7] Roger de Lacy in 1202 successfully pleaded against

---

[1] *Reg. Cantilupe*, p. 296; *Reg. Swinfield*, pp. 28, 38–41.
[2] *Reg. Cantilupe*, pp. 263–4.
[3] For the final settlement see *Reg. Swinfield*, pp. 30, 64.
[4] As at Tynemouth: see p. 30.
[5] *Mon.* ii. 612–13.
[6] *Chron. Iohannis abb. Burgensis*, p. 112: removable priors and obedientiaries of Spalding used to take funds abroad with them.   [7] See pp. 148–9.

the prior of La Charité, before papal judges-delegate, that
priors of Pontefract should be presented to him and made
with his assent, which would agree with canon law because he
was the *dominus possessionis*—a reference to an old canon in
Gratian;[1] and that the priors should be removed only for
reasonable cause and with his counsel and assent, since recent
priors had paid to the prior of La Charité far more than the
1 mark p.a. due, because it was in his power to remove them
arbitrarily.[2] Similarly Roger de Huntingfield, patron of the
Cluniac priory of Mendham, made an agreement with Castle
Acre, its mother-house, that the prior could not be deposed
unless for the canonical causes and with the advice both of the
monks of Mendham and of himself as advocate—if they or
he refused, then only the bishop could depose him.[3]

But in these particular cases the patrons were not asking
for actual election: the priors were still to be appointed by
their superiors; such was the Cluniac custom, and the founder
of Mendham had specified that it was to be subject to Acre as
Acre was to Lewes and Lewes to Cluny.[4] For between the two
extremes, of the true cell so dependent on a not too remote
mother-house that there was little room for ties with either
patron or bishop, and the priory with an elected perpetual
prior, there could be many variations in practice, more or less
illogical; owing to the custom of the order, or local practice
that had never been penetrated by the growing legal orderli-
ness of such relationships, or special arrangements with the
founder[5] or later patron.

So the rights of the patron in elections, usually fixed and
formal for independent houses, remained uncertain and variable for dependent houses. They were a matter for compromise or contention between patron and mother-house,
with the bishop and the monks themselves taking sides in
various combinations. It was by no means certain that the
bishop would side with the mother-house against the layman.
He was likely to be jealous of its authority, which could clash
with his in the sphere of spiritualities where the layman was

---

[1] See p. 40, n. 2.   [2] Duchy of Lanc. 25/46.
[3] *Mon.* v. 59.   [4] Ibid., p. 58.
[5] See Knowles, *M.O.*, p. 156, on the tendency of founders to limit the powers of
Cluniac mother-houses.

clearly excluded; and in some ways his interests ran with those of the patron: a perpetual prior would normally be subject to the bishop's visitation and have to attend his synods. Often agreements were made under the aegis of the bishop that were favourable to the patron and distinctly uncanonical. And the monks of the priory might support their patron against the mother-house for the sake of their own independence.

Barnstaple Priory furnishes an example of common interest between convent, patron, and bishop against the mother-house. In 1233 or earlier the prior and the patron, Henry de Tracy, agreed to press St. Martin-des-Champs to allow Barnstaple a perpetual prior, not removable without reasonable cause, to be elected by the monks with the patron's consent and sent to St. Martin for appointment. This was apparently never granted; but in 1265, after a papal judgement, the prior took an oath of obedience to the bishop of Exeter and promised not to give up office on any persuasion or command— that is, presumably, from the mother-house—and to let St. Martin have only 20s. from the priory. And in 1291 it was alleged at the Cluniac General Chapter that the priors of Barnstaple and Exeter were trying to slip out of the order by promising obedience to the bishop, admitting him for visitation, and paying him procurations.[1]

On the other hand the monks might prefer the distant power (if they were alien) to the nearer one, and there were some advantages in dependence. It might be useful in a civil suit for the prior to plead that he could not answer without his abbot; and the prior of Spalding stressed his subjection to an abbot to excuse himself from attending the Benedictine Chapter.[2] The Chapter also had trouble with alien priories of the 'Order of Bec', for example Stoke and St. Neots—'members of the monastery of Bec', as the abbot called them.[3] And failing such solidarity of a group within the order, the hold of the order itself was strong. Cluniac convents that welcomed or suffered their patron's interference were sometimes careful to excuse themselves afterwards, protesting their innocence and

---

[1] See Graham, '. . . St. Martin-des-Champs and its Dependent Priories . . .', in *Journal of the Brit. Archaeol. Assoc.* III. xi. 41–42.

[2] Pantin, i. 121–6.

[3] Ibid., p. 44; iii. 164. Morgan, pp. 27–28.

loyalty and describing their misfortunes; as did Lewes in
1200, to the prior and convent of Cluny,[1] and Thetford perhaps in 1301, to all Cluniac priors in England.[2]

The trouble about Lewes in 1200 shows the issue clearly.
The patron, Earl Hamelin de Warenne, complained to the
pope that although the prior of Lewes ought to be set up by
the monks' election and the earl's consent, the abbot of Cluny
had intruded a prior, whose removal the earl required. The
monks themselves, despite their later protestations, supported
the earl: asserting that by common law (that is, common canon
law) the election belonged to the chapter with the patron's
assent; that the prior should not be removed without canonical
cause; and that the only service they owed to Cluny was 100
shillings a year. The abbot, on the other hand, claimed the
special Cluniac custom against the common law: the prior of
Lewes, he said, was always appointed by the abbot of Cluny,
as in all Cluniac priories.[3]

The pope ordered the earl to restore all he had taken during
the quarrel, and the monks to obey the abbot's prior while the
case went on;[4] the earl tried to delay obeying this sentence,
shut the abbot himself out of Lewes and Castle Acre, and
obtained a royal prohibition against the judges; the archbishop was preparing to excommunicate him[5] when a settlement was made.

A century later, when such problems might be expected to
have worked themselves out, a similar issue arose at Thetford.
The priors had always been appointed by the abbot of Cluny,
and presented to the earl of Norfolk for the temporalities;[6]
but in 1300, taking advantage of the war with France, the
monks elected one of themselves, supported and perhaps persuaded by Earl Roger Bigod. The bishop took the same side.
Apparently the earl refused to let the abbot's nominee inside
the priory, while the bishop ill-treated the abbot's messengers.

---

[1] Duckett, i. 99–101; Bernard et Bruel, *Receuil des chartes de Cluni*, v. 4398.

[2] Duckett, i. 189–92; Bernard et Bruel, v. 4390. 'Environ 1200' in the latter, but
see pp. 57–58 for possible context.

[3] Duckett, i. 87; Bernard et Bruel, v. 4381.

[4] Duckett, i. 89.

[5] Ibid., p. 95. Bernard et Bruel, v. 4408. Guilloreau, in *Millénaire de Cluny*
(Mâcon, 1910), i. 335–7.

[6] Duckett, i. 116 (1308 inquisition).

The pope ordered that the election be revoked and the earl warned not to interfere;[1] and Archbishop Winchelsey refers to the elected prior as 'intruded . . . by abuse of secular power'.[2]

One solution to this problem which seems to have proved fairly stable though it was certainly not canonical, was that the abbot of the mother-house should name two or three, and the patron should choose one of these as prior. This was the settlement for Lewes in 1201; the abbot was to name two of the best men of the order, except the priors of Cluny and La Charité, and whichever of them the earl's envoys chose was to be accepted as prior and not removed without reasonable cause; while the abbot was to have his full spiritual rights of discipline and correction, but only 100s. a year for all temporal rights.[3] Almost exactly the same settlement (except that two monks were to take part in the choice) was made in 1208 for Farley, between Henry de Bohun and the prior of Lewes;[4] and there are non-Cluniac instances—Lancaster in 1209, between King John and the abbot of Séez (who paid 200 marks and two palfreys for the arrangement)[5] and Tutbury, between the earls of Derby and the abbots of St. Pierre-sur-Dives.[6]

The advantage of this for both sides was that it combined partial appointment by the mother-house with some scope for influence by the patron;[7] it shifted his interest towards the side of the mother-house, and by-passed the question of election by the convent. It was contrary to canon law,[8] and Gregory IX's condemnation of the Lewes settlement[9] was incorporated in the decretals;[10] it was evidently a test case. But there and at Tutbury the arrangement was still in force in the fourteenth century,[11] which shows what irregular prac-

---

[1] *Cal. Papal L.* i. 594–5.

[2] *Reg. Winchelsey*, p. 703. In 1304 the convent again elected a prior with the earl's licence (ibid., p. 792).

[3] *Early Yorks. Charters*, ed. Farrer, viii. 121; Duckett, ii. 92; Bernard et Bruel, v. 4397; *Calendar of Documents . . . in France*, p. 517. See Knowles, *M.O.*, p. 157.

[4] *Mon.* v. 27 (from Lewes cartulary).

[5] *Pipe Roll 11 John*, p. 105.   [6] *Mon.* iii. 395–6.

[7] See p. 64.   [8] See p. 40.

[9] Bernard et Bruel, vi. 4574. The earl appealed against it; see *Early Yorks. Charters*, viii. 122.

[10] Friedberg, ii. 92: I. 6. li. Cf. Cartmel, p. 45.

[11] Lewes, c. 1240, 1298, 1324, 1327: Bernard et Bruel, vi. 4779, 5470 note 2; *V.C.H. Sussex*, ii. 67; Duckett, i. 122. Tutbury, *Mon.* iii. 395–6.

tice remained possible throughout the legalistic thirteenth century.

In many dependent houses, however, where the prior was conventual to the extent of being admitted by the bishop but probably not to the extent of being elected, the patron had a less objectionable part: simply assent to the appointment.[1] Bishops' registers sometimes describe the abbot of the mother-house and the patron of the cell as jointly presenting the prior to the bishop,[2] that is to say, the new prior arrives with letters from both; which implies an earlier presentation to the patron for his assent. Sometimes this assent may have been quite secondary: in 1227 a prior of St. Neots was admitted on the abbot of Bec's presentation 'with the good will' of the earl of Gloucester, but in 1248 one was admitted with merely the note that no objection was raised by anyone that could retard the business:[3] this suggests that while the earl's dissent would be an obstacle his express consent was unnecessary.[4] And when in Bishop Sutton's time a new prior of Minting, sent by the abbot of Fleury, brought letters from the earl of Lincoln which were irregular in form, reference to Grosseteste's register showed that a former prior had been presented by the abbot alone, and it was decided that the abbot's letters would do.[5] On the other hand about the same time a prior of Haugham, cell of St. Severin, could evidently not be admitted without the same earl's letters, which took some time and trouble to obtain.[6] It is likely that in some cases where the patron appears from the bishop's register to have no rights he may have signified his assent to the mother-house before-hand, although it did not have to be addressed to the bishop or was not considered vital enough to record. But some presentations to patrons may have meant simply sending the new prior to do fealty and receive the temporalities, implying assent in practice but not in the technical sense—that is, not

[1] Cluniac examples are Prittlewell (*Close R. 1259–61*, pp. 43, 45, 51–52), Pontefract (ibid., pp. 42–43, 253; and see p. 55), and Barnstaple (1281 inquest: Graham, *Brit. Arch. Assoc.* III. xi. 40).

[2] e.g. Tywardreth (*Reg. Bronscombe*, p. 188), Talkarn (ibid., p. 157), Blythburgh (*V.C.H. Suffolk*, ii. 92, from fourteenth-century Norwich registers).

[3] *Rotuli Hugonis de Welles*, ed. Phillimore and Davis, iii. 54. *Rot. Grosseteste*, p. 295.

[4] But later Earl Gilbert II insisted on his consent being asked (Morgan, p. 29, n. 4).   [5] *Reg. Sutton*, i. 134–7.   [6] Ibid., pp. 131–4.

requiring any expressed assent nor any part in the presentation, if any, to the bishop.[1]

Such routine relationships had not usually been established
at the beginning of the century, which was a time of doubt
and controversy, when the patron might still be claiming to
appoint, the convent beginning to claim to elect, and the
mother-house opposing both. It was then, to clear up such
problems, that some of the uncanonical arrangements were
made between mother-house and patron. The 1208 settlement for Farley ended an involved controversy. Trouble had
begun late in the twelfth century when the prior of Lewes
removed a prior of Farley, contrary to the charter granted to
the founders by an earlier prior of Lewes, which had given
the founders the appointment of a prior (under the name of
'their free election'), allowing them the pick of the monks of
Farley, or of Lewes below the sub-prior, and had undertaken
not to remove the prior without the advocate's advice and
will.[2] Peace was made for the occasion by formally restoring
the deposed prior and removing him again at Henry de
Bohun's request, and a prior was substituted 'by choice and
will' of Henry, according to the charter.[3] The 1208 settlement was anyhow better than this arrangement which gave
all power to the patron and allowed neither the general rule
of election nor the Cluniac custom of appointment by the
mother-house.[4]

At Thetford on the other hand, where no such arrangement
was made, Earl Roger Bigod made trouble in 1237, preventing the abbot of Cluny from visiting the priory, so as to extract

[1] e.g. Modbury; according to 1289 inquisition, the patron (James de Oxton)
and his ancestors always had priors presented to them by the abbot of St. Pierre-
sur-Dives; but in 1275, only the mother-house is mentioned as presenting to the
bishop (Cal. Inqu. Misc. i, No. 1462, and Reg. Bronscombe, p. 207). Examples of
letters of presentation to the patron are Duchy of Lanc. 25/171 and 34/1/3: 1265,
abbot of Lonlay to Hugh de Neville for Stogursey, and 1268, abbot of Sherborne
to Payn de Chaworth for Kidwelly; and a form of words was agreed on, 1255,
between Hugh Peverel and Montacute, for Carswell (Montacute Cart., p. 175). These
all seem to state the bearer's appointment as a fact and ask favour for him but not
written consent.
[2] Acta Stephani Langton, p. 50: Langton's confirmation of Hubert Walter's confirmation of Prior Hugh's charter.
[3] Duchy of Lanc. 27/3: settlement by bishop of Ely, 1189–96.
[4] It is not clear why Langton confirmed his predecessor's confirmation of the
original charter.

from him an undertaking not to make a prior there without
the earl's consent as advocate. The abbot complained to the
king, who ordered the earl to stop preventing the visitation,
since he was exceeding his scope as a layman, and the abbot
to do nothing whereby the earl should lose his advowson.[1]
Negotiations for a settlement were begun, but probably came
to nothing; and the convent was made to acknowledge to
Cluny that no one but the abbot had ever appointed their
prior and that no one else's assent was required for his
appointment or removal.[2]

There was similar trouble in ordinary Benedictine dependencies: for instance, in John's reign, at Binham, where the
abbot of St. Albans deposed what the patron Robert fitz
Walter possessively called 'his' prior. According to Paris's
rather lurid account, Robert used a forged charter by which
no prior could be removed without his consent; and when his
suit in the Curia Regis failed he besieged the priory, but was
chased off by the king, and did not again use the charter, which
was given up to the abbey after his death.[3]

St. Albans had trouble with other cells, and not only at the
beginning of the century. The countess of Arundel challenged
the abbot's right to appoint and recall priors of Wymondham
without consulting her; and in 1264 a startlingly uncanonical
settlement was made, that the countess should choose three
monks of St. Albans, one of whom the abbot would appoint.
This must have become a dead letter, however, after her death,
for the chronicler describing it begins: 'It was once the harm-
ful custom . . .'.[4]

At yet another St. Albans cell, Tynemouth, of royal foundation, arose the common situation of the patron in pursuit of
his rights of licence and assent, backed by the monks making
a bid for independence; but in this case the king, after suing
the abbot,[5] gave up everything, making the priory a true cell

---

[1] *Abbreviatio Placitorum*, p. 106. The word *institucio* is printed in two places
where the context suggests that the word is really, as elsewhere in the passage,
visitacio. The visitation was not adjudged to the prior as stated in *V.C.H. Norfolk*,
ii. 364.

[2] Bernard et Bruel, vi. 4725.

[3] *Gesta Abb.* i. 226–30; *Cur. Reg. R.* vi. 55, 133–4.

[4] *Gesta Abb.* i. 407; ii. 82.

[5] *Select Cases in King's Bench*, ii. 137.

and abandoning its monks to the mercy of the abbot: who promptly put the prior in irons for rebellion.[1]

Sometimes it was the convent that started the trouble, and the patron then gave his support. In 1230 the monks of Spalding opposed an appointment by the abbot of Angers[2] and appealed to the pope; Earl Ranulf of Chester then revoked his letter assenting to the appointment. In the end a different prior was chosen, by election of the abbot and the monks of Spalding, with the earl's licence and assent.[3] Evidently here, as so often, the bishop was on the patron's side; for the earl wrote to thank him for wishing to preserve his right of patronage.[4] Soon after this the earl, the abbot, the bishop, and the priory made several settlements,[5] under the last of which the prior was to be almost wholly conventual: permanent, with full powers in temporalities and spiritualities (except that the abbot was to profess novices and visit at intervals), subject to the bishop's visitation, elected with the patron's licence and assent by his own convent—but the abbot was to take part in the election, provided he arrived within three months.[6] The next abbot of Angers tried to undo this and deposed the prior; but in 1242 a second settlement was made,[7] much as before, with the patroness Margaret de Lacy and her husband Walter Marshal. This Prior Simon was remembered for having thus freed his house from servitude.[8]

But if the patron claimed more than licence and assent the monks might oppose him and uphold their obedience to the mother-house, since they would not have free election in any case. At Hatfield Broadoak in 1235 the earl of Oxford sent an outsider as prior; the monks objected, saying that the abbot of St. Melaine ought to appoint; the bishop of London supported the earl even in this irregular action, and excommunicated the monks. The abbot appealed to the pope, com-

---

[1] *Gesta Abb.* ii. 22.
[2] But in 1284 they exploited their dependence: see p. 56.
[3] *Rot. Wells*, iii. 182–5.
[4] Ibid., p. 185.
[5] Duchy of Lanc. 25/48, 27/31, 25/49. The last (June 1232) is in *Mon.* iii. 220.
[6] The canonical limit within which the election must be made.
[7] *Mon.* iii. 221–2. In force in 1294: *Reg. Sutton*, i. 186.
[8] *Chron. Iohannis abb. Burgensis*, pp. 105, 111–12: a ull and fairly accurate account except for making Simon the originally appointed prior.

plaining that the intruded prior had stolen books and treasure and fed the monks like swineherds.[1] In 1254 the case was settled by the succeeding bishop entirely against the mother-house, making the priory independent and giving the patron the rights which followed from this—not appointing as he originally claimed, but giving licence, having the elected prior presented to him, and presenting him to the bishop. The abbot was merely to receive notice of the prior's death.[2]

In several of these cases, especially if the convent was inclined to oppose him, the patron resorted to force; perhaps preventing communication or keeping out a prior, perhaps seizing property as a kind of distraint, perhaps even besieging and half-starving the monks.[3] 'Lay force' was something of a conventional phrase, and the violence would certainly be exaggerated;[4] but it is obvious that a local noble could do much to exact his rights, or more than his rights, by force or threats of force.

But quiet influence within the framework of the formal rights was probably far more usual. Sometimes a patron's real power might actually be increased by his house's subjection to a mother-house, if he had more influence with the abbot of the mother-house than he would have had with the whole convent. The abbot of St. Albans twice appointed a prior of Wymondham at the instance of the earl of Arundel. The succession of priors here in the few years after 1217 shows the kind of mixed complaisance and resistance that a patron might meet from the mother-house. In 1217 a prior was appointed at the earl's request, but had to be recalled for sheer silliness;[5] the next was recalled for wasting the revenues and courting the earl's favour;[6] the next was objected to by the earl, successfully and rightly, as the chronicler admits;[7] the next, Thomas Medicus, seems to have been chosen because he had a special claim on the new earl's regard, having been on pilgrimage

---

[1] *Cal. Papal L.* i. 152.

[2] *V.C.H. Essex*, ii. 108; *Hist. MSS. Comm.* viii. 632.

[3] Robert fitz Walter and Binham (*Gesta Abb.* i. 226–7). Earl Warenne and Lewes (Duckett, i. 87). Earl of Oxford and Hatfield Broadoak (*Cal. Papal L.* i. 152). Earls of Norfolk and Thetford (ibid., pp. 594–5, and *Abbrev. Plac.*, p. 106).

[4] All the accounts come from the mother-house.

[5] *Gesta Abb.* i. 260.

[6] Ibid., pp. 272, 274.

[7] Ibid., p. 274.

with the earl's father and brought his body home from Italy.[1]
All this is influence quite apart from his formal powers. Later
in the century the countess had a formal share in the appointment,[2] and this led to the appointment of one, Adam Poleyn,
who died in 1303, who inclined more to the patron's will than
to the abbot's, and allowed the patron to have his own way
and to injure the priory.[3]

Such influence was less likely with foreign abbots; yet even
they had interests in England and hence a motive for not
offending a great man and his friends, and the patron of a rich
and famous monastery like Lewes would certainly take an
interest in appointments there. Archbishop Pecham wrote
to the abbot of Cluny in 1285 urging him to make a good
appointment at Lewes, pointing out, amongst other considerations, that if the Earl Warenne were offended, 'being
a much-loved prince, you will offend all the princes and prelates of England', and asking him to consent to the earl's
wishes 'if he asks to have someone preferred there of the English tongue'.[4] But there seems to have been no response to
this, for a Frenchman was appointed who was already known
as one who 'sells and alienates whatever he can'.[5]

There remains the broader question of how far patrons of
independent houses were likely to go in open interference
after John's promise of free elections, and how much real
influence their formal part in elections carried with it. The
second question is probably insoluble, but it is inherently
likely that there was a lot of unspectacular influence which
would leave no trace: too informal to involve documents, too
questionable to be mentioned in their own chronicle, not out-
rageous enough to provoke protest or scandal. We are more
likely to hear of what was probably exceptional—any clumsy,
overt interference or serious blow to free election.

Unwillingness to have an enemy as tenant might provoke
interference. In the first 'free' election at Barking John insisted that the nuns should elect one of four whom he named,

---

[1] *Gesta Abb.* i. 275.   [2] See p. 61.
[3] *Gesta Abb.* ii. 82.   [4] *Reg. Peckham* (R.S.), iii. 904.
[5] John de Chartres, formerly prior of Bermondsey, Northampton and Wenlock
(see R. Graham, *English Ecclesiastical Studies*, pp. 105, 122). In 1324 Edward II
wrote to the abbot suggesting two candidates for presentation to the earl (*V.C.H.
Surrey*, ii. 71).

but in any case not the sister of Robert fitz Walter.[1] Later such open interference is rare; but there is one outstanding case, when King Henry in 1246 forbade the election of a particular nun as abbess of Shaftesbury. This was Agnes de la Ferere, related to the traitor William de Mariscis.[2] She had already been one of the rivals in a disputed election in 1243;[3] this was probably how the king's attention had been drawn to her. On the day, 14 May, that he gave the nuns licence to elect,[4] he ordered the custodian to announce publicly that they must not elect Agnes de la Ferere, coming of the stock of the king's enemies and totally unacceptable to him.[5]

But from this high ground the king quietly climbed down, although he might quite canonically have refused assent on the ground that the elect was his enemy.[6] By July he had accepted the possibility of her election, but had arranged with the bishop of Salisbury that should she be elected a royal clerk should take part in the bishop's examination of the election.[7] In the autumn this was done;[8] and in January the king gave his assent, in the regular way, to Agnes's election.[9] Perhaps he had decided that his suspicions were groundless; but probably a factor in his decision was the force of custom, unwillingness to do anything so drastic as to refuse assent; public objection beforehand had been unusual enough. Incidentally, Shaftesbury was one of the small group of great royal nunneries which owed knight-service, which perhaps helps to explain the king's concern. But much more common than fear of an enemy would be objection to an incompetent man who would not be a good tenant,[10] or even, one may conjecture, to a disagreeable man who would not be a good host.

Apart from this negative interest, there was the positive interest in gaining the place for a friend or servant. This element of favour or reward could not be so effective for religious houses as for other benefices, once there was some degree of free election, especially since choice was virtually restricted to the religious of the same order. But a patron

[1] *V.C.H. Essex*, ii. 116, from the close rolls.
[2] *Cal. Pat. R. 1232–47*, p. 489. See Powicke, ii. 755–6.
[3] *Close R. 1242–7*, p. 28.   [4] *Cal. Pat. R. 1232–47*, p. 480.
[5] *Close R. 1242–7*, p. 424.   [6] Hostiensis, p. 145*v*.
[7] *Cal. Pat. R. 1242–7*, p. 484.   [8] Ibid., p. 489.
[9] Ibid., pp. 495, 497.   [10] See pp. 147–9, 154–6.

might interest himself in the advancement of a friend or relative already in the convent or a neighbouring convent; and the king could go further than this, having so many houses of his patronage, and being great enough to keep prelates in his service away from their duties, even against their Rule.[1] If the prior of one house had served him well, he could put him forward for the next vacant abbacy of the same order. This was obvious in the days of open royal appointment; Roger Norris of Evesham was accused of boasting that he did not get his abbacy from those 'dogs', the monks, but from the king for his service.[2] But even after 1214 there are occasional open attempts to use abbacies to reward or secure good service. In 1215, before free election had had time to become standardized, John asked the convent of Ramsey to elect one of three whom he named—all outsiders—as they were of good fame and would be useful to him in the kingdom.[3] But in fact they elected their own prior Hugh Foliot, who had the king's assent apparently without difficulty.[4]

Later there is a clear case of such intentions on Henry III's part, though again ineffective. In 1253, on his way to Gascony, he wrote to the guardians of the realm: 'As the king has not yet had respect unto Elerius, abbot of Pershore, according to his merits . . . he commands them that, as soon as an abbey of the order of St. Benedict fit for so great a man falls void . . . they are to endeavour by such means as seem most efficacious to promote him thereto.'[5] Elerius was escheator citra Trent, and an important minister of the king;[6] yet in spite of this letter he was still abbot of Pershore eleven years later, when he resigned. Both these cases show that it was conceivable that the king could induce even a great and rich convent to elect a nominated outsider, but by no means certain.

A far more discreditable use of influence is attributed in the Dover chronicle to the Lord Edward just before he became king. A monk of Reading, imprisoned and excommunicated by his abbot for getting into arrears as an obedientiary, had sent £100 to Edward for his crusade. For this,

---

[1] See p. 120.   [2] Chron. Evesham, p. 241.
[3] Rotuli Litterarum Patentium, ed. Hardy, p. 183. The words sound like an echo of the legate's instructions the previous year.
[4] Rot. Lit. Pat., p. 187.   [5] Cal. Pat. R. 1247–58, p. 211.
[6] He had also been bailiff of Fécamp and prior of Cogges: see Reich, p. 330.

Edward not only got him out of prison, but privately told his servants 'that if they saw any vacant place of an abbey or priory, they should provide him to it'. In consequence this 'vagabond monk' got a letter from the chancellor, at the suggestion of the constable of Dover, presenting him as prior to the monks of Dover—who accepted him, in the absence of their real prior with whom they were quarrelling about their subjection to Christchurch, Canterbury.[1] (The Crown's claim to the advowson, implied by this presentation, was probably the vacancy of the archbishopric; its practical power was that the constable had taken custody of the priory for its protection.)[2] The account both of the intrusion and of the intruded prior's background may be malicious; but the story implies a belief in the availability of abbacies and priories.

The most acceptable man might be elected without the need for a word to be spoken. Paris says that Henry III's great friend and servant Richard of Crokesley was unanimously elected abbot of Westminster, for fear that otherwise the king might abandon their half-built church.[3] The hope of favours to the abbot which would benefit the convent might have the same effect. The election at Peterborough in 1299 of Abbot Godfrey, who was favoured by the king, was followed by three benefits carefully noted by the chronicler: Edward's gift of a cup, 'a very great sign of love from so great a lord'; his personal warning to the abbot to get a certain fine paid quickly because there would shortly be a change of coinage; and his allowing the abbot a confirmation of charters for the chancery fee alone, when, as the treasurer remarked, 'if he were not your friend, he would not have got away for less than 1000 marks'.[4]

But in any case the king (or other patron) had a weapon in his hold on the temporalities before and after the election. There is one apparently gross case (probably highly coloured by Paris) of unfree election, at Peterborough in 1249: King Henry was angry with the convent for opposing the former abbot, a partisan of his; his custodians were extortionate; so to avoid the total confiscation of their goods, they elected

[1] *Gervase of Cant.*, ii. 267. He seems to disappear from the scene after this.
[2] See p. 96. [3] *Chron. Maj.* iv. 589.
[4] *Hist. Burgensis*, Whytesley, p. 153.

vellent nollent at the king's command John de Caux, prior of Winchester—although he was of another house and a foreigner.[1]

This emphasizes how the king could really make use of abbacies and priories for his servants and supporters only if there were some degree of interchange between houses. For bishoprics, where the range was far wider, direct requests and indirect pressure on elections were far more frequent.

It might not require much pressure to induce a convent to elect a relation of the patron. There is a strong suggestion of pleasing the patron, Earl Roger Bigod, in the election[2] of an outsider to the Cluniac priory of Thetford in 1304; the new prior was a monk of Walden, a whole county away and not even Cluniac; but his name was Thomas Bigod.[3] A younger son of Vitalis Engayne, patron of Fineshed Priory, was prior there 1226–33;[4] the prioress of Sinningthwaite about 1219 was descended from the founder Bertram Haget;[5] a member of the Scales family, patrons of Blackborough, was prioress in 1238.[6] There are probably many such cases.

In the baronial complaint against papal provisions after the Council of Lyons, before it was realized that provisions would not be made to churches of a layman's advowson, it was pointed out on behalf of king, barons, and knights as patrons of churches, including abbeys and priories, that in England it was the custom that younger sons should take orders and be admitted to dignities and benefices, by election, presentation, or collation.[7] This shows that election to the headship of a monastery, as well as presentation to ordinary benefices, was an accepted means of providing for cadets of noble families.

Free election remained, then, a live issue after 1214, since there were always ways of exerting influence[8] and advantages

---

[1] *Chron. Maj.* v. 84–85. The Peterborough chronicler says he was elected 'regis interveniente favore', and praises his rule (*Hist. Burgensis*, Whytesley, pp. 128–9).

[2] See p. 58, n. 2. [3] *Reg. Winchelsey*, p. 792.

[4] *V.C.H. Northants.* ii. 135–6. [5] *V.C.H. Yorks.* iii. 176, n. 3.

[6] *V.C.H. Norfolk*, ii. 351.

[7] H. Cole, *Documents illustrative of English History in the 13th and 14th Centuries*, p. 360.

[8] There was probably an extra loophole for outside influence when the election was made by compromission; in 1233 at Glastonbury the compromissors chose one, at the wish of the bishop (who was then patron), whom the other monks disliked—he had been chaplain to their old enemy Bishop Savary (Domerham, p. 478).

in doing so. In a vacancy at Tewkesbury in 1231, during the
wardship of Richard de Clare, an appeal was made in chapter
that no one should be elected under pressure from the king
or the justiciar, and the decree of the Fourth Lateran Council
against elections by abuse of secular power was read aloud:
this suggests that special precautions were needed when the
patronage of this rich abbey was for once in the king's hand.[1]
Miss Gibbs quotes the opinion of the canons of Wells in 1244,
about 'the power of the magnates who will intrude themselves
into any election. All the churches of England, in spiritualities
and temporalities, have suffered much and are in great danger
. . . from these great men.'[2] Edmund of Abingdon was apparently more concerned about delays than about interference:[3]
but the bishops complained in 1253 that 'no one can be promoted in cathedral or conventual churches unless intruded
by the king',[4] and in 1257 to the same effect.[5] This was fairly
true of cathedral churches,[6] but much exaggerated for monasteries. But there was some interference, and Paris says that in
the discussion on free election in 1256 King John's grant was
of little use because even the pope took the line that it was not
expedient to offend princes.[7] Nor was free election safe in
Edward I's reign: the First Statute of Westminster includes
the clause 'Because elections ought to be free, the king forbids
upon forfeiture that any great man or other by arms or by
menace disturb free election being made.'[8]

But the king and his magnates must have accepted the
canonical position in principle to make this statute; and in
fact obvious cases of interference are rare, and not always
successful.

On the whole the value set on the formal rights of licence
and assent suggests that there was not much really formidable
power outside them; had there been, the forms would not
have mattered much. As it was, the forms were very important; in Bishop Bronscombe's quarrel with the monks of
his priory of Plympton, licence and presentation were made

[1] *Ann. Mon.* i. 83.
[2] *Wells MSS.* i. 117. Gibbs and Lang, p. 90.
[3] Ibid., p. 142.   [4] *Chron. Maj.* v. 373.
[5] Ibid. vi. 353–4.   [6] Gibbs and Lang, pp. 90–91.
[7] *Chron. Maj.* v. 540–4.
[8] *Statutes*, i. 26 (c.v.). Cf. 1309 grievances: *Reg. Winchelsey*, p. 1030.

the criteria of their submission to their patron.[1] In the same way licence and assent were, with custody, the key points of the quarrel between the king and the bishop of Bath and Wells over Glastonbury. King Edward gave the abbot a mandate not to get licence to elect from anyone but the king;[2] and two years later the monks were particularly careful to get his licence and assent instead of the bishop's;[3] these were the marks of patronage, and to establish himself in seisin of these two rights was half the battle.

The king kept a personal hold on the giving of licence and assent for the greater houses; when he went abroad they had to seek him abroad, unless they were specially excused;[4] but the smaller houses could usually go more cheaply to the guardian of the realm, as a matter of government routine.[5] Some other patrons allowed their monasteries to resort to their stewards in their own absence abroad;[6] and Earl Henry de Lacy, one of the greatest lay patrons, commissioned his mother, in his absence abroad, to present to benefices and give licence for and consent to the elections of abbots and priors.[7] To the king, and probably to many other patrons, fees had to be paid for the letters of licence and assent; with travelling besides, it was an expensive business.[8] The head of a poor house might as a favour be excused from coming in person even within England.[9] And it was not even yet so automatic that it might not need some string-pulling to help it on: in 1304 Bishop Pontissara promised the nuns of Winchester that he and his friends would try to further the business

---

[1] *Reg. Bronscombe*, p. 225.   [2] Domerham, p. 537.

[3] Ibid., pp. 538–9. *Wells MSS.*, pp. 166, 476.

[4] e.g. Wherwell, 1262: abbess to be admitted and have her fealty taken by the justiciar and chancellor because of the king's long absence—not to be a precedent (*Close R. 1261–4*, p. 162). Adam Marsh asked the archbishop to get this favour for Osney, 1254 (*Monumenta Franciscana*, ed. J. S. Brewer, R.S. 1858, p. 85).

[5] 1242, all abbeys and priories worth over 50 marks a year had to go to the king abroad (*Cal. Pat. R. 1232–47*, p. 290). 1253, certain named abbeys had to go abroad (ibid. *1247–58*, p. 206). But 1262, the elect of Tavistock was sent to the king though the house was poor, 'since we have no power to admit any elect or give assent to elections on your behalf' (*Close R. 1261–4*, p. 132).

[6] See p. 46, n. 6, p. 47; Nostell, Barnwell.

[7] *Reg. Sutton*, i. 100, 120, 131–4.

[8] See *Close R. 1261–4*, pp. 132, 147; correspondence about Tavistock.

[9] e.g. Bishop Simon de Ghent's request to the king for the prioress-elect of Bromhale: the nuns were poor, and sited in the conventional 'loco horroris et vaste solitudinis' (*Reg. Gandavo*, ii. 732–3).

of obtaining royal licence, and hoped they would remember him in their prayers for this.[1]

But whatever trouble, expense, or delay[2] there might be, it seems that actual refusal of licence or assent, by the king or by other patrons, was very rare indeed: King John's promise that they should not be refused was effective. This seems to show that these rights represented no real power to veto the election, but were signs of patronage, carrying with them opportunity for informal influence. Patrons were not concerned to withhold licence and assent, but rather were anxious to grant them—to keep seisin of these formal rights by exercising them. I have found no case of licence being refused; and the one or two cases of refusal of consent seem to be caused not by objection to the person elected, nor even by the desire to prolong the vacancy (this would be done, if at all, by delay, not refusal), but by offence at omission to obtain licence beforehand or obtaining it from the wrong person. In 1247 Giles de Argentein perhaps refused outright to accept, anyhow 'began to oppose', an election at Wymondsley Parva, *sed nihil profecit*:[3] his reason may have been that after a disputed election was cancelled a new election had been made with licence from the bishop;[4] it looks as if Grosseteste had been ignoring the lay patron. More clearly, in 1296 Philip d'Arcy refused consent to an election at Nocton Park, explicitly because the canons had not asked licence. It was argued that they were exempt from this,[5] and d'Arcy provisionally gave in; but when the election was quashed as irregular and another one ordered, he refused again on the same grounds; the election was completed none the less, and it seems probable that he gave way eventually.[6] The trouble, in fact, was about the formal rights, not about the election itself.[7] The 1201 agreement between Nostell Priory and Roger de Lacy allowed the

---

[1] *Reg. Pontissara*, i. 182. [2] But see pp. 75–76.

[3] *Ann. Mon.* iii (Dunstable), p. 175. (The elect was a canon of Dunstable.)

[4] *Rot. Grosseteste*, p. 292.

[5] Licence was given in 1240 (ibid., p. 53) but not in 1286 (*Reg. Sutton*, i. 85).

[6] Ibid., pp. 209–11.

[7] One might compare the Lord Edward's actions at Chester just after its surrender in August 1265. He was angry with the new abbot of St. Werburgh's for being elected with Earl Simon's licence instead of his own, and excluded him for a day, but the next day admitted him, and restored the wine consumed by his (Edward's) household (*Annales Cestrienses*, ed. Christie, pp. 92–96).

patron to contradict the election of an unsuitable person, in which case the matter was to be taken before an ecclesiastical judge;[1] but it is doubtful whether even this would have been considered at all normal later in the century: it was the bishop's job to break elections of bad prelates, and the patron's mild influence would usually serve to prevent elections of unwelcome ones.

Trouble about the formal rights sometimes broke out when the bishop provided a head, after breaking an election either because the elect was not fit or because of a technical fault in procedure. In the latter case he might appoint the elect,[2] and there would then probably be no trouble from the patron. But if he appointed a different man, it was an injury to the patron that the election which had his authorization should be broken and an appointment made for which his authorization was perhaps not asked.[3] Philip de Kyme, patron of Kyme Priory, objected when Grosseteste broke an election made there with Philip's licence; the bishop wrote to Philip justifying his own action in instituting a prior; he insisted that Philip had no ground for complaint, since the new prior was more suitable 'and if I am not mistaken, more useful to you yourself'; in any case the patron had no right to be consulted, and he had himself broken elections even in houses of royal foundation.[4]

Similar trouble arose over Luffield Priory in 1285, between King Edward and Bishop Sutton. After the resignation of Prior Adam, the convent elected a new prior, with the king's licence and consent; but the bishop quashed the election, and reappointed Adam, without renewed licence or assent;[5] that was the critical point. The escheator was ordered to deliver

---

[1] See p. 45.

[2] e.g. Elstow, 1249 (*Rot. Grosseteste*, p. 335). Selby, 1270 (*Reg. of Walter Giffard*, p. 217). Woodchurch (= Flamstead), 1255 (*Rot. Henrici de Lexington* [with *Rot. Grosseteste*], p. 511).

[3] e.g. apparently at Nutley, 1236 (*Rot. Grosseteste*, p. 343), Newstead-by-Stamford, 1285 (*Reg. Sutton*, i. 70–71). But at Nocton Park in 1286, when attempts at an election had failed, Bishop Sutton provided a prior with the consent of the patron Norman d'Arcy (ibid., p. 85).

[4] *Rot. Grosseteste*, p. 11. *Roberti Grosseteste . . . Epistolae*, ed. Luard, p. 116.

[5] Cf. Edward I's assent 'by special grace, for this occasion' to an abbot of Abbotsbury provided by the bishop on breaking an election (*Mon.* iii. 58); and to provision of abbot of Faversham (*Cal. Close R. 1272–9*, p. 253).

the temporalities to Adam 'late' prior, for a limited term;[1] but later they were restored to him without term,[2] as if it had been only a formal protest and the matter had been put right.

Two years earlier, more serious trouble had arisen when the pope provided to the exempt house St. Augustine's, Canterbury. The late abbot had gone on a pilgrimage; on his way he went before the pope and resigned, without consulting the king; the pope then provided a monk of the abbey as abbot; the vacancy was not announced to the king, nor licence asked of him, nor assent.[3] When five weeks later the new abbot informed the king of his creation,[4] Edward took the abbey into his hands for four months, and finally pardoned the monks for a 300 marks fine on condition that in future they must announce vacancies and apply for licence and assent.[5] But there was no question of having the new abbot removed or even re-elected; the chief point was probably that the king had not had custody for the whole of the vacancy.[6]

But the king's insistence on treating provisions by ecclesiastical superiors like elections did not go unchallenged in principle: in their articles of 1257 the bishops condemned Henry's attempt so to extend his privilege of being asked for licence to elect.[7]

There are rare references still to the right of investing with the pastoral staff;[8] or the patron might claim what was certainly the bishop's function, that of installing the abbot or prior.[9] When a new prior of Newnham was installed on the bishop's mandate, the patron William de Beauchamp and his wife Ida, *vehementer indignati*, forced the prior by threats to come outside the priory gate and ask installation from them; then de Beauchamp led him to the choir and installed him

---

[1] *Cal. Fine R.* i. 210. [2] *Cal. Pat. R. 1281–92*, p. 160.

[3] Thorne, col. 1938. Cf. papal appointments of bishops (Powicke, i. 263).

[4] This was on 19 June (Thorne) and the sheriff's order to take custody was on 21 June (*Cal. Fine R.* i. 186), which suggests that this was the king's first news of the vacancy.

[5] *Cal. Fine R.* i. 192, 197.

[6] The abbot had to account, with the sheriff and custodians, for issues from the beginning of the vacancy.

[7] *Chron. Maj.* vi. 354.

[8] At Nutley in John's reign (see p. 99, n. 5), Tewkesbury in 1231 (*Ann. Mon.* i. 83).

[9] The king claimed that in royal free chapels induction by lay power was customary (*Reg. Winchelsey*, p. 1019).

again.[1] This couple always pressed hard for their rights; seven years earlier Ida and her steward had punished the canons and laid waste their property for electing without reference to her husband, who was overseas;[2] but in this matter of installation they were clearly going beyond a layman's rights, and this was later admitted to the bishop by their chaplain, who undertook that his master would not in future interfere with the spiritualities.[3]

But formal difficulties were only occasional, and the cruder irregularities were rare; patrons' rights in the choice of prelates were formal and recognized, though with room for variation and disputes and for an amount of peaceful influence which is necessarily incalculable.

---

[1] *Ann. Mon.* iii (Dunstable), pp. 191–2 (1254).
[2] Ibid., p. 172.
[3] Harl. MS. 3656 (cartulary), f. 54. See Fowler and Chambers, 'The Beauchamps of Bedford', in *Beds. Hist. Rec. Soc.* i. 10.

V

CUSTODY

THE feudal right to take custody of the house's possessions during a vacancy[1] was one of the most solid and
valued rights of a patron. It was the only occasion
when land granted away in mortmain could yield appreciable
profits: the value of an advowson was sometimes equated with
the value of the vacant temporalities.[2] Custody was one of the
lay interests involved in the programme of the Second Council of Lyons[3] which the baronage felt concerned to safeguard.[4]

In its fullest form, it meant administration of all temporalities and receipt of all issues; a custodian was put in as soon
as the vacancy was known of, and ordered to hand over as
soon as the new head was confirmed. There was an obvious
temptation to delay giving licence or assent in order to prolong the vacancy, as King John was said to have done at St.
Albans in 1214, 'knowing its custody was profitable to him';[5]
but this temptation does not seem during the rest of the century to have led to outrageously long vacancies in royal houses
(the evidence for others is scanty).[6] Grants of exemption sometimes allow for vacancies of several months, or over a year.[7] But
in fact in Henry III's reign custody usually lasted between a
fortnight and six weeks, counting from the order to take custody, or from the receipt of formal news of the vacancy, to the
order to restore the temporalities or related orders such as
that to the tenants.[8] Custody was sometimes ordered a few
days before the monks' announcement of the vacancy,[9] but

[1] See Knowles, *M.O.*, pp. 612–14.
[2] e.g. Ronton, for Richard de Harecourt (*Inquisitions Post Mortem, Staffs.*,
William Salt Soc. Collections, 1911, p. 213). Barnwell (implication that advowson
had no monetary value because there were no rights in vacancies: *Liber Mem.*, p. 53).
[3] See pp. 16–17.
[4] Cole, *Documents*, p. 359 (points to be made on behalf of the community by
messengers sent to Lyons).   [5] *Gesta Abb.* i. 250.
[6] See Morgan, p. 29, on St. Neots. Sir John Dinham's extraordinary and not
necessarily ancient claims on Hartland in 1427 (see p. 45) included custody for four
months at every vacancy.
[7] See St. Albans and Burton, pp. 85, 86.
[8] *Cal. Pat. R.* and *Close R. passim.*
[9] e.g. Peterborough (*Cal. Pat. R. 1247–58*, p. 56). See Reich, p. 301, for the case
of Shaftesbury when there was in fact no vacancy.

often on the same day or a day or two later.[1] Licence to elect
was usually granted on the day that the vacancy was announced
or custody ordered or both,[2] or a few days later,[3] rarely more
than a week. So if the king substantially lengthened vacancies
it must have been by delaying not licence but assent or the
restoration of temporalities; but to ascertain this one would
have to know the dates of the actual election and of the
bishop's confirmation, besides allowing for travelling time.

The very short vacancies naturally occur chiefly when the
king was fairly near at hand, as when the monks of Winchcombe came to him first at Clarendon and then at Woodstock;[4]
but the monks of St. Benet's, Holme, twice managed vacancies
of about a fortnight though the king was two counties away at
Westminster and Windsor.[5] The longer vacancies of two or
three months can usually be explained by the king being overseas[6] or by the need for exempt houses to get the pope's confirmation.[7] Vacancies at Evesham reached the exceptional
lengths of eight and six months in 1229–30 and 1255.[8] Early
in the century there was some idea at Evesham, put forward
by Marlberge, that in exempt houses, requiring papal confirmation, custody should only last till the election;[9] but it
became normal for the elect to get royal assent, then papal
confirmation, and then restoration of the temporalities,[10] as in
houses which only had to resort to the local bishop.

But even if custody rarely exceeded a few weeks its profits
need not be negligible, and in any case it was a criterion of
patronage, along with licence and assent: inquests about the

---

[1] e.g. Bury, Evesham, Thorney, Croyland, Battle, St. Frideswide's (*Cal. Pat. R.*
1225–32, pp. 250, 320, 193; *1232–47*, pp. 158, 115, 117).

[2] e.g. Ramsey, Reading, St. Albans, St. Benet's, Faversham, Muchelney,
Thorney, York (ibid. *1225–32*, pp. 440, 18; *1232–47*, pp. 95, 183, 85, 105; *1247–
58*, pp. 373, 630–1).

[3] e.g. Evesham, Godstow, Shaftesbury, Wilton (ibid. *1247–58*, pp. 454, 11–12,
629–30, 148–9).

[4] Ibid., *1232–47*, pp. 504–5.

[5] Ibid., pp. 183, 185, 186; *1247–58*, pp. 470, 472.

[6] e.g. Ramsey, 1253 (ibid., pp. 221, 241, 223), 1254 (ibid., pp. 374, 386, 392).

[7] e.g. Battle, 1235 (ibid. *1232–47*, pp. 115, 117, 130). Bury, 1233 (ibid., pp. 26,
27; *Close R. 1231–4*, p. 373). Westminster, 1246 (*Cal. Pat. R. 1232–47*, pp. 495,
499).

[8] Ibid., *1225–32*, pp. 320, 321, 392; *1247–58*, pp. 454, 479.

[9] *Chron. Evesham*, pp. 258–9.

[10] Ibid., pp. 272–4, 279.

patronage of monasteries usually ask who has custody and from whom the convent asks licence and assent;[1] and when Bishop Pontissara took custody of Southwark Priory in 1283 it was expressly to conserve his right of patronage.[2] For this reason, as well as the profit, it was often over custody that disputes about patronage broke out. In 1279 the bishop of Exeter excommunicated certain people who had expelled his custodians from St. German's Priory; these were probably the king's servants, for in the same year and probably occasioned by the same vacancy, an inquisition had found that the priory held in chief of the king, being founded and enfeoffed by the kings of England.[3] The bishop, however, said that it was well known all over Cornwall and the diocese that the priory, both temporalities and spiritualities, and its custody when vacant, belonged to the bishop.[4] To have custody this time would be both the most profitable consequence of having the patronage and the most convincing kind of seisin.

Custody was a key point in the struggle for the patronage of Glastonbury in 1274, between King Edward and the bishop of Bath and Wells. The abbot was dying; the bishop was abroad, but his proctors were on the alert; the king was known to be preparing, with the monks' goodwill, to claim the patronage. The day after the abbot's death, but before it was published, the dean of Wells and the bishop's steward and bailiffs came demanding to see the abbot if he were still alive. Evidently they had heard the rumour of his death and were determined to take custody at once if it were true. Next day, after the official announcement of the death, they took fealty of the *ministeriales* and put bailiffs into the manors. It was not until that evening that the custodian of Bristol castle, less quick off the mark, arrived to take seisin for the king; but he won by prestige or a show of force, for the bishop's men fled and lost the advantage of being first on the scene.[5]

[1] e.g. *Cal. Inqu. Misc.* i, Nos. 181, 1462 (Haghemon, 1235; Modbury, 1289).

[2] *Reg. Pontissara*, i. 275.

[3] *Cal. Inqu. Misc.* i. 344.

[4] *Reg. Bronscombe*, p. 247. Cf. the same bishop's efforts to get the custody of Barnstaple against Henry de Tracy, and of Hartland against Oliver de Dinham (ibid., p. 273; Oliver, pp. 208–9).

[5] Domerham, pp. 537–8. But Edward at one point ordered his custodian to let a man assist him on behalf of the bishop, until the right of the king or the bishop should more fully appear (*Cal. Close R. 1272–9*, p. 74).

While the importance of custody as a sign of patronage was constant, its extent and character varied widely. It was of course only the office of abbot or prior which fell vacant, and only the possessions belonging to the abbot or prior, his barony if he held in chief, which were taken into custody. Sometimes this was the whole of the house's possessions; the head was regarded as the tenant, the monks were dead in law.[1] But by the thirteenth century there had been in most important houses a separation of the head's property from the convent's; the convent was regarded as able to hold land, and since it was immortal, its lands did not come into the patron's custody.[2] These separations were stimulated by the patron's right of custody;[3] and since his interests were affected, his consent to a new division or allotment was apparently necessary in the thirteenth century.[4] Occasionally an escheator seized the convent's goods, but he was normally ordered to restore them;[5] though Bury in 1279 could get no redress in this situation 'for prayer or payment',[6] and had to pay 1,000 marks two years later for confirmation of the separation.[7]

A special class of separation was that between the goods of a cathedral priory and the bishopric, which is analogous to separation from the abbacy.[8] As late as 1299 the prior of Ely paid a fine of 1,000 marks for a charter that in vacancies of the see the king should not have the keeping of the priory.[9] This was after Archbishop Winchelsey had twice written to complain that the king had taken custody of the priory, not itself vacant, in a vacancy of the see, though the king, he says, must be aware that a vacancy of the bishopric does not imply a vacancy of the priory, which has separate possessions.[10] The

---

[1] Pollock and Maitland, i. 433–8.

[2] See Westminster, 1252; confirmation to prior and convent of free administration of their separated goods (*Cal. Pat. R. 1247–58*, p. 150). Cf. St. Benet's, Holme, 1303 (*Mon.* iii. 93, inquisition).

[3] Knowles, *M.O.*, pp. 405, 436, 614–15.

[4] See charters of St. Albans (*Gesta Abb.* i. 370–3) and Bury (*Cal. Charter R.* ii. 259). See pp. 156–7.

[5] St. Albans, 1290 (*Gesta Abb.* ii. 5). Cf. Westminster, 1258: order to guardian to respect separation (*Close R. 1256–9*, p. 249).

[6] *Bury Memorials*, iii. 33.

[7] *Cal. Charter R.* ii. 259.

[8] Knowles, *M.O.*, p. 625.

[9] *Cal. Fine R.* i. 419. See Knowles, *R.O.*, p. 273.

[10] *Reg. Winchelsey*, pp. 253–4, 258. See R. Graham, 'Administration of the diocese

application of this charter is seen three years later. The keeper of the vacant bishopric removed the porter of the priory, to maintain the precedent, and tallaged the priory tenants with the bishop's;[1] but an inquisition showed that the king ought not to interfere with this or other offices; this had been done only before the priory's separation from the bishopric by the present king's charter.[2] On the other hand at Winchester in 1239, before there had been a firm separation, the property of the priory, not itself vacant, was included in that of the vacant bishopric.[3]

This is of course distinct from the question of custody in vacancies of the cathedral priory itself, which would normally either be taken into custody by the bishop as patron,[4] or else would be in his hands as abbot. At Winchester in 1255, before the separate patronage of the cathedral priory was in question, Henry III declared that 'the temporal goods of that priory are known to be of our barony and held of us' (that is, presumably, by the bishop) 'and when there is no prior the custody of the goods belongs to the bishop, or if there is no bishop, to us'.[5] Later, when Edward I claimed the patronage and therefore the custody of the priory, one of Bishop Pontissara's arguments was that if the king were to have custody of a cathedral priory and its offices in the bishop's lifetime he should equally have it in the deaneries and prebends of secular cathedrals, which was never the case; implying that the bishop and not the prior was tenant-in-chief of the cathedral monastery.[6] Finally custody was allowed him on the grounds not that he was abbot but that he was patron.[7] On the other hand in 1271, when a prior of Ely died in the lifetime of the bishop, the escheator took the priory into the king's hands, and only after the lapse of some weeks was ordered to restore it as wrongly seized.[8]

of Ely during vacancies . . . 1298–9 and 1302–3', in *Trans. R. Hist. Soc.* 4th Ser. xii. 52–56.

[1] *Hist. MSS. Comm.* vi (Appendix), p. 290 (from Ely Priory register).

[2] *Cal. Inqu. Misc.* i, No. 1877.

[3] See *Cal. Liberate R. 1226–40*, p. 433.

[4] e.g. Durham (*Scriptores Tres*, Graystanes, pp. 53–54), Worcester (*Acta Stephani Langton*, pp. 160–2. *Reg. G. Giffard, passim*). See pp. 48–52.

[5] Prynne, *Records*, ii. 832–3, from the patent rolls (forbidding the sequestration of the priory's goods on a papal mandate).   [6] *Reg. Pontissara*, ii. 678–9, 686.

[7] *Cal. Charter R.* ii. 287–9. See pp. 9 and 52.   [8] Bentham, *Ely*, p. 218.

If not the whole convent but the obedientiaries had separate sources of revenue, these were often exempt from custody. Glastonbury Abbey settled with the bishop of Bath and Wells, then patron, that in vacancies he would not take away the possessions of obediences;[1] and in 1274 when the king had custody he ordered his keeper not to intermeddle with manors belonging to obedientiaries, but to let them have free administration—prior, chamberlain, sacristan, infirmarer, and mead-maker.[2]

Lands given by and held of lords other than the patron would be taken into custody by those lords, or relief paid to them; Godstow, for instance, holding some land from Adam de Stratton, owed him 1 mark at a vacancy 'in name of custody'.[3] Royal houses holding by knight-service would be exceptions; for the king claimed wardship of all the lands of a tenant-in-chief by knight-service, of whomsoever they were held, except lands held of a few great lords.[4]

The king had custody of lands in England held in chief by foreign abbeys;[5] he took the new abbot's fealty and gave him seisin on receiving letters of confirmation from the foreign bishop; this part of the interplay between church and lay powers in creating an abbot belonged logically to all lords, not only to the patron who had given licence and assent.

On this principle the patron of a cell which had been given as property to its mother-house would probably have custody of it at vacancies of the mother-house, since he was the lord of whom the mother-house held that cell's land (the abbot of Lonlay calls Hugh de Nevill 'our lord and advocate of Stoke

---

[1] Domerham, pp. 550–1.

[2] *Cal. Close R. 1272–9*, p. 81. Cf. St. Peter's, Gloucester: order to custodian, 1243 (*Close R. 1242–7*, p. 117), and inquisition, 1287 (*Gloucester Cart.* iii. 19).

[3] *Mon.* iv. 367. Cf. Bruton: royal custody of one manor (*Close R. 1268–72*, p. 340). Cf. also 100s. due to Mohuns as relief for Taunton Priory; and the memorandum that for lands given to Cleeve they took nothing and did not interfere in vacancies (*Honour of Dunster*, ed. Maxwell-Lyte, p. 58). Reliefs were due to lords other than patrons by Colne and Stratford Langthorne—probably socage reliefs, since they were equal to a years' rent (*Essex Feet of Fines*, ed. Kirk, Essex Archaeol. Soc., 1899), i. 178–9). See Colvin, p. 248, for other examples.

[4] *Statutes*, i. 266. *Reg. Winchelsey*, p. 878.

[5] e.g. Holy Trinity, Caen (*Cal. Fine R.* i. 273), St. Stephen's, Caen (ibid., p. 291), Grestain (*Cal. Pat. R. 1281–92*, p. 185), Cluny (*Close R. 1259–61*, pp. 20, 66–67, 224). If the vacancy had been overlooked a fine could be taken afterwards: *Close R. 1261–4*, p. 159.

RESERVE FOR

Edwin Thompson

Name

Address

Phone No.

Notified

Reserve until

GAYLORD 117

...ntury inquisition it was found ...ities of Horsley Priory at every ...t belonged;[2] Horsley being a ...t. This might turn on whether ...t of the property or a mere ...es claimed to be a perpetual ...nto whether he or the king ...ll in a vacancy of Fécamp Abb...

It ... the patron of the mother-house ... ith a cell held of a different patron ... th his special prerogative over la... ub-escheator in charge of St. Alb... ession of Binham Priory as vacan... s removed the sick prior of Binh... of the Fitz Walters' advowso...

In a va... itself, custody some-times belo... es to the abbot of the mother-ho... on how far the prior was the rea... doing fealty for it[7] and answerable ... as a perpetual prior. Thus in 1230 the custody of Lancaster Priory, in the king's hands, was to be given up to the abbot of Séez if his claim that the prior had no perpetuity was true: however, an inquisition presumably occasioned by this claim showed that, although the abbot appointed and removed the prior, the king had custody.[8] On the other hand the abbot's custody might be no indication of the dependent status of the cell but the result of a grant by the

---

[1] Duchy of Lanc. 27/71, 72.

[2] *Bruton Cart.*, p. 93.

[3] *Close R. 1256–9*, p. 396.

[4] *Gesta Abb.* ii. 16.

[5] e.g. the alien priories of Modbury (James de Oxton), Tywardreth, and St. Michael's Mount (Earl of Cornwall): *Cal. Inqu. Misc.* i, No. 1462, *Cal. Inqu. P.M.* iii, p. 476.

[6] e.g. the abbot of St. Albans appointed custodians for Tynemouth Priory in 1266 (Hill, *Letter-books*, p. 88), before the king had quitclaimed his patronage to the abbot (see p. 30).

[7] e.g. St. Neots, 1262, in wardship of Gilbert de Clare: royal custody, and fealty from new prior (*Close R. 1261–4*, pp. 159–60).

[8] *V.C.H. Lancs.* ii. 169. *Close R. 1227–31*, p. 460. Cf. Wilsford (Morgan, p. 81).

patron;[1] or it may indicate that the patronage itself belongs to the mother-house.[2] There might be joint custody, as at Ewyas Harold where the Tregoz lord and the abbot of Gloucester each sent a man in a vacancy.[3]

In this last case the custody was nominal: the patron took no issues. This drastic limitation on custody is quite common for independent houses, as may be seen from inquisitions into a patron's rights when they had come to the king by wardship or escheat. The main question was usually whether the patron had any government or profit during vacancies; the answer was often that the patron took no issues, but only put in a gate-keeper who should have his keep from the house and must leave as soon as the new head was confirmed.[4] This is usually said to be a sign of dominion; in one case, to guard against robbers. Another way of signifying lordship, when the patron had no real custody, was to send a sergeant to take simple seisin at the gates and to go away at once.[5]

This very limited custody, or total exemption, was some-times specified at the foundation[6] and sometimes granted later.[7] Gilbert Pecche's 1256 charter for Barnwell included the undertaking that he and his heirs would not waste the priory's goods in a vacancy by selling or scattering them; and so as to have no occasion for such waste, he would only send one servant with horse and groom, to have simple seisin in recognition of his patronage, but also to take part with the house's officials in preserving its goods.[8] A similar agreement

[1] e.g. Isabel de Forz allowed Lire Abbey the custody of Carisbrooke (*V.C.H. Hants.* ii. 230).

[2] The bishop of Carlisle's quitclaims to St. Mary's, York, about Wetheral Priory perhaps involved surrendering the advowson (*Wetheral Reg.*, pp. 73–77).

[3] *Cal. Inqu. P.M.* iii, p. 455.

[4] e.g. Langley (*Mon.* iv. 223), Frithelstock, Prittlewell, Holy Trinity at York, Bolton, Nunmonkton (*Cal. Inqu. Misc.* i, Nos. 1401, 1885, 1958 and 1983, 1985, 2019), Bromholm, Eye (*Cal. Close R. 1307–13*, p. 526; *1313–18*, p. 9), Winchester after 1284 (*Cal. Charter R.* ii. 287–8).

[5] e.g. Campsey nunnery's arrangement with Robert de Valognes (*Mon.* vi. 1. 587). Cf. royal houses, p. 85, n. 1.

[6] e.g. Alcester: Ralph Butler's foundation charter of 1140 (*Mon.* iv. 175). Raven-stone, founded by the king and his treasurer Peter Chaceporc: royal charter of 1271 (*Close R. 1263–72*, p. 370).

[7] e.g. Reginald de Mohun II to Bruton, 1237 (*Bruton Cart.*, p. 3). King John to Battle, with grant of free election (*Mon.* iii. 247).

[8] *Liber Mem.*, p. 49. Cf. similar grant by Isabel de Forz to Christchurch, Twynham (*Cal. Charter R.* ii. 469).

was made in the 1230's or 40's between Missenden Abbey and Joan de Sanford; she was to put in a servant with custody of only those things 'within the orbit of the abbey', 'ad conservandum et congregandum, nequaquam ad dispergendum vel alienandum'.[1] A little earlier, William de Cantilupe allowed Studley Priory to have custody by the sub-prior and cellarer,[2] not even sending a servant.

Apart from such specific grants, exemption from custody was implied in proven frankalmoin tenure, and must have been a really important consequence of that tenure, which cannot therefore be held to have had no practical meaning at the end of the thirteenth century.[3] This is shown at Wymondham Priory in 1303: in the minority of Robert de Tateshall's heir, the king's escheators took custody in a vacancy; the monks objected that they held in pure alms; and after examination of documents, presumably proving this, the escheators were forbidden to interfere.[4]

Similarly at St. Werburgh's, Chester, in 1291, custody was taken in error,[5] and the issues were restored next year, because the exchequer rolls and an inquisition showed that after the earldom of Chester escheated King Henry or the justice of Chester had taken nothing in vacancies and only put in a sergeant who had two keepers under him, at the gate and in the cellar—supervision, in fact, but no profit; this proved the custom, while the earl's charters[6] reserving nothing but prayers proved the right.[7] In the abbey's chronicle, commenting on an incident in 1265,[8] a different hand adds: 'By which it appears that the lords of Cheshire at a time of vacancy of the abbey of St. Werburgh ought to have nothing at all from the issues, because the abbey is founded on no barony,

---

[1] *Missenden Cart.*, p. 38.

[2] *V.C.H. Warwicks.* ii. 95. Cf. agreement between Canonsleigh and John de Clavill, 1282: patron to appoint the canons' own porter or other servant to guard their goods against spoliation (C. S. Perceval, 'Remarks on some early charters . . . relating to the Priory . . . and Abbey . . . of Canonsleigh', in *Archaeologia*, Soc. of Antiquaries of London, xl; London, 1871; p. 441).

[3] See pp. 13–14, 34–35. [4] *Gesta Abb.* ii. 83–86.

[5] For the second time: cf. 1249–50 (*Close R. 1247–51*, pp. 221, 204, 206, 272).

[6] Cf. *Cal. Charter R.* ii. 371: Inspeximus of confirmation charter.

[7] *Cal. Pat. R. 1281–92*, p. 471. *Cal. Inqu. Misc.* i, No. 1546. Cf. Frithelstock and Nunmonkton, *Cal. Inqu. Misc.* i, Nos. 1401, 2019.

[8] The Lord Edward's compensation for wine consumed by his household before he had accepted the abbot-elect (see p. 71, n. 7).

but everything belonging to it was given in pure and perpetual alms.'[1]

Cistercian, Carthusian, Premonstratensian, and Gilbertine houses were free from even nominal custody, though mistakes might be made: at the death of an abbot of Netley in 1260, the escheator took the abbey into the king's hands, but was ordered to restore it at once (though not explicitly because it was Cistercian).[2]

Early in Henry III's reign the burden of custody was sometimes lightened for royal houses which were not exempt from it, by allowing the monks, or one or two of them, to act as custodians themselves, though answering to the king for the issues: the king still had the profits but the house was not under the control of his potentially dishonest bailiffs. St. Augustine's, Canterbury, asked the legate for this in 1220, when their abbot was dying; custody was actually given, not as they had asked to the monks in general, but to one of them, William, who was the legate's penitentiary. The advantage of having one of themselves as custodian was that he regarded himself as there 'to exonerate, not to burden', and was economical.[3] There are many other cases in the 1220's where one or both of the custodians were obedientiaries of the house, perhaps combined with a royal clerk.[4] This practice may have been continued by the two escheators, who took over much of this work in 1234. It is paralleled by the common employment on lay lands, in wardship or escheat, of one of the tenant-in-chief's own household,[5] and was probably as much a matter of convenience as of benefiting the monastery.

But John occasionally[6] and Henry III frequently allowed the prior and convent to buy the custody of the abbacy for a particular occasion;[7] not merely managing the estates themselves but taking all the issues, for the next vacancy or one

[1] *Ann. Cestrienses*, p. 96.
[2] *Close R. 1259–61*, p. 24 (in any case the bishop of Winchester was probably patron).
[3] Thorne, cols. 1871–2, 1892. *Cal. Pat. R. 1216–25*, p. 254.
[4] e.g. Abingdon, Westminster, Merton, Selby, Whitby, Shrewsbury, Bardney (*Cal. Pat. R. 1225–32*, pp. 298, 330, 339, 369, 374, 381, 379).
[5] N. Denholm-Young, *Seigneurial Administration*, p. 162.
[6] C. R. Cheney, 'King John's Reaction to the Interdict', in *Trans. R. Hist. Soc.* 4th Ser. xxxi. 137: Peterborough, Battle, Bury, and St. Augustine's, Canterbury.
[7] See Reich, p. 305.

just begun;[1] or sometimes to buy back the issues of a past vacancy.[2] Occasionally the issues of a vacancy might be given back to the house on the grounds of its poverty, as at Elstow in 1259, where the king kept only 10s. as a sign of seisin.[3] Or the fine paid might be applied to benefit the house: of Westminster's fine of 1,100 marks in 1258, 1,000 marks was spent on the fabric of the church, 100 marks to pay a debt of the late abbot's;[4] but Westminster under Henry III is a special case.

Later, custody might be granted for all future vacancies.[5] At St. Albans the prior and convent bought custody of the abbacy for the 1235 vacancy for 300 marks,[6] and in 1260 for 600 marks.[7] In 1290 King Edward refused to let them make fine beforehand, and they only got custody by buying it from the escheator when he had already, by their account, done much damage.[8] Finally in 1301 the abbey paid 1,000 marks for several charters, the chief of which allowed the prior and convent custody of the abbacy in every vacancy, for 1,000 marks each time, and more if the vacancy lasted more than a year. When the abbot died that same year, the sub-escheator came to take seisin; the prior and cellarer had the charter read to him, and he left the barony in the monks' hands.[9] For less rich abbeys, the original payment might cover all future vacancies, without payments for each occasion.[10]

[1] See *Close R.* for Henry III, *passim*; and *Cal. Fine R.* i. 3–4, 196, 269, 485–6, 526. Foreign abbeys might fine for the custody of their English lands: e.g. Bec, 1266 (*Close R. 1264–8*, p. 188). An exempt house might buy custody after the royal assent and pending papal confirmation: e.g. Bury, 1229 and 1256 (*Cal. Pat. R. 1225–32*, p. 255; *1247–58*, p. 546); Westminster, 1258 (ibid., p. 650). When custody had been bought a clerk or sergeant might be sent to take simple seisin: e.g. St. Mary's, York, 1258 (ibid., p. 630); or the escheator might do so: e.g. St. Albans under 1301 charter (*Gesta Abb.* ii. 34), St. Benet's under 1305 charter (*V.C.H. Norfolk*, ii. 333).

[2] e.g. Tavistock, 1260; Glastonbury, 1274 (only certain issues); Hyde, 1282 (*Close R. 1259–61*, p. 294; *Cal. Close R. 1272–9*, p. 291; *Cal. Pat. R. 1272–81*, p. 83; *Cal. Fine R.* i. 166).

[3] *Close R. 1254–6*, p. 402. Cf. Bicknacre (ibid., p. 69), where the issues were to be kept 'to the utility of the house, which is poor'.

[4] *Cal. Pat. R. 1247–58*, p. 650.

[5] Knowles, *R.O.*, pp. 278–9: early fourteenth century, Bury, St. Albans, Evesham, Hyde. [6] *Gesta Abb.* i. 306. [7] Ibid., p. 398.

[8] *Gesta Abb.* ii. 3, 6. [9] Ibid., pp. 32–34, 52.

[10] e.g. St. Benet's, 1305 (*V.C.H. Norfolk*, ii. 333). St. Benet's had tried to get permanent exemption in the 1250's (*Chron. Johannis de Oxenedes*, ed. Ellis, p. 298). Waltham had it as early as 1253 (ibid., p. 196).

Since there was a permanent body of men with an active substitute head in the prior or sub-prior, custody in a vacancy was not a practical necessity as it might be for a layman's fief.[1] It might pay the patron to accept a lump sum and give up the troublesome administration of the issues, and still more to take ready money rather than wait for the vacancy; Henry III was said to have been angry when the abbot of Abingdon died only a fortnight after the king had short-sightedly sold the custody for a mere 500 marks.[2]

Fines made during or after the vacancy are likely to be nearer the actual value of the issues during that time, and failing an extensive study of unprinted pipe rolls are probably the best indication of the profits of custody. The sums range from 10 or 20 marks from smaller royal houses[3] to 200, 500, or 1,000 marks from the greater.[4] Sometimes a time limit was set: Burton Abbey in 1281 arranged to pay £40 for any vacancy up to two months, and £20 a month after that.[5]

These royal grants nearly always made certain exceptions: the king was still to have the advowsons, the service from knights' fees, and the feudal incidents of wardship, marriage, relief, and escheat on the free tenants.[6] The bishop of Worcester, allowing his cathedral priory custody in 1224, reserved these same things.[7] Sometimes the incidents were allowed while the advowsons were reserved:[8] for the presenta-

---

[1] But the grant of custody might be dependent on unity in the election; e.g. Selby, 1223 (*Pat. R. 1216–25*, pp. 367, 369), Wilton, 1271 (*Cal. Pat. R. 1266–72*, pp. 584, 612; *Close R. 1268–72*, p. 384), Shaftesbury, 1290 (*Cal. Fine R.* i. 269); either because of danger of waste by a disunited convent, or perhaps because the election might not be confirmed by the bishop or pope (Marlberge thought custody in an exempt house should end 'statim post concordem electionem': *Chron. Evesham*, p. 258).

[2] *Chron. Maj.* v. 567. The grant was made on 25 May and licence to elect was granted on 11 June (*Cal. Pat. R. 1247–58*, pp. 476, 480).

[3] e.g. Holy Trinity (London), Newstead (Notts.), Lilleshull, St. James at Northampton, Grimsby, Nunnaminster (*Close R. 1263–72*, pp. 16, 209, 307, 330, 378, 528).

[4] e.g. St. Albans, above; St. Augustine's, Canterbury (*Close R. 1251–3*, p. 365); Evesham (ibid. *1261–4*, p. 260); Westminster (*Cal. Pat. R. 1247–58*, p. 650).

[5] *Burton Abbey*, Staffs. Rec. Soc. 1937, p. 82.

[6] A. M. Reich points out that the grant to Bury in 1248 excepted, perhaps uniquely, tallages, assize rents, and the profits of jurisdiction (Reich, p. 305).

[7] *Acta Stephani Langton*, pp. 160–2.

[8] St. Augustine's, Canterbury, 1273 (Thorne, col. 1921). Perhaps Bury, 1256 (*Cal. Pat. R. 1247–58*, p. 546).

tion to livings which fell in during a vacancy was a much valued right. On one occasion a clerk presented by the late prior of Bermondsey but not yet instituted at the prior's death was ousted in favour of the king's presentee.[1]

This presentation was part of the recognized 'common right' of a monastery's patron, and was claimed as such in 1304 in a plea *quare impedit* brought against the sub-prior and monks of Huntingdon by the earl and countess of Gloucester, about a church which was in their presentation because the priory was vacant and in their custody. Against the monks' plea that the earl had no custody beyond putting a man at the gate, the patrons claimed 'common right'.[2]

A general assertion of this right was made by the king's Council on 14 March 1258 for some case involving Walter de Merton. It laid down that, since in England an advowson normally goes with a manor, the presentation to benefices of a vacant bishopric or abbey always belongs to the king or magnate who has custody of the manors, although the right of institution belongs to the appropriate ecclesiastical authority. So that although bishops, and even some abbots having pontifical rights,[3] can collate to churches of their manors, because for them patronage and the right of instituting go together—that is, the same person is both patron and ordinary —nevertheless, they have the right of patronage not by reason of their pastoral office but by reason of their manors or baronies, and the patronage goes with these—that is, to whoever has custody.[4] The point seems to be to prevent the

[1] *V.C.H. Surrey*, ii. 67. In 1245 Henry III warned the convent of Lewes (in his hands in the wardship of the Warenne heir), in threatening terms, not to present to any churches vacant since they had no head (*Close R. 1242–7*, p. 285). See writ of prohibition against a convent's presentee suing the king's presentee (*Close R. 1251–3*, pp. 242–3) and a form of prohibition given by Bracton (*De Legibus*, iv. 258). There was a test case in 1234 (Reich, pp. 307–8; *Select Cases before the King's Council*, p. lix).

[2] *Year Bks. 32, 33 Edw. I* (R.S.), pp. 208–12. Their plea against the bishop of Lincoln (ibid., p. 176) concerns the same benefice: 'Lincoln' Priory is a mistake for Huntingdon (Common Pleas, Easter, 32 Edw. I, m. 34d). Cf. Earl Warenne's plea against the sub-prior and convent of Lewes, 1258 (Curia Regis, Mich. 42–43 H. III, m. 27 d). Professor Plucknett implies that in a vacancy the patron had the advowsons even of other lords' donation (*Legislation of Edw. I*, p. 101, n. 2), but in the cases he cites (see p. 158, n. 5) the patron was the king, so that prerogative wardship might apply (see p. 80).

[3] See Knowles, 'Monastic Parish Organization', in *Downside Review*, li (1933).

[4] *Cal. Pat. R. 1247–58*, pp. 619–20.

ecclesiastical authority on whom institution devolved from exercising the patronage as well;[1] or possibly to combat a papal provision made on the grounds that the patronage was in ecclesiastical hands: the lay power was perhaps asserting that in a bishopric's or monastery's vacancy its livings were not at the pope's disposal, because they were temporarily of a layman's advowson.[2]

A right related to this was the presentation to the next benefice to fall vacant after the new prelate had succeeded.[3] This seems to be the nearest thing to a relief normally paid by royal houses, though other patrons sometimes took ordinary reliefs.[4] But the king took a kind of heriot like the continental 'spoils'[5] from the goods of the late prelate, normally a cup and a palfrey,[6] but sometimes a large-scale seizure of movable property: at Westminster the kings before Edward I used to take the abbot's oxen, horses, stored corn, silver vessels, jewels, and books.[7] A private patron might have a similar right: in 1329 Robert fitz Walter of Daventry quitclaimed to Daventry Priory his right of custody including the prior's and cellarer's horses.[8] It was doubtful whether charters of exemption from custody covered this due: in 1302 the monks of St. Albans

---

[1] It is tempting to suppose that vicarages of appropriated churches were in question (see pp. 157-8); but there is no mention of appropriations, but only of benefices in a bishop's or (rarely) an abbot's collation.

[2] See p. 152 for protests about the depreciation of custody by provisions.

[3] See pp. 113-14.

[4] e.g. quitclaim of relief (with other dues) to Langdon by Nicholas de Crioil (Exch., King's Remembrancer Misc. Books 29, ff. 11*v*-14**v*). At Bolton a relief was due to the earls of Albemarle at the prior's installation (*Cal. Close R. 1272-9*, p. 158). Eye paid 5s. or an ox to the patron's gatekeeper at the installation, perhaps as a relief (ibid. *1313-18*, p. 9). Isabel de Forz promised that custody should end without payment at Christchurch, Twynham (*Cal. Charter R.* ii. 469). William de Fauconberge's renunciation of any secular right such as a palfrey due at a vacancy or a new creation at Welbeck (Colvin, p. 248, n. 1) suggests a right more like the king's cup and palfrey: see below.

[5] Lunt, *Financial Relations*, pp. 506-7.

[6] e.g. Osney, 1255: 'cum ex consuetudine approbata et obtenta habere consueverimus palefridos et cuppas episcoporum et abbatum regni nostri cedentium vel decedentium' (*Close R. 1254-6*, 167). The claim was disputed at Peterborough, 1263 (*Hist. Burgensis*, Whytesley, p. 132); St. Benet's, 1303 (*Mon.* iii. 93: inquisition).

[7] *Mon.* i. 311. Cf. order to escheator at Bury in 1257 to restore to the convent the silver vessels and kitchen utensils of the late abbot, the prior's and sacristan's horses, and the abbot's cart and cart-horses which ought to go to the sacristan (*Close R. 1256-9*, p. 118).

[8] Daventry cartulary: Cott. MS. Claud. D. xii, ff. 11-12.

and of Waltham claimed exemption on this ground from paying a ring, cup, palfrey, and pack of hounds of the late abbot's,
and the question was referred to Council at the next parliament.[1] On the same occasion the new abbot of St. Albans
failed to get exemption from giving a benefice to a royal clerk.[2]

Where the patron had full custody, both administering and
receiving issues, his bailiff or custodian needed knowledge
and skill. When the obedientiaries' revenues were not free
from custody, the custodian would probably appoint his own
men temporarily to the more mundane offices, since to him the
obedientiary was primarily a receiver of revenue. So in 1303
at Wymondham the escheators put in keepers to the cellar,
the gates, and other offices.[3] Sometimes some secular offices
might be bestowed by the custodian or the patron: at Christchurch, Canterbury, in vacancies of the archbishopric, analogous to vacancies of an abbacy, the king could confer the
keeping of the great gate and the stewardship of the hall,[4]
offices which the archbishop normally filled.[5] But the patron's
powers over obediences and other offices were sometimes controversial. When the bishop of Durham had custody as patron
of the vacant cathedral priory, the monks maintained that he
should only put in a clerk for their defence, and contested his
custodian's claim to interfere with their household by demanding an oath of fealty from marshal and porters and the power
to remove them.[6]

The patron or his custodian took the prelate's place in
certain respects. The tenants usually did fealty to the custodian. The escheator at St. Albans in 1290 claimed the same
status for the king as the abbot had, in temporal things.[7] Odd
duties might thus come in the custodian's way: in 1242

---

[1] *Cal. Close R. 1296–1302*, pp. 512–13.
[2] See p. 114.
[3] *Gesta Abb.* ii. 83–86. Cf. St. Albans in 1290: p. 93.
[4] *Cal. Pat. R. 1266–72*, pp. 503, 528, 577.
[5] *Reg. Winchelsey*, pp. 400, 401, 490.
[6] *Ann. Dunelm.*, pp. 31–35. *Scriptores Tres*, Graystanes, pp. 53–54. Cf. agreement
between Missenden and Joan de Sanford (*Missenden Cart.*, p. 38); the free servants
were to take oath before the custodian and the prior that they would fulfil their
offices and be faithful to the patron while the abbey was vacant. Any dilapidator
amongst them was to be removed and replaced by the custodian with counsel and
consent of the prior and convent.
[7] *Gesta Abb.* ii. 4.

Robert Passelewe, as keeper of Shaftesbury, was ordered expressly to take the abbess's place in supervising the election of a prioress, since the king would not tolerate the election of an abbess when there was no prioress.[1]

But the custodian's main task was to administer the revenues: to collect them, spend them on the house's affairs and on local royal expenses, and pay the rest into the Exchequer. The issues he received[2] would be chiefly rents, sale of crops or wool, pleas and perquisites of courts, and tallages; the normal revenues of the abbot or prior, in fact; with the possible addition of abnormal sales of stock and timber, or extortions from tenants.

Out of this he was expected, if the convent had no separate revenues, to provide reasonable food and clothing for the monks, and wages for their servants; in any case, for any wages which the abbot normally paid; for necessary repairs to buildings, and for the expenses of agriculture, which he was to see properly carried on.[3] These duties are stressed in various mandates of Henry III's, such as that to the keeper of Bardney in 1244 to keep the abbey as well as it would be kept under an abbot, lest the buildings should fall and the land lie barren.[4]

Then he would have to pay any normal charges on the revenues, such as corrodies; and he would also, like any other collector of the king's revenue, receive orders for payments to merchants; for gifts, perhaps to the house itself;[5] for consignments of beasts for the king's household when he travelled that way;[6] for extra corrodies, not always for the king's men (the keeper of Ramsey in 1253 was to provide for an old servant of the abbot who was not to be deprived of his living);[7]

---

[1] *Close R. 1242-7*, pp. 75, 77.

[2] See Ramsey accounts (*Cartularium mon. de Ramseia*, ed. Hart and Lyons, i. 227–30; iii. 11–12, 215. *P.R. 4 John*, p. 138; *9 John*, pp. 110–11; *10 John*, p. 189). Hyde (*P.R. 8 John*, pp. 45–46). St. Augustine's, Canterbury, 1283 (Thorne, col. 1939).

[3] A crop sown during custody belonged to the king whenever it was harvested, and was often sold to the new abbot (Reich, p. 303); sometimes apparently for the cost of cultivation only (see below, pp. 94–95).

[4] *Close R. 1242-7*, p. 178. Cf. mandates for Thorney, Evesham, Bardney, Malmesbury (ibid. *1234-7*, p. 497; *1242-7*, pp. 24, 33, 67, 399, 401).

[5] e.g. Thorney, 1237, £10 for a lawsuit (*Cal. Lib. R.*, p. 290); Winchester, 1239, gift of wine (ibid., p. 433).

[6] e.g. Hyde Abbey, 1248; order to send fat sheep, oxen, and salt meat to Winchester for Whitsun; 10 days later, 22 bullocks and 40 sheep (*Close R. 1247-51*, pp. 42, 110).   [7] *Close R. 1251-3*, p. 503.

hospitality for the king's guests;[1] above all, lodging for his servants and horses. A grant of King Henry's in 1253, that Barking was not to be burdened with lay brothers and royal messengers, makes the reservation 'while the house is not in the king's hands in a vacancy'.[2]

The kinds of expense are shown in accounts for Ramsey Abbey in its two vacancies during John's reign. Most of the long second vacancy was during the Interdict, but the custodians' actions do not seem to have been abnormal on that account, apart from the major point that the convent's property was included.[3] In 1202 the custodian spent £23. 7s. on wages, building, and necessary expenses within the abbey, except the monks' chamber and cellar—presumably provided for by property in the convent's or obedientiaries' hands; £6. 10s. on the manors—presumably wages and upkeep; 6s. 2d. on clothes; and £10 on travelling expenses of monks going overseas to the king about their election. There was also £6. 15s. on the Holy Land Fortieth, 10s. for a messenger taking three palfreys to the king (perhaps his own stabled there for a time, perhaps due from the dead abbot), and the extraordinary sum of 80 marks on a 'corrody' due to the king. Since the receipts came to nearly £400, this leaves a large balance for the Exchequer.[4] In later accounts the expenses are heavier and more interesting. In 1206–7 normal expenses for the house itself (including the convent this time), repairs, wages, pittances, and so on, came to just over £100; over £26 was spent on keeping horses for the king, with grooms, for varying periods—some for six months; £97 had already been paid to the king in his Chamber; and over £40 was spent on expenses authorized by royal writ, mainly robes and liveries for people staying at the abbey; some of which may of course have been due anyhow, such as £2. 10s. to John de Kemeseye 'which he used to get from the abbey'.[5]

In 1207–8 £112 was apparently spent on genuine expenses, including repairs and buying plough-oxen; whereas £128

---

[1] e.g. in 1182 the archbishop of Trondhjem was accommodated at the king's order in the vacant abbey of Bury (*Jocelyn of Brakelond*, ed. Butler, p. 15).

[2] *Cal. Pat. R. 1247–58*, p. 180.

[3] Cheney, in *Trans. R. Hist. Soc.* 4th Ser. xxxi. 143–4.

[4] *Ramsey Cart.* i. 227, and *P.R. 4 John*, p. 138.

[5] *Ramsey Cart.* i. 230–2; *P.R. 9 John*, pp. 110–11.

was spent mainly by royal writ on liveries, for instance to two
'men of the queen's nurse'; the support of grooms, horses,
and dogs; and hospitality to the abbot of Angoulême and his
retinue, accounting for over £50 of it.[1] Then in 1211–12
expenses for the house come to £148, again including repairs
to mills and buying oxen, horses and ploughs; while liveries
to men staying, sometimes for a stated number of days (therefore not regular corrodians), keeping horses, and clothing a
hostage, come to £51—less than usual.[2]

These Ramsey accounts may be compared with those of
Hyde in 1206. Here, of £375 receipts, about £42 came from
the sale of stock—not necessarily waste, for much stock
always had to be sold or slaughtered in the autumn. Over £40
of the expenses were for horses and servants of the king, or
his guests—three burgesses of Niort for two days, with their
horses and men. On the other hand nearly £100 was spent on
ordinary expenses of the monastery; nearly £19 on buying
oxen and cattle; and over £100 on paying the abbot's debts.[3]

The profits, then, were large, including as they do much
that was spent on the spot for the king's advantage; but (failing a detailed comparison with the normal revenues and expenses) the accounts do not suggest crude, short-sighted waste;
apparently stock was bought and repairs done. Perhaps waste
was less likely the longer the custody.

But there were substantial opportunities for the custodian
himself to make profit, by cutting down on repairs or the
monks' food and by wasting timber and stock, and then falsi-
fying the accounts; and even an honest custodian might be
extortionate out of official zeal. The monks of St. Albans,
after obtaining exemption from custody in 1235, 'rejoiced
that they were not to be entangled in the nets of the king's
satellites'.[4]

There are royal writs (presumably obtained by the monks)
in general terms not to damage a vacant monastery,[5] or in
particular not to sell or waste woods without the king's command;[6] not to take tenants' rents early[7] to be sure of getting

---

[1] *Ramsey Cart.* i. 229; *P.R. 10 John*, p. 189.   [2] *Ramsey Cart.* iii. 215.
[3] *P.R. 8 John*, pp. 45–46.   [4] *Gesta Abb.* i. 306.
[5] Alcester (*Close R. 1251–3*, p. 64).   [6] Bury (ibid. *1256–9*, p. 118).
[7] Abingdon (ibid. *1259–61*, p. 102).

them before the vacancy ended; to restore 100 sheep and some corn taken without the king's command.[1] A keeper of Wenlock Priory was afterwards made to pay the prior and convent 70 marks for the damage he had done.[2] A bad custodian might be removed by the king in his own interest; Henry III, hearing that the keeper of Evesham had taken horses, meat and wine for his own use, ordered that he be removed and made to render account—he was not to grow fat on the abbey's goods at the king's expense.[3]

An example of excessive zeal rather than dishonesty was the behaviour of the escheator at St. Albans in 1290, when, according to the chronicler, in spite of the royal promise that the escheator should do them no harm, he occupied the abbey forcefully and impatiently, seized the keys and put in his own officials, imposed tallages on the serfs, openly took the convent's goods as well as the abbot's, seized stock which the prior had been afraid to sell in advance (an obvious way to cheat the custodian), and even sold tithes, which as spiritualities were outside his province.[4] Some of these things were within his rights; the trouble was partly that the monks were not used to them, having made fine in the last two vacancies, and partly perhaps in the escheator's hasty and forceful manner. But selling tithes and seizing the convent's goods were certainly oppressive.

Matthew Paris (who of course had an eye for such things) gives several instances of abuse of custody for which he holds the king or guardians of the realm responsible: as at Bury, where he accuses the king of extorting 1,200 marks;[5] Peterborough, where extortionate custody forced the issue of the election;[6] Ramsey, where the keepers seized silver vessels, horses, wine, and game for the guardians of the realm, and worse, extorted from the tenants whom they should have protected.[7] In his amusing story of Henry's chagrin when Abingdon fell vacant unexpectedly soon after he had allowed the monks custody, he makes the king say he could have got 1,000

---

[1] Gloucester (ibid. *1227–31*, p. 62).
[2] Ibid. *1259–61*, pp. 476–7.   [3] Ibid. *1242–7*, pp. 24, 33.
[4] *Gesta Abb.* ii. 3–6.   [5] *Chron. Ma* . v. 40 (1248).
[6] Ibid. v. 84–85 (1249).
[7] Ibid. v. 394 (1253). Cf. St. Augustine's, Canterbury, 1253: the king's satellites seized the goods *quasi exterminando* (ibid. v. 362).

marks or more in a few days from the abbey's woods alone[1]—
which, however exaggerated, shows that devastating inroads
on capital might be feared.

Paris's spectacular instances do not of course show how
widespread such abuses were.[2] Nor does the dismal picture of
royal custody drawn by the bishop of Winchester to dis-
courage his monks from seeking royal patronage;[3] nor the
general complaints which were made: by Grosseteste, for
instance, who complained that when the king had custody of
vacant sees and monasteries he 'enormously diminishes their
goods, and burdens the poor tenants with intolerable tallages';[4] backed by extracts from canon law made by Robert
Marsh, to prove that patrons having custody must be moderate
and not oppressive.[5] The bishops in 1257 complained that
lands were left uncultivated, woods and fisheries wasted,
buildings neglected, goods seized, villeins impoverished and
ill-treated, and supplies that should have fed the convent
taken.[6] The Convocation of Merton next year made a general
charge of waste against the king and his bailiffs, referred to
Magna Carta, and required offenders to be excommunicated;[7]
the Council of Lambeth in 1261 did the same, accusing magnates as well as the king, and listing much the same abuses as
in 1257.[8] Amongst the grievances of 1300, repeated in 1309,
were the same complaints;[9] the king's answer that the writ *de
vasto* was available was held insufficient, and they asked that
custodians who put in irresponsible underlings should be held
responsible for the damage they did. Further, the bad cultivation was to the damage of new prelates who bought crops
sown but not harvested during a vacancy,[10] and were forced to

---

[1] *Chron. Maj.* v. 567 (1256).

[2] The Dunstable annalist, who has in general a just tone, remarks that the custodian in 1280 'did not burden us at all, and did not oppress our tenants' as if this
were remarkable (*Ann. Mon.* iii. 284).

[3] *Reg. Pontissara*, i. 683. The king would take their goods at his free will, including timber and the contents of their barns; allow them only the bare necessities of
life; take 'recognitions' from their men, bond and free; so that a run of vacancies
would reduce the monks and their tenants to extreme poverty.

[4] *Ann. Mon.* i (Burton), p. 423.

[5] Ibid., p. 429.

[6] *Chron. Maj.* vi. 353.   [7] *Ann. Mon.* i (Burton), p. 420.

[8] *Concilia*, i. 752–3. Cf. the grievances of uncertain date in Cole, *Documents*,
p. 356.   [9] *Reg. Winchelsey*, pp. 1018–19.

[10] See p. 90, n. 3.

pay a fixed price for them: so it was asked that the old custom
should be kept by which they paid only the cost of cultivation.[1]
And apparently as an afterthought[2] they asked that chapters
and convents should be allowed to buy custody, in the king's
interest as well as the Church's, since custodians often did not
pay the king one-third of their gains.

A special complaint, made in 1257, 1261, 1280 (repeated
in 1309), and still being made in 1327,[3] was that custodians
interfered with spiritualities, taking tithes and oblations of
appropriated churches,[4] and even (according to the 1300
grievances)[5] presenting to them.[6]

Apart from exploitation, custody provided opportunities
for influence which the patron enjoyed at no other time. It does
not seem to have been much used to force elections;[7] but at
Bardney in 1243 the king interfered through his custodian on
behalf of a deposed abbot, and was crisply reprimanded by
Grosseteste. The bishop writes that he has heard that the king
has ordered his custodian to provide better for the ex-abbot
Walter and his party than for the other side, and to allow him
free ingress and egress to the church. Thus to prefer rebels is
preferring darkness to light. Even if the deposed abbot had
rebelled rightly, this is a matter for ecclesiastical judgement,

[1] It is not entirely clear from the register that this request refers to the grievance
about prelates buying crops, because of a long intervening passage; but part of this
is an insertion (see next note); and a different version runs: 'non est sufficienter
responsum quo ad gravamen compulsionis prelatorum quod solvant certum precium
pro fructibus terrarum suarum de quibus in articulo fit mencio, cum antiquiter
solerent [? tantummodo] solvere custagia culture et seminis earundem terrarum'.
This is in an earlier draft of the 1300 grievances, attached to a draft of the collected
grievances: Dean and Chapter Library, Canterbury, Cartae Antiquae C. 256.

[2] This passage, from 'et quia communiter contingit' to 'custodia concedatur', is
not in the Canterbury draft (see last note), and in Winchelsey's register (f. 2) it is in
the margin, though not so marked in *Reg. Winchelsey*, p. 1018 (but see Wilkins,
Concilia, ii. 316–17). I have to thank Mr. Dodwell, Librarian of Lambeth Palace
Library, for kindly looking at the MS. and informing me on this point.

[3] *Chron. Maj.* vi. 353 (cf. London Convocation of 1257, *Ann. Mon.* i. 406, where
lay patrons other than the king are mentioned); *Concilia*, i. 752–3; *Reg. Winchelsey*,
p. 1017; *Rotuli Parliamentorum hactenus inediti*, ed. Richardson and Sayles, p. 108.

[4] Cf. the complaints of St. Albans in 1290 (see p. 93); and the king's orders to
the keepers of St. Augustine's, Canterbury, 1283, not to lay hands on spiritualities
otherwise than was usual (*Cal. Close R. 1279–88*, p. 213).

[5] *Reg. Winchelsey*, p. 1019.

[6] See pp. 157–8. The question of abuse of custody is discussed in chapter ii of a
thesis by Miss Ursula Henriques on clerical *Gravamina* (particularly of 1309).

[7] But see p. 67, Paris on Peterborough, 1249.

not for the lay power; and even if the lay power acts so out of
devotion, he is no better than the well-meaning Uzzah who
touched the Ark of the Lord.[1]

The king had, in fact, ordered the custodian to provide
necessaries for Walter and his supporters,[2] and had ordered
that no monks were to be captured because of any sentence
passed on them by any bishop of the province of Canterbury;
action was to be delayed till his return.[3] From his own point
of view the king was probably simply trying to exercise his
right of custody impartially; from Grosseteste's point of view
he was abusing that right to interfere in spiritual matters.

The king did in fact claim some powers of interference and
protection in the churches of his realm, in special circumstances of discord or danger; and the method he used was
commonly to take custody although there was no vacancy,
and to have the issues applied to the good of the house.

This might be done if there were serious dissension in the
house, endangering its possessions, as at Beeleigh in 1269;[4]
or enmity from without, as Quarr in 1282 was taken into the
king's hands to protect it against its own patron, Isabel de
Forz.[5] Dover Priory was taken into custody in 1271 for both
reasons—to protect it against the monks of Canterbury, who
were claiming dominion over it,[6] and because of internal discord resulting from this.[7]

But by far the commonest occasion for this protective custody was debt; in the late thirteenth century the king frequently took over the affairs of embarrassed monasteries, and
had their goods administered to pay off their debts. In all this
he was on the whole acting as king, not as patron. Miss Wood-
Legh has shown that in the time of Edward III there was a
regular statement that the house taken over was of royal
patronage, or that the patron was in wardship;[8] but in the

---

[1] *Grosseteste, Epist.*, pp. 308–9.
[2] *Close R. 1242–7*, p. 131.   [3] Ibid., p. 66.
[4] *Cal. Pat. R. 1266–72*, pp. 390, 392. Cf. Lenton, 1258 (*Close R. 1256–9*, p. 459).
[5] *Cal. Pat. R. 1281–92*, p. 39; *Select Cases in King's Bench*, i. 120.
[6] Christchurch had for years been claiming dominion, partly as mother-house,
partly as patron in vacancies of the archbishopric (C. R. Haines, *Dover Priory,
passim*).
[7] *Cal. Pat. R. 1266–72*, pp. 613, 631, 694, 700; *Close R. 1268–72*, p. 389. *Gervase
of Cant.* ii. 262–3.
[8] Wood-Legh, *Church Life . . . under Edward III*, p. 4.

thirteenth century this was not so; the houses taken into royal custody might be of anyone's patronage.[1] Indeed in 1267 Spalding Priory was taken into royal custody at the request of the patron, Henry de Lacy.[2]

On the other hand this royal protection was a kind of general patronage; and there was an added motive for it if the house were actually of royal foundation.[3] Edward I took Leominster Priory into his hand 'as belongs to its patron', to relieve the debt of its mother-house Reading Abbey, which he was bound to help considering his ancestors' pious intention in founding it;[4] here he helps the mother-house by taking custody of its cell, explicitly as patron of both. A patron other than the king might take the same steps: Archbishop Winchelsey appointed a custodian for the temporalities of St. Gregory's, Canterbury, not then vacant, because of its debts.[5] But this seems exceptional: in the 1290's the archbishop of York was actively concerned for Fountains as its patron,[6] but it was the king who took custody.[7] Probably royal custody was more effective than any other, for protecting a house against its enemies or creditors, corrodians or guests, or against itself or its prelate.

Similarly alien priories were taken into custody in time of war, for security and profit, irrespective of who was patron; the orders for this in 1295 say nothing about whether or not the priories concerned were of royal patronage.[8] In this year Henry de Lacy wrote to the king about the seizure of Spalding Priory of his patronage, explaining that all but three of the monks were English and that the prior was elected and perpetual, and asking for their possessions to be restored, saving to the king the right to forbid aliens to stay there and the £40

[1] e.g. Fountains, 1274, 1291 (*Cal. Pat. R. 1272–81*, p. 59; *1281–92*, p. 431): see of York not vacant. Newborough, 1281 (ibid. *1272–81*, p. 437); Roger de Mowbray not a minor. Missenden, 1281 (ibid. *1281–92*, p. 2): Joan de Sanford's heirs already had seisin (*Cal. Fine R.* i. 149). Flaxley, 1281 (*Cal. Pat. R. 1281–92*, p. 4): Humphrey de Bohun not a minor. St. Augustine's, Bristol, 1285 (ibid., p. 198): Thomas de Berkeley not a minor.

[2] *Cal. Pat. R. 1266–72*, p. 109.

[3] This was claimed for Dover (see p. 96), probably at the suggestion of the monks who obtained the writs, although the archbishop was in fact patron.

[4] *Reg. Cantilupe*, p. 37.   [5] *Reg. Winchelsey*, p. 299.

[6] *Fountains Memorials*, i. 179–81.

[7] Ibid. i. 181, and *Cal. Pat. R. 1281–92*, p. 431.

[8] *Cal. Fine R.* i. 362–6.

which normally went to Angers. This was granted, not because the priory was of someone else's patronage, but because it was not really alien.[1]

This royal custody in special circumstances might often be disliked by the patrons. At the beginning of the Interdict some patrons obtained from the king the custody of their monasteries' confiscated goods:[2] others may have felt a grievance. But beyond this, both John and Henry III were accused of taking custody of houses not of their patronage even in ordinary vacancies. Magna Carta laid down that barons who had founded abbeys, and whose titles were attested by royal charter or ancient possession, were to have their wardship when vacant;[3] and the Barons' Petition of 1258 included the complaint that the king had demanded custody in vacancies of abbeys and priories founded in the fiefs of earls and barons, 'so that they cannot elect without his will' (presumably his licence and assent); this was to the barons' prejudice, since they as *medii* bore the service due from these houses to the king.[4]

Cases which might provoke such protests (especially from bishops as patrons) can be found,[5] but neither they nor the terms of the protests suggest that the king had been claiming to be universal patron or aiming at becoming it. There are hints in Richard I's reign of an idea that all *abbeys* should be in the king's gift. According to the Walden chronicle[6]

---

[1] *Mon.* iii. 225–6. Cf. Edmund of Cornwall's recovery of the custody of Eye Priory, seized as alien while vacant in his hands. He charged the priory £100 for expenses of litigation and travelling (Midgley, *Accounts of the Earldom of Cornwall*, p. 156).

[2] Cheney, in *Trans. R. Hist. Soc.* 4th Ser. xxxi. 134, 136, n. 1: Geoffrey fitz Piers (Walden, Shouldham, and Hurley) and Henry Hussey (Durford: *Rot. Lit. Claus.* i. 110b). When Kenilworth Priory was in John's hands, services due to the *dominis fundorum* (the Clintons, presumably) were paid (*P.R. 12 John*, p. 6).

[3] Stubbs, *Charters*, p. 298 (c. 46). The 1217 reissue uses the terms 'patrons' and 'advowson': ibid., p. 343 (c. 40). See McKechnie, *Magna Carta*, pp. 506–7.

[4] Stubbs, *Charters*, p. 375 (c. 11).

[5] e.g. Eynsham: according to the Barnwell chronicler, one of John's misdeeds was to take its custody while vacant during the Interdict, though its advowson belonged to the bishop of Lincoln (*Walter of Coventry*, ii. 213). For the royal claim to advowson, see p. 29. Thorney: Henry III took custody, &c., while the bishop of Ely claimed the advowson by John's grant (*V.C.H. Cambridge*, ii. 214). Glastonbury in 1274 (see p. 77). St. German's, 1279 (see p. 77). Binham, 1290 (not claiming to be patron, but as patron of the vacant mother-house: see p. 81).

[6] Arundel 29, f. 11v.

Richard I's inquiries before making Walden an abbey were not only whether the revenues were adequate and whether it was free of subjection to any other house, but also whether King Henry had had the last donation.[1] Further, Richard did in fact retain its advowson after making it an abbey; but John restored it to the new earl of Essex as having been wrongly retained.[2] Similarly, in Richard's dispute with St. Hugh of Lincoln over Eynsham, the bishop was warned that Henry II had decreed 'that every abbey in his kingdom should remain in the king's gift';[3] but the bishop won his case in the Curia Regis.[4] Thus the idea was abortive.[5] Thirteenth-century kings were rather pressing home any claims that they had to particular advowsons. Besides disputed claims for which there is evidence, the king had in his possession several advowsons which might well have been claimed by someone else,[6] and this would come to light chiefly at vacancies. In any case, the escheator might take custody of a vacant monastery in the absence of any other claimant, and give it up if successfully challenged.[7] In fact, the king as such claimed custody only in

[1] The answer is not clear: the chronicler says the prior's institution *omnibus liquido patet*.

[2] See p. 169, n. 6.

[3] *Magna Vita*, p. 190: see Reich, p. 309.

[4] See p. 29.

[5] In 1200 John granted William Marshal the privilege of bestowing the pastoral staff of Nutley Abbey, in his fief (Rymer, *Foedera*, i. 81); however, this may mean not that the king had hitherto done it, but rather that actual lay investiture was so rare that it needed royal sanction. It certainly does not show, as McKechnie claimed, 'that John forbade appointments without royal licence' (*Magna Carta*, p. 507).

[6] Especially the earls of Leicester and Winchester; three Beaumont foundations were in the king's hands: Alcester Abbey by 1216 (*Pat. R. 1216–25*, pp. 2–3); Luffield Priory by 1231 (ibid. *1225–32*, pp. 432, 436) and perhaps late in Henry II's reign (Browne-Willis, *Mitred Abbeys*, London, 1718–19, ii. 24–25, from Luffield register); Leicester Abbey by 1178–9 (*P.R. 25 Henry II*, p. 115; *34 H. II*, p. 215). Of these, Leicester at least may have been retained by Henry II out of property restored to Robert Blanchesmains after his rebellion in 1173. Cf. Whitby (royal by 1180: *P.R. 27 H. II*, p. 50; *28 H. II*, p. 62; *7 Ric. I*, p. 28. See A. H. Thompson, in *Yorks. Archaeol. Journal*, xxvii. 402; *Cartularium abbathiae de Whiteby*, ed. Atkinson, i. xxxvi–xxxix, ii. 688; *Percy Cartulary*, ed. Martin, No. 4623). Selby (royal by 1214: *Rot. Lit. Pat.*, p. 125. See Knowles, *M.O.*, p. 402; *Selby Coucher Book*, ed. Fowler, pp. 291, [25]). Darley (see *Darley Cartulary*, ed. R. R. Darlington, Kendal, 1945, ii. 571, and introduction, pp. iii–iv).

[7] e.g. Wintney: royal claim disproved by inquest (*Reg. Pontissara*, ii. 509). But cf. Alcester; royal claim (after seisin throughout the thirteenth century) unsuccessfully challenged in 1300 by a descendant of Ralph the Butler, joint founder with his lord the earl of Leicester (*Cal. Chancery Warrants*, i. 125). Cf. Pontefract, 1259,

exceptional circumstances of war, danger, or debt; ordinary custody in vacancies was the patron's right, in all its variations from full exploitation to posting a man at the gates.

where the monks obtained an inquest on whether the escheator had wrongly taken custody, on the grounds that the Lacys were patrons (*Close R. 1216–19*, p. 457): though the escheator seems to have acted correctly, since the heir was a minor.

VI

EXPLOITATION

A RELIGIOUS house could be far more to its patron even
at a mundane level than an establishment which occasionally applied to him about its election, which rendered rent or service, and to which he sent a bailiff in vacancies.
The monks were his dependants and neighbours, and he could
expect from them many useful services and incidental gains.

The monastic obligation to general hospitality had led to
monasteries being treated as convenient lodgings for royalty
and nobility on their travels. At Dunstable Priory, placed as
it was on the way between London and Northampton, King
Edward's visits were frequent enough to make it worth building him a special room.[1] Hospitality to ladies might entail
a modification of discipline; rules had to give way before the
habits of aristocratic society. The English Benedictine Chapter
made statutes against women coming in after dinner, but
exceptions might be made for noblewomen.[2] By the Cistercian statutes women were only allowed in during nine days at
the time of the church's dedication, obviously a social occasion; they were on no account to spend the night.[3] But privileges to visit were sometimes granted to great ladies with their
waiting-women.[4] The Premonstratensian statutes excepted
none but foundresses, who might enter the cloister only.[5]

This hospitality, not to poor travellers but to the noble and
exacting, was amongst the monasteries' heaviest expenses.
Grosseteste complained that the king burdened religious
houses by staying in them, and although he was sometimes
invited, 'fear, not love, is the spur of such an invitation'.[6] And

---

[1] *Ann. Mon.* iii. 276. Several other monasteries had royal chambers; e.g. Winchcombe, where a corrodian was given a room under the king's room 'provided that
his comings and goings . . . were decent' (*Landboc sive registrum mon. de Winchelcumba*, ed. Royce, i. 344).

[2] Pantin, *Chapters*, i. 42, 72.

[3] Fowler, *Cistercian Statutes 1256–88*, p. 22.

[4] e.g. 1243, the queen (*Foedera*, i. 252); 1290, Countess Joan of Gloucester (*Cal.
Papal L.* i. 525).

[5] Lefèvre, *Les Statuts de Prémontré*, p. 134. The Gilbertines apparently made no
exceptions to their limit of three days for a woman's stay: see p. 104, n. 2.

[6] *Ann. Mon.* i (Burton), p. 424.

there were improper motives subtler than fear; a willingly hospitable abbot might be accused, like Abbot John I of Fountains, of too much concern to win the 'favour of the people, friendship of powerful men, and grace and familiarity of the king'.[1] A bishop's injunctions for economy might include limitations on hospitality: Archbishop John le Romeyn forbade Marton Priory to receive secular persons and their dogs to stay, except at the patron's request.[2]

The interest of king and magnates in this was not altogether opposed to that of the Church; they had an interest in protecting houses of their own patronage against impoverishment by others. Royal commissions for the custody of houses in debt often include orders to turn out guests and not to receive any more;[3] and the first clause in the First Statute of Westminster forbade anyone to demand hospitality at a monastery not of his own advowson. Further, no one was to hunt, fish, or eat in the lands or houses of prelates or religious men against their will; nor to harm them for denying food or lodging—this was to bind the king's counsellors and justices[4] like anyone else; nor to send men, horses, or dogs to stay in religious houses or their manors. The statute was not intended to authorize withdrawal of hospitality from the needy, or, on the other hand, burdensome demands by *avouwez*.[5]

This shows that while magnates habitually stayed in monasteries not of their own patronage, it was only the patron who had a definite claim to hospitality at the monastery's cost. How much he imposed on the house probably depended on custom and goodwill. Late in the twelfth century Bishop Hugh of Coventry and Lichfield, giving Buildwas Abbey of his patronage a lodging in Lichfield as a friendly return for the hospitality they owed him, stated this as unlimited: 'Because the abbey was founded by one of my predecessors, I can and ought to go to those brothers whenever I wish, more certainly than to others.'[6]

---

[1] *Mon.* v. 305 (from chronicle). He was abbot 1203–9.

[2] *Register of John le Romeyn*, ed. W. Brown, i. 160.

[3] Wood-Legh, pp. 7, 8.

[4] The Dunstable annals record that in 1247 the justices were there for two days at the prior's cost; and that in 1254 the prior was 'much oppressed by expenses of the justices' (*Ann. Mon.* iii. 174, 192).   [5] *Statutes*, i. 26–28.

[6] i.e. probably others in his diocese but not of his patronage. *Mon.* v. 359.

But there may sometimes have been a defining custom; Bishop Pontissara wrote to Titchfield Abbey, founded by one of his predecessors, that he intended to come to stay with them, for by ancient custom they received the bishops of Winchester returning from abroad 'for rest from their labours'. He added that as he was coming from the court of Rome he should be entertained by exempt houses even if they were not of his patronage.[1] The letter has a note of assertion, as if he expected to be resisted or received grudgingly (and in fact the bishops were perhaps no longer technically patrons).[2]

The patron might have a defined right to stay at a manor belonging to the house. Lewes Priory held the manor of Walton in Norfolk of the Warennes for the service of two *hospicia* in the year, on the way to Yorkshire and back; if they stayed more often they were to pay.[3] This manor, now West Walton, would obviously be a convenient lodging for the Warennes; it lay near the roads from King's Lynn and their own Castle Acre to Wisbech at the lowest crossing of the river Nene, where they would have to go on their way round the Wash to their lands in the north.

Any such defined service might be repudiated on the grounds of frankalmoin tenure. In 1298 the steward of Edmund of Cornwall claimed entertainment at a manor of St. Frideswide's when a court was held there; not that the earl was patron, but St. Frideswide's held this land of him. An inquest held by the earl's own order found that the manor was held in alms and therefore the steward had no right to stay there, though he had been invited by the prior on occasion.[4] As a rule hospitality was undefined, not a detailed, regulated *droit de gîte* like that of the French advocate.[5]

The Quincys stayed so often at their alien priory of Ware, partly to hold courts for Ware manor, that Countess Margaret built herself a hall, chamber, and chapel in the priory, which her successors used and enlarged.[6] Sometimes the

[1] *Reg. Pontissara*, i. 267.   [2] See pp. 19–20.

[3] The condition is attributed to the first earl in one of the forged foundation charters (*Chartulary of Lewes Priory*, ed. Saltzman, i. 2–7. See *Early Yorks. Charters*, viii. 57).

[4] *Cart. of the Monastery of St. Frideswide*, ed. Wigram, ii. 310–12.

[5] Senn, *L'institution des avoueries* . . . , p. 135. *Dictionnaire d'histoire . . . ecclésias-tique*, v. 1235.   [6] *V.C.H. Herts.* iv. 455.

patron or one of his family might stay for a long stretch: in 1279 the Cluniac visitors reported that Thetford was embarrassed by the residence of the advocate,[1] the earl of Norfolk's brother, who cost more than the whole convent and prior put together.[2]

Probably such continual residence was unusual; more often the patron would be the chief amongst those occasional guests whose arrival crowded the stables and called for entertainment at the abbot's own table; he would have a stronger right than others to come often, and probably a social duty to come sometimes.

Sometimes the patron would pay a ceremonial visit, and be met in procession as was his right in canon law;[3] often this would be for a special occasion like the dedication of a rebuilt conventual church or the installation of an abbot; or he would stay there for a feast of the Church. In 1266 King Henry spent a week over Christmas at Osney, 'with all cheerfulness and gaiety', before returning to the campaign against the Disinherited.[4] In 1278 King Edward and Queen Eleanor spent a week at Easter at Glastonbury; they and the archbishop of Canterbury, who accompanied them, were received one by one in solemn procession. The archbishop held an ordination in the abbey, ordaining the king's treasurer and vice-chancellor. The guests were shown Arthur's tomb, and the king arranged for it to be put before the high altar.[5]

Although it was obviously fitting that the patron should celebrate a festival and be shown the sights at his own monastery, it might cause some anxiety. Adam de Domerham's account of this visit to Glastonbury shows, besides the honour and excitement of a visit by the court, some preoccupation with expense and jealousy for the abbey's liberties. These liberties are presumably those of the Twelve Hides within which no royal servant could enter to perform his functions,

---

[1] See p. 18.

[2] Duckett, ii. 142–3. Cf. the master of Sempringham's complaint of oppression, and the king's intervention, when Agnes de Vescy stayed at Watton several times, and beyond the three nights' limit required by their order, with a crowd of women with dogs, &c. (Bodl. MS. Laud 642, Alvingham cart., f. 36). This is a rare example of patronal claims on a Gilbertine house: see p. 5.

[3] See p. 127.   [4] *Ann. Mon.* iv (Osney), p. 197.

[5] Domerham, pp. 587–9.

nor could even the king himself do justice.[1] Before the king's
arrival the Earl Marshal's substitute came to arrange about
lodging the magnates; but the monks would not let him interfere, as it was against their liberties; they insisted on doing
everything themselves, and the abbot's own marshal carried
the marshal's rod in the king's presence. This was evidently
something of a triumph. On Easter Monday another trouble
rose and passed: the king had arranged to hear the assizes at
Glastonbury, but when the abbot and convent begged him not
to do so, he assured them that he had no wish to derogate
from their liberties, and held the assizes at Street instead.

A more awkward situation arose at St. Augustine's, Canterbury, where the royal family stayed on their return from Gascony in 1289. Edward invited Archbishop Pecham to dine
with him at the abbey on Sunday. This apparently harmless
invitation raised a hornet's nest. The monks feared for their
exemption if the archbishop came with cross erect, and the
archbishop would not come except in proper state. After
elaborate negotiations the king took the line of least resistance,
respecting the monks' prickly caution as he had done at Glastonbury: he told the archbishop to eat at home at the king's
cost. Pecham was naturally offended, and blamed the abbot
and monks; after the royal visit was over he summoned them
to show their privileges; the abbot appealed to Rome; and so
a formidable lawsuit was started by the king's wish as a guest
at the abbey to entertain a guest of his own.[2]

But a commoner worry than endangered privileges was the
plain expense. Domerham records as if with relief that for the
first few days of their Easter visit the king and queen stayed
at their own expense; though on the Tuesday the whole court
was there at the monastery's charge.[3] When the royal family
came to Dunstable in 1247, the prior and canons gave gilt
cups to the king and queen, and gold buckles to the Lord
Edward and Princess Margaret; and though the chronicler
seems proud of these gifts, he remarks carefully that they cost
the priory 22 marks apart from all the other expenses of the
visit.[4]

---

[1] *Glastonbury Cart.* i. 220.   [2] Thorne, cols. 1951–4.
[3] Domerham, pp. 587–9.
[4] *Ann. Mon.* iii. 173. When the queen received confraternity at St. Albans in

Presents were of course made both ways; on this occasion at Dunstable the king gave 100*s.* for a pix and a thurible, and some precious cloths. It seems, too, that the king sometimes arranged for large offerings of candles to be made on his behalf when he came to a monastery for a festival, which would reduce the expenses of the sacristan; in 1242 and 1244, for instance, the local sheriffs were to spend a few pounds on having large numbers of candles made and sent to Bury or St. Albans 'against the king's arrival'.[1]

Despite the expense and anxiety, occasional visits by the patron were not likely to be resented;[2] what would cause more ill-feeling would be the casual and impersonal use of the house as lodgings for his servants, or as stables and kennels. This would be a steady drain on a house's resources; a measure of economy which the king enjoined on Reading Abbey in 1275 was to turn out all horses and sergeants, both the king's and others'.[3]

King John sent sick horses to Milton;[4] and Henry III sent horses belonging to various servants of his[5] to different monasteries for forty days at a time: not just for summer grazing but for stabling and fodder, for they were sent in November and February.[6] Two of the houses concerned were not of royal patronage,[7] which shows how this kind of request was not made only by the patron;[8] but it was more normal, and harder to refuse, if it was the patron who asked. Hugh de Courtenay, patron of Ford Abbey, forced the monks to keep two horses, their grooms, and a hound with her puppies;[9] and Robert Boutevileyn claimed that Pipewell Abbey should keep his hounds and one horse indefinitely.[10]

1299, the less cheerful side of the picture was that she stayed three days 'with too big a following' (*Rishanger,* p. 194).

[1] *Cal. Lib. R. 1240–5,* pp. 114, 115, 244.
[2] See Powicke, ii. 721.
[3] *Cal. Pat. R. 1272–81,* p. 81.
[4] *V.C.H. Dorset,* ii. 59. But the abbey was vacant.
[5] They include Nicholas the Usher; Richard Oysel, sometimes sent on errands by the king (*Close R. 1254–6,* pp. 11, 15, 17); John de Stratford, a royal clerk (ibid., p. 3) and Geoffrey de Lucy, the king's valet (ibid. *1256–9,* pp. 272–3).
[6] *Close R. 1256–9,* pp. 197, 282.
[7] St. Osyth's and Kingswood.
[8] This is implied in Archbishop Romeyn's order to Marton Priory (see p. 102).
[9] *Mon.* v. 380 (chronicle).
[10] *Mon.* v. 437 (chronicle).

The presence of the patron's servants could be more troublesome than the mere stabling of one or two extra horses. In 1276 the canons of Dunstable had the king's falconers lodged with them; one night the falconers started a brawl, which worked up until the prior could hardly prevent his men and the townspeople, for once allied, from lynching the falconers. Apparently no violence was done them, but they went next morning to complain to the king at Wallingford; and only after two stringent inquests were the canons, their servants, and the burgesses acquitted of injuries to the king's servants.[1]

These falconers were probably lodged at Dunstable because the king intended to hawk in the neighbourhood; but often servants were sent to monasteries for longer spells—for intervals between service,[2] as it were on half-pay, or perhaps when their work lay near by. King Henry sent his servant Robert le Blund, with a horse and a boy, to convalesce at St. Albans;[3] King Edward sent his man Wobodus to Abingdon, with two horses and two grooms, to stay eight months.[4]

But frequently royal servants were lodged in monasteries for life, on retirement, with a corrody in food and clothing.[5] This was amongst the services most often required in the second half of the century by the king. It is not so much a branch of hospitality as a kind of patronage belonging to the house which could be exercised in favour of its lord.

The close rolls, late in the century, contain many requests to religious houses to admit some man, the king's sergeant, often with a horse and groom, and find him the necessities of life according to his station;[6] sometimes it is stated that he has served the king long and faithfully but is not yet provided for. These requests were frequent before they were regularly enrolled; the patent rolls, from about 1267, contain grants to

---

[1] *Ann. Mon.* iii. 273.

[2] In the late twelfth century Boxgrave Priory was endowed by its patron William de St. John for the support of his chaplain, who was to be maintained there like a monk, except when the lord or lady was living at Halnaker (their nearby residence); i.e., while the family was away, the chaplain lodged in the priory (*Mon.* iv. 646: charter). The editors of the *Monasticon* misunderstood this as providing for one of the monks to act as chaplain, a mistake reproduced in *V.C.H. Sussex*, ii. 56.

[3] Hill, *Letter-books*, p. 100 (No. 99).

[4] *Cal. Close R. 1288–96*, p. 507.

[5] See Reich, pp. 311–12.

[6] e.g. *Cal. Close R. 1288–96*, p. 279; *1296–1302*, pp. 188, 308, 597, 606.

various houses that as they have admitted a sergeant of the king's they need not be burdened with any more corrodies while this man lives.[1] Earlier than the 1260's the evidence is scanty, but such corrodies were certainly sometimes asked for; in 1249 King Henry ordered Muchelney to support Ralph de Hele and his wife and to restore the house and land whence they had ejected them;[2] and in 1251 the king wrote thanking the monks profusely for keeping his servant Ralph de Hele for several years, and relieving them of their charge from next Easter when Ralph would be sent elsewhere.[3]

The kind of men sent is sometimes shown by their surnames or descriptions: blacksmith, painter, surgeon; 'of the chamber' and 'of the pantry'; 'once the king's porter' or 'sergeant of the kitchen'. Most of them have a horse and groom; some two, and some none. The houses concerned were almost always of royal patronage. They include Cistercian houses;[4] although these escaped the regular consequences of having a patron, they were liable to these occasional requests.

It was an excellent way for the king to provide decently for his old servants, but a burden to the monasteries. The monks might try to withdraw a corrody; in 1297 Edward wrote thanking the monks of Abbotsbury for admitting Henry Lumbard, but insisting that they restore to him certain necessities which he complains they have withdrawn.[5] Henry wrote similarly to Muchelney in 1255 on behalf of Ralph de Hele and his wife, still on their hands, whom the monks 'have many times provided with necessaries, out of love for the king, for which he thanks them', but who had lately been 'driven hither and thither' and deprived of their portions of food and clothing. Evidently Ralph still had periods of work, for the king states that he sends him back now since he is not strong enough for his usual labours.[6]

---

[1] e.g. *Cal. Pat. R. 1266–71*, pp. 49, 241, 370, 462, 507, 528, 654, 695.

[2] *Close R. 1247–51*, p. 546.

[3] Ibid. *1251–3*, p. 175. He was still there in 1255, however: see n. 6. Another early case is a corrody to Philippa de Rading (not explicitly a royal servant) and her daughter, at Barking in 1253; meanwhile, the abbey was not to be charged with lay-brothers, messengers, &c. (*Cal. Pat. R. 1247–58*, p. 180).

[4] e.g. Stanley or Stoneleigh, Woburn, Coggeshall, Meaux.

[5] *Cal. Close R. 1296–1302*, p. 123.

[6] *Cal. Pat. R. 1247–58*, p. 436. In 1260 Henry III tried to make Colchester Abbey give Henry Prat a letter patent from the chapter confirming his livery; after some

The monasteries often put up some resistance to demands for corrodies, sometimes successfully, despite the king's promises of favour and threats of displeasure, which seem almost a matter of form. The grants of exemption during the life of the present corrodian reflect the monks' attitude. That to Woburn in 1272 relates that the king has several times asked the monks to take William Blacksmith; now, presumably after several refusals, he concedes that if they take the man they shall be charged with no more while he lives.[1] This principle of one at a time seems to have been accepted as fair.[2]

Some of these old men were sent backwards and forwards between the court and various monasteries for months before they finally settled down. It seems that the man himself carried the application, and carried back the letters of excuse.[3] For example, amongst several old servants sent to monasteries in the spring of 1303 were William the Surgeon and Roger the Usher.[4] King Edward sent William to be maintained with horse and servant at Ramsey, promising the monks his favour if they complied. The abbot, calling himself the king's 'humblest chaplain', sent the man back and begged to be excused, as they already had two such old servants to support, and they never used to have more than one. The king then changed his promises to mild threats of diminishing his favour, while the chancellor warned the abbot that he would incur the king's anger.[5] Yet they escaped the burden; for on 20 June William the Surgeon was sent to the canons of Butley.[6] But these, meanwhile, had also been excusing themselves from corrodies; earlier in the year Roger the Usher had been sent to them, with two horses and grooms,[7] but they had evidently sent him back, for Roger was sent to Bury; the Bury monks

resistance, the abbot confirmed it under his own seal (*Close R. 1259–61*, p. 108; *1261–4*, p. 102).

[1] *Cal. Pat. R. 1266–72*, p. 695.

[2] In 1302 Gilbert del Bed, the king's 'sumeter', asked for a letter to some religious house not otherwise burdened by the king. Later he specified Bardney or Leicester (*Rotuli Parliamentorum*, i. 156).

[3] J. C. Cox (*V.C.H. Berks.* ii. 55) suggested that when a man had letters to several houses he got corrodies from several, in a money commutation; but the cases he cites show an interval between one letter and the next: probably one application had failed.   [4] *Cal. Close R. 1302–7*, p. 86.

[5] *Ramsey Chron.*, pp. 381–3 (letter-book).

[6] *Cal. Close R. 1302–7*, p. 91.   [7] *Ibid.*, p. 86.

also asked to be excused, since they already had one William of the Chamber. On 17 August Roger was sent back to Bury, but this time it was conceded that the monks need only support a single horse and groom for him. They must have excused themselves again, for on 4 September Roger the Usher was sent to Ely, in his reduced state with one horse;[1] at Ely it seems he stayed.

On the same day Ramsey was again asked to support an old servant, Stephen de Meen; and the abbot again asked to be excused, naming the same two who already had corrodies.[2] His excuse was accepted again, and Stephen was sent to Peterborough.[3] Meanwhile William the Surgeon was still on his travels; the Butley canons had said they could not take him, because of their debts and losses from floods; but on 4 September the king sent him back, rejecting their excuse.[4] Even so, they must have got rid of him somehow, for in November the abbot of Ramsey was once more trying to avoid taking him, asking the queen and the princess for their support and promising 'to pray for you the more heartily'.[5] He may have settled at Butley in the end, for in 1312 the canons there were asked to take a corrodian instead of William le Leche, now dead.[6] Evidently there was no clear right on either side; the matter was settled by adjustment of pressure between the king's tenacity in asking and the monks' tenacity in excusing themselves. He could not absolutely command, and they could not absolutely refuse.

A special kind of corrody for which King Henry asked was the maintenance of Jewish converts; but whereas requests for corrodies for old servants were in this period almost entirely limited to houses of royal patronage,[7] converts were sent to any house. Prynne prints an enrolment of these requests on the dorse of the fine roll for 1254-5: out of more than a hundred requests either to take new converts for two years, or

---

[1] *Cal. Close R. 1302-7*, p. 104 (all Roger's moves August–September).
[2] *Ramsey Chron.*, p. 385 (letter-book).
[3] *Cal. Close R. 1302-7*, p. 104.   [4] Ibid., p. 107.
[5] *Ramsey Chron.*, pp. 383-4 (letter-book).
[6] *Cal. Close R. 1307-13*, p. 450. For corrodies at Butley see Myres, in *Oxford Essays . . . to H. E. Salter*, pp. 193-4. It may have been considered as of royal foundation in the interval between William de Auberville's quitclaim of the advowson and Eleanor Ferre's claim to it.
[7] But not under Edward II: Reich, p. 312.

to keep those already sent, only about half are to royal houses. But it is perhaps significant that while almost half the houses receiving first requests refused and were asked again, about two-thirds of these were non-royal.[1]

The monks' unwillingness to take in converts gave scope for a kind of blackmail; in 1254 the abbot of Hyde gave 1 mark to a Jew, Martin le Cumvers, to buy him off when he arrived with letters requiring maintenance; actually Martin was a fraud, and had obtained the letters by deception. A little later he posed as a convert at St. Swithun's, pretending that he had been christened Henry after the king.[2] Probably he had not aimed to be actually received into the monastery and live there; he would be too readily found out; he must have been going the rounds of the Winchester houses to collect money, rightly expecting them to be willing to pay him to go away with his letters.

Places in the convent itself might be filled at the patron's request. Rarely, the patron had definite control over the admission of new members. Roger de Thony's foundation charter for Flamstead Priory, about 1150, had required the patron's consent for the admission of new nuns;[3] and the nuns of Burnham told Archbishop Pecham (who had asked for a place) that the earl of Cornwall forbade the reception of new nuns without his consent.[4] Pecham professed not to believe this, and anyhow denied that the earl had any voice in the matter; but at least the nuns thought it a plausible excuse. This sort of control was probably meant chiefly to prevent the house being overburdened with numbers,[5] and could well be not a regular right but a temporary order; but probably it could also be used to put in the patron's own candidates.

Sometimes a benefactor intended his gift for the support

[1] Prynne, ii. 835–40. For an earlier example see the king's release of Thorney in 1253 from a corrody already granted to a convert and his family (*Close R. 1251–3*, p. 457). For later examples see St. Osyth's (ibid. *1265–8*, p. 109), West Dereham (ibid. *1268–72*, p. 524).

[2] *Close R. 1253–4*, p. 121 (mandate for his arrest).

[3] *Mon.* iv. 300. The archbishop of York's injunctions to St. Oswald's, Gloucester, in 1250 stipulated for his consent to the admission of new canons (*Reg. W. Giffard*, p. 204), but his position here was exceptional.

[4] *Reg. Peckham* (R.S.), i. 189.

[5] In 1267 Henry III forbade Acornbury to receive new nuns without his consent, because of debts (*Cal. Pat. R. 1266–72*, p. 109).

of one or more monks or canons whom he was to nominate; at Blackmore Priory Gilbert Basset, uncle of the patron's son Alan de Sanford, made grants for Alan's soul and had in return the right to present one canon, to be called the Basset canon.[1] But such definite arrangements do not normally seem to have been made with the chief patron. The patrons might endow an addition to the convent's numbers, as the St. Johns did for Boxgrave in the twelfth century, but apparently without a right of nomination;[2] while on the other hand the Says had the right to have a nun maintained at their foundation Westwood, but there is no mention of a special endowment for this.[3] At a few royal houses in the next two centuries the king nominated a nun at each accession to the throne, or sometimes in a vacancy.[4] Far more usually, probably, than any defined rights the patrons would occasionally ask for a place;[5] as in 1294 Margaret, grand-daughter of Alice de Luton, had letters from the king asking Romsey Abbey to admit her as a nun.[6]

But perhaps the favour most commonly asked was a benefice of the monastery's advowson. When it was reported that a certain rich church in St. Albans' gift had fallen vacant, the abbot and convent presented to it hastily; meanwhile the king asked for it for a chancery clerk, and the pope provided to it; in the chronicler's words, they were 'crows waiting for a corpse'.[7] Benefices, like corrodies and places, were of course not only asked for by the patron. His relationship in these matters was not unique, but was repeated in a vaguer form with all sorts of neighbours, benefactors, and magnates.[8] The

---

[1] *Catalogue of Ancient Deeds*, i. A. 501. Cf. Reginald de Cornhill and Prittlewell, 1203 (*V.C.H. Essex*, ii. 139). For several interesting cases in Premonstratensian houses see Colvin, pp. 304–5.

[2] *Mon.* iv. 646, 647.   [3] *V.C.H. Worcs.* ii. 148.

[4] Power, *Medieval Eng. Nunneries*, p. 189. According to *V.C.H. Cambridge*, ii. 220 the bishop of Ely could nominate a nun at the succession of a new abbess of Chatteris, as patron; but the reference (*Reg. Winchelsey*, pp. 324, 711–12) suggests that it was as diocesan (see Power, loc. cit., for another example).

[5] In 1273 Carrow Abbey had a papal privilege not to receive new nuns, being burdened by the requests of nobles who could not be resisted because of their power (*Mon.* iv. 71).

[6] *Cal. Close R.* 1288–96, p. 382.   [7] *Gesta Abb.* i. 346–9.

[8] The *Letters of Edward Prince of Wales*, 1304–5, ed. H. Johnstone (Cambridge, 1931), contain many such requests made by the Prince of Wales, mostly to royal houses; e.g. pp. 7–10, 39, 48, 51–56.

letter-book of Ramsey Abbey illustrates this: not only the king and queen but prelates and royal servants asked for corrodies and livings, a pension for an old lady or a job for a man with a good voice.[1] Some of these requests were refused, others granted. The patron would ask with most force, but even he could not demand such favours outright. In 1301 the queen asked the Ramsey monks for some living for her treasurer, who would be useful to them in any business with the king;[2] apparently the monks had said that they would more readily advance such a man. There might be a definite agreement that the monastery would present its patron's presentees to certain churches, as between Walden Abbey and Geoffrey fitz Piers for his and his eldest son's lifetimes;[3] but this seems exceptional.

Sometimes the monastery would present its patron's younger son or brother. In 1242 the abbot of Tewkesbury consulted Bishop Grosseteste on whether he should present to a benefice a minor, Gilbert de Clare.[4] This was presumably the younger brother, then aged thirteen, of the patron Earl Richard of Gloucester; if the earl had asked for a benefice for him, this would account for the abbot's embarrassment. The bishop's advice was to present someone else, and to give Gilbert 26 marks a year until he should obtain another living; so even the strict Grosseteste recognized the expediency of doing something for him.

This practice of granting a pension to a clerk until there was a living available was common and must have been expensive. St. Augustine's, Canterbury, had a privilege from Innocent III that they were to grant no more pensions to clerks, since the monastery was too much burdened with them by the prayers and sometimes threats of powerful men.[5] In Henry III's reign houses of royal patronage commonly gave a pension and then a benefice[6] to one of the king's clerks after the creation

---

[1] *Ramsey Chron.*, pp. 374, 377, 390, 403. [2] Ibid., p. 372.

[3] Harl. 3697 (cartulary), f. 20. Cf. the similar concession to the previous earl, William de Mandeville (ibid., f. 19).

[4] *Ann. Mon.* i (Tewkesbury), p. 122.

[5] Thorne, col. 1868.

[6] If the clerk refused an adequate benefice, the monks were no longer bound to pay the pension, but might be asked to do so: e.g. in 1280 Richard Inge had a 40s. pension from Dunstable; in 1282 he refused a benefice; at the chancellor's request the canons paid the pension *donec de artibus inchoasset* (*Ann. Mon.* iii. 264, 284, 289).

of an abbot. Sometimes the king promised this in advance; in 1242 Nicholas de Bolevill was promised that as soon as an abbot of Evesham was made, the king would ask the abbey for a benefice when there was one vacant, and meanwhile a pension, for one of Nicholas's brothers;[1] and in the same year Henry undertook to present his clerk Geoffrey de Wulward to the first benefice of Shaftesbury's advowson to fall vacant while the abbey was in his hands, and failing that, to ask the future abbess to provide for him.[2] Possibly the custom arose through the king promising more livings during a vacancy than actually fell in, and having to ask the new head for one to fulfil his promise.

By the end of the century this was considered a standard custom in royal houses, and also in foreign houses holding English lands in chief,[3] unless exemption were proved. In the discussion of King Edward's rights in a vacancy at St. Werburgh's, Chester, the abbot had to show why he refused to grant such a pension and benefice 'when bishops and any prelates who hold of the king . . ., by reason of their new creation, ought to do this and are bound to it'.[4] But an inquest proved that the king had not this right, just as he had no custody.[5] Indeed the two were sometimes held to go together, this 'grace due by reason of new creation' being a kind of relief: the abbot of St. Albans in 1302 claimed to be exempt from giving such a pension by the fine recently made for custody in vacancy. But his claim was not allowed.[6]

This shows how this sort of custom was coming to be considered a matter of right, a definite feudal service. St. Werburgh's exemption went with, if it was not a consequence of, tenure by prayers alone. In the fourteenth century the grant of a corrody was regarded in this light: Edward III sued the abbot of Ramsey for refusing a corrody to a man sent with royal letters, but the abbot maintained successfully that corrodies given hitherto were given by courtesy only, and that the

---

[1] *Cal. Pat. R. 1232–47*, p. 351. Calendared as '. . . as soon as he is made abbot of Evesham', but this must be a mistranslation for 'as soon as an abbot of Evesham is made'. Nicholas was a king's clerk, not a monk.

[2] Ibid., p. 324.

[3] e.g. Mont St. Michel, 1265 (*Close R. 1264–8*, p. 128); Grestain, 1285 (*Cal. Chanc. Warrants*, i. 26).   [4] *Rot. Parl.* i. 80–81, 89.

[5] *Cal. Pat. R. 1281–92*, p. 471.   [6] *Gesta Abb.* ii. 62. See pp. 88–89.

king could not thus burden the abbey as of right, for it held by no such services, but free from all tributes.[1] (This is odd, since the abbey held by knight-service). It is all neater and more theoretical than the empirical give-and-take of request and refusal at the turn of the century.

The keeping of horses and dogs, too, might be turned into a fixed service; the Ford monks complained that Hugh de Courtenay had exacted this although they held in frankal-moin.[2] William de Braose, lord of Bramber, gave an interesting charter to Sele Priory about 1260; in this he recognized that though the prior and monks had often 'of their mere courtesy, at our request' taken care of young horses and brought up young hounds and harriers for him, and given corrodies or liveries to his men, they were not bound to such services and he could not claim them as of right.[3] This shows once again that there was danger of such customs turning into fixed services (in which case the obvious counter-claim was tenure quit of all earthly service), but that normally they had to be asked for and might be refused. The charter also shows some of the common royal requests listed, as if standard, by a small patron; and there is in the Sele cartulary a grant of a livery to a chaplain 'at the request of our lord William de Braose'.[4] In fact though the bulk of the evidence relates to the king it seems likely that much the same pattern of services was rendered, friendlily or grudgingly, to most patrons, great or small.

Probably the king's and others' use of the monasteries' hospitality, or indirect exercise of their patronage, came to be resented as burdens the more they were demanded as due. Amongst the newly proposed grievances of 1309 were requests that the king abstain from asking for corrodies, pensions, or *perhendinaciones* from religious houses, by which they were impoverished; and that founders and others be careful not to burden the religious by staying with them or sending horses.[5]

---

[1] *Ramsey Cart.* iii. 99–108. Cf. Waverley, 1334, 1340 (*V.C.H. Surrey*, ii. 85).

[2] *Mon.* v. 380.

[3] *Chartulary of the Priory of Sele*, ed. Salzman, p. 49.

[4] Ibid., p. 73. Cf. Humphrey de Bohun's grant to Walden, 2 Edw. II, that the corrody to his valet (with horse and groom) was not to be a precedent (Harl. MS. 3697, f. 27v).   [5] *Reg. Winchelsey*, pp. 1029–30.

There could be other miscellaneous gains or services for the patron. The priory of Ewyas Harold provided the Tregoz family with a monk or chaplain to celebrate daily in the chapel of the castle;[1] and Robert fitz Roger (Clavering) arranged in 1278 to have a chaplain celebrating daily at Walberswick from the canons of Blythburgh, instead of an old custom whereby they gave his men of Walberswick a Christmas feast.[2] Robert de Tateshall, patron of Wymondham Priory at the end of the century, succeeded in recovering a livery of bread and ale which the former abbot of St. Albans (the mother-house) had withdrawn.[3] Robert Boutevileyn claimed from Pipewell Abbey, besides stabling and kennelling, a winter gown and four bloodlettings a year.[4] Oddest of all, the patron of Harrold Priory claimed to 'give the holy water', until in 1268 Ralph Morin surrendered this right to the nuns, in an agreement otherwise concerned with such straightforward matters as commons, a right of way, the diversion of a brook.[5] It seems most likely that the Morins had had at their disposal the benefice of holy water clerk, perhaps in Harrold parish.[6] Then there might be money dues, not only ordinary socage rents[7] but dues such as the 3s. owed specifically *de recognitione fundi* by the Markyate nuns to their patrons the dean and chapter of St. Paul's.[8]

Occasional demands for money gifts or aids were made, at least by the king; and one chronicler saw the feudal aids paid by an abbot in much the same light as his personal gifts of jewels and horses.[9] Henry III demanded taxes from the religious not specifically as patron nor only of royal houses, but

[1] *Cal. Inqu. P.M.* iii, p. 455. Cf. the arrangement between the Pomerays, patrons of Tregony, and its mother-house Le Val (*Reg. Coll. Exon.*, p. 321).

[2] *V.C.H. Suffolk*, ii. 92.

[3] *Gesta Abb.* ii. 23, 63–64.

[4] *Mon.* v. 437.

[5] *Records of Harrold Priory*, ed. Fowler, pp. 27–28.

[6] The parish church, though not identical with the conventual church, was appropriated to the nunnery and the vicar was of their household (Fowler, ibid., p. 11). A holy water clerk received alms for taking holy water round to the houses of parishioners in general or of those who could not attend mass; the benefice was supposed to be reserved for poor clerks or scholars (Du Cange, i. 342–3).

[7] e.g. Maiden Bradley to the Bisets (*Inquisitions Post Mortem for Worcs.*, ed. Willis-Bund, Worcs. Hist. Soc., Oxford, 1909, ii. 16).

[8] *Mon.* iii. 372.

[9] *Hist. Burgensis*, Swaffham, p. 119.

sometimes using the name of patron as an argument. In 1256
the Cistercian abbots refused to contribute for the Sicilian
project. According to Matthew Paris, Henry asked the abbot
of Buildwas, who happened then to be at court, why the abbots
had refused—for 'am I not your patron?'. In this he seems to
express the idea that he was in some sense the general patron
of churches in England; Buildwas itself was almost certainly
not of royal patronage.[1] The abbot acknowledged the king as
patron and defender, 'but you ought not to harm us by extorting money, but rather with devotion ask for our prayers', like
King Louis. Henry said he wanted both the money and the
prayers, and the abbot argued that this was impossible—'You
must do without one or the other. For if you violently extort
from us our little substance, how can we pray for you devoutly
and with sincere hearts? Prayer without devotion is of little or
no use.'[2] Though this improbably neat conversation, so vic-
torious for the abbot, may be largely Paris's invention, it is
none the less expressive of the monks' idea of what they did and
did not owe to a patron. Stiffer and more hostile arguments for
their purely spiritual obligations, emphasizing the rights
of other patrons, are attributed to the Cistercian abbots facing John's demand for aid in 1210: they were only stewards
of the alms of the faithful, given to God for their souls and
their ancestors' and childrens' souls, for the use of the religious and for the poor and sick, widows and orphans, not for
the king's revenues and knights' wages.[3]

Sometimes the house might help the patron out of debt, or
redeem a mortgage for him, in return for some confirmation or
privilege. When Henry d'Oilly, patron of Osney early in the
century, confirmed a manor to the canons, they gave him 300
marks and so freed him and his lands from 'the hard hand' of
David, a Jew of Oxford, 'because they did not wish to be found
ungrateful or illiberal to me their patron in my necessity'.[4]

[1] See p. 102.
[2] *Chron. Maj.* v. 553-4.
[3] Stanley chronicle, in *Chronicles of . . . Stephen, Henry II and Richard,* ed.
Howlett, ii. 510.
[4] *Cal. Charter R.* i. 49. Cf. Norman d'Arcy, benefactor of Barlynch Priory: in
1268 he changed the canons' tenure to frankalmoin, for 31 marks to ransom his
lands in his great need (ibid. ii. 395). In 1281 Easby Abbey lent money to Roald,
descendant of the founder Roald the Constable and probably the patron, on the
security of certain wardships and marriages (*V.C.H. Yorks., North Riding,* i. 234).

The credit of a house might well be of more use to its patron than its actual wealth. Hence one possible service was to raise a loan for the patron, or to stand surety for him when he borrowed—to be *fidejussores*. In 1243 the abbot and convent of Tewkesbury stood as *fidejussores* to the earl of Cornwall for a loan of £100 to their patron, the earl of Gloucester, who gave them a charter of indemnity;[1] in 1249 they borrowed 100 marks from the Jews for the earl,[2] just before he started on pilgrimage, and probably to pay for it. In 1252 the heads of three Clare foundations—Tewkesbury, Keynsham, and Stoke—went to the king on the earl's behalf about the money to be put down as security for his son's marriage to the king's niece; presumably they guaranteed or lent it.[3] In October 1307 the heads of Tewkesbury, Keynsham, Walsingham, Anglesey, and Tonbridge acknowledged a debt of 2,000 marks to Earl Henry de Lacy;[4] since they were all Clare foundations, this was probably a debt incurred for the young Earl Gilbert, perhaps for the expenses of his relief and coming of age.

Standing as *fidejussores* for anyone was forbidden repeatedly in the Cistercian statutes,[5] and in the chapters of the English Benedictines in 1249, 1253, and 1277.[6] This, together with particular papal privileges, and rulings in the decretals,[7] gave the royal abbeys strong grounds for resistance when the king required them to bind themselves for him.

A classic occasion was the visit of Simon Passelewe to various royal abbeys in 1258, a few years after some of the Benedictine statutes against standing surety, to ask them to stand surety for the king for 2,500 marks. At each house he concealed the last refusal and pretended to have come straight from court, but this ruse was useless because Waltham sent warning to St. Albans and St. Albans to Reading ahead of him. His main argument was 'You have nothing but what the king or his ancestors have given you; so you are bound, by right,

---

[1] *Ann. Mon.* i. 134.

[2] Ibid. i. 137. Cf. Thetford, which the Cluniac visitors in 1275–6 reported in debt for 400 marks borrowed for the patron, the Earl Marshal (Duckett, ii. 127).

[3] *Ann. Mon.* i. 151.   [4] *Cal. Close R. 1307–13*, p. 42.

[5] Fowler, pp. 90, 120, 121.   [6] Pantin, i. 35, 50, 65.

[7] Used respectively by St. Albans and Waltham in argument with Passelewe: see below.

to help him in so hard a case, since "all things are the prince's".'
To this the monks of St. Albans replied that all things belonged
to the prince for protection, not for destruction, according
to the coronation oath. At Waltham, Passelewe urged the
example of Westminster, the one house that had agreed; but
the canons of Waltham maintained that Westminster had an
obligation to King Henry above other royal houses, since he
was in a special sense their patron—'they of necessity favour
the lord king, and ought to obey him even in difficult things,
as the restorer of their church'.[1] Where there was no such
personal tie the monks could not feel strong personal reasons
for helping the king; their attitude was more remote, that of
the unwilling lender or grumbling tax-payer.

In an undated letter which must fall between 1238 and
1260, Abbot Richard of Reading wrote to Abbot John of
St. Albans thanking him for his advice and warning; he knows
that this advice is sound, and according to what was laid down
in General Chapter, that abbots and priors should not *fide-
jubere* for anyone or bind themselves by charter, unless with
the General Chapter's consent. He adds that he has already
excused himself to the king and queen on these grounds on
another similar occasion.[2] It seems very likely that this letter
was in answer to the abbot of St. Albans' warning mentioned
by Paris, during Passelewe's round of visits. The monks of
St. Albans themselves wrote to the king, after Passelewe had
left, excusing themselves 'moderately and amicably'.[3] It seems
clear that if the monasteries held together, and all made their
stand on the statutes of the order, they could evade such
requests by the king; the monks of Westminster were looked
on rather as blacklegs—'infatuated with false promises' and
setting a 'pernicious example'[4]—but it was admitted that they
had special obligations.

Sometimes the head of a house went on business for the
patron; the abbot of Tewkesbury went to Glamorgan in 1242

[1] *Chron. Maj.* v. 682–8, and *Gesta Abb.* i. 374–9.
[2] Pantin, i. 56.
[3] *Chron. Maj.* v. 687.
[4] Ibid., p. 682. And recording the death in the same year of Abbot Crokesley of
Westminster, Paris says that amongst all his virtues and accomplishments he had
the great fault of giving in to the king's demands when others stood out (ibid.,
p. 700).

for Richard de Clare, with 'several others of his special friends', to help quieten the country;[1] and in 1299 a monk of Hailes had royal permission to go abroad for the earl of Cornwall.[2] Kings, of course, found it useful to send heads of royal houses on diplomatic business, or to employ them as justices; there is no need to multiply examples of this.[3] Monks thus employed include Cistercians—in 1260, for instance, the abbot of Coggeshall went overseas as the king's envoy.[4] This was against their statutes, which forbade them to go on princes' affairs against princes or to mix in secular business;[5] but such isolation from affairs was impossible. In 1272 the abbot of Furness had himself taken off the commission of justices at Lancaster; but the others, it was said, 'did everything with the abbot's counsel'.[6]

In 1218 the abbot of St. Augustine's, Bristol, went on business to Ireland for the Earl Marshal,[7] who was not patron but had similar relations with the house. His niece had married the patron Robert de Berkeley, and through him Robert had just been reconciled after his rebellion.[8] The abbot wrote an account to his canons of how he had progressed in making peace for the earl in a lawsuit with the bishop of Ferns about lands in Leinster; the abbot explained that he had not taken any payment from the earl's steward, considering that if the earl won his cause they could freely and boldly ask for what they had spent; whereas if he lost, *quod absit*, he would have no cause for resentment against them. The abbot reminded them how the earl had helped them in their affairs, and how tangled their own Irish business would be without his advice.[9] When the Earl Marshal died he made the abbot of St. Augustine's one of his executors.[10] This was a connexion of friend-

---

[1] *Ann. Mon.* i. 122.

[2] *Cal. Chanc. Warrants*, i. 103.

[3] See Knowles, *R.O.*, pp. 276–7 (on, for example, Richard Crokesley of Westminster and Richard le Gras of Evesham), and Reich, pp. 328–32 (especially on Elerius of Pershore).

[4] *Cal. Pat. R. 1258–66*, pp. 83, 86. Cf. the first abbot of Beaulieu, whose worldliness consisted partly in being King John's agent, and who became bishop of Carlisle after his deposition (Knowles, *M.O.*, p. 658).

[5] Fowler, p. 70.

[6] Furness chronicle, in *Chron. of Ste., H. II and Ric.* ii. 561.

[7] *Cal. of Documents relating to Ireland*, p. 122.

[8] Smyth, *Lives of the Berkeleys* (Gloucester, 1883–5), i. 96–97.

[9] Hill, *Letter-books*, p. 232 (given in full).   [10] *Close R. 1227–31*, p. 505.

ship and mutual service, though not technically of patronage.

There were many occasional friendly services which the convent or its head could do. In 1268 the prior of Dunmow gave evidence for the young patron, Robert fitz Walter, in proving his age, and showed entries in the priory's annals as evidence.[1] Just after the Barons' Wars William de Esseby, the young patron of Catesby Priory, was pardoned for a man's death at the instance of the prioress.[2] Abbot Peter of Tewkesbury married Isabel de Clare and Richard of Cornwall in 1230;[3] and in 1258 a monk of Tewkesbury accompanied the patron's daughter overseas to her marriage.[4] In 1301 the abbot of Tewkesbury was one of Gilbert de Clare's executors,[5] as, lower in the social scale, the prior of Canons Ashby was for the patron Bartholomew de la Legh, about 1228.[6] Two of Isabel de Forz's three executors were the priors of Breamore and Christchurch, Twynham, of her patronage.[7]

So the patron of a monastery had numerous claims on it, which might be moderately or oppressively exercised, and which acted more perhaps than any other single influence to interweave monastic life and the social life of the country. Where the patron had no fixed right or established custom, he could always ask; he could resort to the monastery for a benefice for a clerk, or provision for a dependant; for stabling his horses, or a few days' entertainment for himself; to raise a loan, or for a solid and circumspect agent to go on special business.

[1] *Mon.* vi. 1. 148 (chronicle).
[2] Farrer, *Honours*, i. 170.
[3] *Ann. Mon.* i. 78. By this he presumably risked the king's displeasure.
[4] Ibid., p. 162.
[5] *Reg. Winchelsey*, p. 741.
[6] Farrer, i. 70.
 Reg. Romeyn, i. 320–1.

VII

FRIENDSHIP AND CONFRATERNITY

At the back of the hospitality and odd services from a house to its patron lay a personal relationship; it was part of his countryside and social circle. And at the heart of the value set on the patronage in the assumptions of the time, however conventional and perfunctory in individuals, lay the sense of belonging to the house and sharing in its spiritual benefits; though at another level this could be regarded simply as part of the feudal bargain, the services in exchange for the original grant.

There might be a whole network of kinship and friendship between the members of the convent as individuals, particularly the head, and the neighbouring gentry, particularly the patron. In a nunnery the patron's own nieces or daughters might take the veil.[1] The royal family had its special refuge, Amesbury in Wiltshire;[2] here the second Eleanor of Brittany, and the queen-mother Eleanor, became nuns,[3] and King Edward's daughter Mary together with thirteen daughters of noblemen.[4] It was an aristocratically select nunnery, and these royal nuns did not live the routine cloistered life, for they had private incomes.[5] But a house so neatly reduced to a family affair is exceptional. Other royal ladies became abbesses of famous nunneries: Abbess Mary of Shaftesbury was probably Geoffrey Plantagenet's natural daughter, and so King John's aunt;[6] while the abbess of

---

[1] e.g. two grand-daughters of Countess Ela of Salisbury entered her foundation Lacock (*Mon.* vi. 1. 501: history of founders). Two grand-daughters of one of the Lacy of Trym coheiresses entered the Lacy foundation Acornbury (ibid., p. 135: chronicle of Llanthony II).

[2] See Knowles, *M.O.*, p. 204.

[3] *Ann. Mon.* iii (Dunstable), pp. 326, 366. *Mon.* ii. 338. Eleanor of Brittany became abbess of the mother-house, Fontevraud (H. F. Chettle, 'English Houses of the Order of Fontevraud', *Downside Review*, lviii, 1940, p. 42).

[4] *Ann. Mon.* iv (Worcester), p. 491.

[5] Princess Mary had £100 p.a. for her chamber, 40 oaks for a fire in her room, 20 tuns of wine; later exchanged for manors. Eleanor of Brittany had a manor and the advowson of Poughley Priory given by the queen-mother (her grandmother) to Amesbury for her support (*Mon.* ii. 337–8).

[6] C. J. Fox, 'Abbess Mary of Shaftesbury', in *E.H.R.* xxvi (1911). John in making a gift to the abbey referred to her as *carissima amica*, or more probably *amita* (*Mon.* ii. 482).

Barking in the middle of the century was Henry III's sister Maud, to whom he gave silver vessels for the use of future abbesses.[1]

A distinguished abbot might be asked to be godfather to a child of the king or of some magnate. John of Sawtry, abbot of Ramsey, was a friend of the king and queen and stood godfather to Edmund of Woodstock.[2] Cistercians were forbidden to do this; but exceptions could be made for someone who could not be denied without scandal;[3] such, in fact, as a great man of the neighbourhood.

Noblemen and knights would meet the local abbots and priors on social occasions, and could do business informally. After Robert de Tateshall had quarrelled with the abbot of St. Albans about a livery due to him from the cell of Wymondham, they met at the inauguration feast of a new abbot of Bury, and settled the matter there.[4] And the prior of Barnwell, when his house passed into royal patronage from that of the Pecches, a local family, regretted the days when the prior could talk on equal terms with the patrons.[5]

But besides contingent and personal links there might be a more general and more standardized friendship between monastery and patron: a sense of belonging to the house, on the patron's side, that might take the form of explicit admission to confraternity; and, on the monastery's side, a sense of obligation, an interest in the patron's fortunes, gossip about his family, perhaps sympathy with his politics. The chronicle of Tewkesbury is full of the births, marriages, and deaths of the Clares and their connexions, and of their part in affairs. It ends with a separate account of the fight for the Provisions,[6] whose partisan tone is of course to some extent the common attitude of the religious; but it seems likely that Tewkesbury had an extra interest through the Clares. The chronicler is savage about those who deserted the Provisions in the early stages; but his treatment of the time between the Oxford Parliament and the departure of Archbishop Boniface is very cursory, with no reference to the breach between Simon de Montfort

---

[1] *Close R.* 1256-9, pp. 464-5 (order to custodian to recover them after alienation by Maud's successor).

[2] Hill, *Letter-books*, p. 200.   [3] Fowler, p. 24.

[4] *Gesta Abb.* ii. 64.   [5] *Liber Mem.*, pp. 51-52.

[6] *Ann. Mon.* i. 170-80, beginning in 1258, after entries for 1262 in the chronicle.

and the old earl;[1] and the account breaks off before the breach with the young earl. But it concludes with a letter of advice to the baronial party, criticizing Earl Simon, which seems to be a 'manifesto . . . from the entourage of Gilbert de Clare' early in 1264.[2]

One may compare the brief annals of Little Dunmow which include, along with the elections and deaths of priors, the births, deaths, marriages, and knightings of their patrons the Fitz Walters;[3] while almost their only mention of public affairs is the naïve account of Robert fitz Walter's quarrel with King John, making that quarrel centre wholly on John's designs on Robert's daughter, and making the breach with the barons centre wholly on that quarrel.[4] Where the Tewkesbury chronicler is well informed and has a wide view, the Dunmow chronicler is parochial and writes from a backwater; but both make their patron's affairs a main point of contact with the outside world. The heads of houses may sometimes have been kept informed by letters from their patrons: in 1257, after Richard of Cornwall and Countess Sanchia had been crowned in Germany, she wrote a brief account of their journey and reception to the prior of Wallingford (probably of their patronage), who seems to have lent it to Matthew Paris.[5] Many monasteries, including Cistercian houses,[6] kept a genealogy (often inaccurate) or quite a long history of the family, sometimes incorporated in the cartulary;[7] the house was a repository of family tradition.

A good idealized account of this kind of relationship is in

[1] *Ann. Mon.* i. 175. There are then one or more missing leaves; but unless Boniface's departure is out of order these would have covered events after Earl Richard's death.

[2] Powicke, ii. 444, n. 2, 452.

[3] Cf. the Cistercian house Croxden: deaths and successions of Verduns amongst those of the abbots (*Mon.* v. 661).

[4] *Mon.* vi. 1. 147.

[5] *Chron. Maj.* vi (Additamenta), p. 366. A much longer account (ibid., pp. 366–9) was sent by Richard to various people (see N. Denholm-Young, *Richard of Cornwall*, p. 92).

[6] e.g. Meaux: earls of Albemarle and lords of Holderness (*Mon.* v. 392). Stanlaw: Lacys (*Mon.* v. 647). Byland: Albinis and Mowbrays (*Mon.* v. 346). Tintern: Clares (*Mon.* v. 269–70). Sibton: Cheneys (*Mon.* v. 559). Also Ros, perhaps from Rievaulx or Kirkham (*Mon.* v. 280). A Premonstratensian example is Alnwick: Vescys and Percys (*Archaeologia Aeliana*, iii. 1844, pp. 33–44).

[7] This shows that such histories, even if often commissioned by the patron, interested the monks.

the history of the founders of the Cistercian abbey of Ford;
full of the descent, inheritances, and marriages, the fortunes
and misfortunes of the Courtenays of Okehampton.[1] The
details begin with Reginald de Courtenay, late in the twelfth
century, who promoted the monks' good, gave them money
and jewels, trusted in their prayers more than in worldly goods,
and it seems had all a patron's desirable virtues. Then came
his son Robert, from 1194 till his death in 1242. He protected
the monks and did them no harm; 'he often called the monks
his fathers and patrons, to whom he was himself a true patron'.
He was buried in the abbey, and was succeeded by his son
John, who like him was upright and strenuous in arms, and
no less devout and kind to the abbey. He confirmed their
freedom from suit and service, trusted them fully and 'set
their prayers before all his doings'. They had a story (closely
paralleled at Dieulacres about Earl Ranulf of Chester)[2] of
how when in danger of shipwreck he saved the ship by his con-
fidence in the prayers of 'monachi mei' for 'eorum servulo'—
prayers which must have effect, since 'ego eos, et illi me dili-
gunt', for all the arguments of his despairing companion who
pointed out that the monks were in bed and asleep. Perhaps
these elegant sentiments hardly represent John de Courtenay's
language under stress of shipwreck; but they show the monks'
idea of a good patron's attitude. When he had come safely
home and told the monks of this incident, he was more generous
to them than ever, and was admitted to their fraternity; in
1273 he died and was buried there. After this the abbey was
less fortunate in its patrons; perhaps this heightened the affec-
tionate enthusiasm with which they remembered Reginald,
Robert, and John.

In much the same way one of Walden's chronicles speaks
of Beatrice de Say, sister of the founder, Geoffrey de Mandeville, and for a short time their patron,[3] who in her old age con-
trasted favourably as friend and neighbour with the present
patron, Geoffrey fitz Piers. She lived at Rickling, a few miles
from Walden, looking after the local poor as the great lady of
the countryside; meanwhile she gave gifts to the monks of

---

[1] *Mon.* v. 377–80.
[2] Ibid., p. 628: account of foundation.
[3] Harl. MS. 3697 (cartulary), f. 19*v*.

Walden, went over on feast-days to see 'her sons', and finally died and was buried at the abbey.[1]

There might be a special bond in the patron's devotion to the saint of the house. Gifts were made to God, the saint, and the monks; and the saint would have his shrine and his special masses, and be considered particularly powerful on behalf of that house and anyone who helped it and was prayed for there. This is evident in some old and famous royal abbeys, where the king might have a special reverence for the patron saint; as for St. Edmund at Bury, himself a king; King Henry was asked by the abbot of Bury to call his second son Edmund, and he wrote to tell the abbot of the prince's birth, saying that he had had the antiphon of St. Edmund sung just before the good news reached him.[2]

St. Alban, too, was a favourite saint of the royal family, as the protomartyr of the realm;[3] the queen in 1257 gave a thank-offering to him at the abbey for her recovery from illness;[4] King Edward in 1299 came there to get St. Alban's help against the Scots, and a special mass and collect were instituted for the king and queen.[5] Then there was St. Cuthbert at Durham; in the monks' account of Edward's intervention between them and the bishop in 1300, they repeatedly stress his devotion to the saint; he weighed against the bishop's services to him the fact that he had 'often experienced the patronage and help of St. Cuthbert in various troubles and dangers, through your prayers'.[6]

There would probably be a specially close relation between a house and its actual founder while he lived, or a patron who had rebuilt extensively. The Westminster monks were looked on as peculiarly beholden to Henry III;[7] and the Glastonbury monks spoke to John of their rebuilder Henry II as

---

[1] *Mon.* iv. 146–7.   [2] *Bury Memorials*, iii. 28. When Henry extorted from Bury in a vacancy, Paris condemned him for forgetting his reverence to the martyr 'whom he was specially bound to venerate' (*Chron. Maj.* v. 40). Cf. King John (Cheney, in *Trans. R. Hist. Soc.* 4th Ser. xxxi. 131–2).

[3] *Chron. Maj.* iii. 337.   [4] Ibid. v. 653–4.

[5] *Rishanger*, p. 193.

[6] *Gesta Dunelmensia*, ed. Richardson, in *Camden Miscellany*, xiii. 16–17. Cf. St. Wulstan of Worcester—before his last Welsh campaign Edward promised 'St. Wulstan and the prior and convent' an appropriation, for three extra monks and two candles burning before the saint's shrine (*Reg. Swinfield*, pp. 421, 432).

[7] See p. 119.

dulcissimus patronus noster.[1] Any patron in the line of succession could thus by some special generosity revive the special friendship with which the house and his family must have begun their connexion.[2]

During his life, then, the patron could have if he chose this kind of spiritual anchor: the convent's prayers for his welfare, perhaps extra ones for a special need;[3] and sometimes a definite grant of *consortium* or *confraternitas*,[4] by which a benefactor was ceremonially admitted to be 'partaker of those good things which God has given us to accomplish', a formalization of the idea of vicarious merit.[5] At intervals he would visit the house, and perhaps be ceremonially received and given the 'honour of procession' mentioned in canon law.[6] In 1259 Earl Richard de Clare went to Tewkesbury and 'asked for a procession'; after that 'he gave the kiss of peace to all, great and small, for which sign everyone rejoiced'. This followed a time of recurrent friction between the earl and the abbey; perhaps he came to make a solemn reconciliation.[7]

A hollower welcome, after more serious quarrels,[8] was that accorded to Geoffrey fitz Piers at Walden. There is a vivid account of this, which, while stressing that the whole solemn occasion was a dismal mockery, at the same time describes the festivity with which a patron would be received on a formal visit, and implies by contrast the genuine welcome which

---

[1] Domerham, p. 446.

[2] Cf. King Edward's words explaining his protection of Reading Abbey in time of debt: 'not only because that house was founded for [. . . our ancestors . . .] and us and our successors, but also so that we may be made sharers and authors in the new foundation or relief of that house' (*Reg. Cantilupe*, p. 37).

[3] e.g. in 1282 Bury promised the king extra masses and psalms for him, his family and household, and all those fighting in Wales, while his army was in Wales (*Foedera*, ii. 604).

[4] e.g. Queen Eleanor in 1242 at Winchester (*Ann. Mon.* ii. 89). Queen Margaret in 1299 at St. Albans (*Rishanger*, p. 194). John de Courtenay at Ford, above. The patron of a dependency might be given confraternity at the mother-house: e.g. Hugh de Nevill and his wife in 1263, at Lonlay, as patrons of Stogursey (Duchy of Lanc. 27/72); Odo de Dammartin, 1217, at Merton, as founder of Tanridge (A. C. Heales, *History of Tanridge Priory*, London, 1888, p. 102).

[5] E. Bishop, *Liturgica Historica*, ch. 16, esp. pp. 352, 357. Coulton, iii. 346–52.

[6] Clement III's definition of the patron's position (Friedberg, ii. 617: III. 38. xxv) allows him 'the honour of procession'; and Hostiensis, glossing this, says that the patron may be met processionally, or have first place in procession or in the lay congregation (*Commentaria*, pp. 146*v*–7*r*).

[7] *Ann. Mon.* i. 167. [8] See pp. 167–70.

ought to have underlain it. The earl arranged at last to visit
the monks as their lord and patron, and they undertook to
pay him all due honour. Cheering crowds collected from the
villages; the outer gates were thrown open, and the place
would hardly hold them all. Monks and people met their lord
in procession, wearing white and purple vestments and carrying gilded texts of the gospels, precious vessels, and banners.
Some of the brothers 'with downcast faces, pretending to sing,
wept bitterly; others forcing back their tears, sang more with
the mouth than the heart'. Geoffrey fitz Piers proceeded to
the church, and offered a silver cup; then the Te Deum was
sung. Thence he went to the chapter-house, with a crowd of
varying rank; at this point he was expected to make some great
gift or concession to the abbey; everyone swarmed up to hear
what he would give. To the general surprise and disapproval,
he neither gave nor promised anything; but only, with an arro-
gant air, had read aloud the royal charters conferring on him
the donation of the abbey.[1] After that he had a private interview with the bed-ridden abbot, heard mass, and went away.
Clearly such a first formal visit was an important social occasion, and in ordinary circumstances would have been a cheerful one.[2]

Late in the thirteenth century a canon of the Premonstratensian abbey of Dale recalled how in his early days there 'the
noble matron Lady Maud de Salicosamara, foundress of our
church, whose memory is blessed, came to us ... old and full
of days; and knowing the time of her summons out of this
world was approaching rapidly, proposed to commend her
departing to the prayers of such holy men of God'. The convent gathered round her, and she told the story of the foundation, beginning long before her own time with the hermit who
was first directed to Depedale in a vision. All this is used as a
literary device to introduce a long and elaborate history of the

---

[1] See p. 10.

[2] *Mon.* iv. 148 (Walden chronicle). One may compare with this the procedure laid
down about three centuries later at Marrick nunnery for receiving a new patron (of
the Askes): 'The forme of takyng the fownder' (Bodl., Yorks. Charter 26b). He
and his lady were to be met in solemn procession, while the bells were rung; he was
to ask and be granted, in set terms, admission as their founder and a share in their
prayers and good works (exhaustively listed), in exchange for a promise of protection; the prioress then cast holy water and censed them, and they processed into
church, with specified psalms, for a service beginning with the Te Deum.

foundation; but it seems to be based on a true incident, of the old lady paying a last visit and treating the new generation of canons to her reminiscences.[1]

A patron might choose to stay at his monastery when he was ill; Bishop Richard le Poer died at his foundation, Tarrant Keynes nunnery.[2] In old age or when widowed the patron might actually join the convent; Countess Ela of Salisbury became a nun at her own foundation, Lacock, and was abbess there for many years.[3]

Usually the patron would choose his monastery as his burial place; or if he were patron of several houses, would choose that which family tradition or his own favour put first; or he might arrange for his heart to be sent to one and his body to another.[4] This choice of burial-place was very important, both to the family and to the monastery. The kings who lay in Westminster Abbey had something in common with such country gentlemen as Alan de Sanford who chose to be buried near his ancestors at their little priory of Blackmore.[5] There is something intimate and domestic about the Westminster monks' opinion that Edward I favoured them (in allowing a franchise) because the bodies of his father and father's children lay there, and because he himself had been baptized, confirmed, and crowned there.[6]

Most of the Clares were buried at Tewkesbury, sometimes when they had died hundreds of miles away. The body of Earl Gilbert I, who died in Brittany in 1230, was brought solemnly to Tewkesbury by way of Cranborne in Dorset, another Clare foundation and a dependency of Tewkesbury, conveniently on the way from Plymouth.[7] Nearly a century later the body of the last Earl Gilbert, killed at Bannockburn at the age

---

[1] Chronicle of Thomas de Musca, *Derbysh. Archaeol. Journal*, v. 4.

[2] *Chron. Maj.* iii. 392.

[3] *Mon.* vi. 1. 501 (history of the founders). Countess Isabel of Warwick probably entered her foundation Cookhill (*V.C.H. Worcs.* ii. 157). But the formerly accepted identification of the first prioress of Castle Hedingham with the widow of the founder, Aubrey de Vere, was mistaken (*Complete Peerage*, x. 207, note b).

[4] See Coulton, iii. 47–63, on the commercial aspect of burials, and on some contemporaries' disapproval of dividing bodies and Boniface VIII's condemnation of the practice as impious and horrible.

[5] *Cat. Anct. Deeds*, i. A. 501.

[6] *Flores Historiarum*, ed. Luard, iii. 50.

[7] *Ann. Mon.* i (Tewkesbury), p. 76.

of twenty-three, was taken all the way south to Tewkesbury, 'the place of his fathers'; a formidable journey, and a measure of the importance of the matter.[1]

Sometimes compromise was necessary; the first Earl Gilbert's widow, Countess Isabel, had, according to the Tewkesbury chronicler, wished to be buried there with her first husband, but was buried at Beaulieu by the wish of her second husband, Richard of Cornwall, who shared King Henry's interest in their father's foundation. Her heart was sent to Tewkesbury and her intestines to Missenden;[2] the Tewkesbury monks consoled themselves with the thought that where the heart was there was the affection.[3]

This was before Earl Richard had founded his own abbey of Hailes, as a daughter-house to Beaulieu; he himself was buried there, as were his second wife Sanchia, his son Earl Edmund, and Henry of Almain, whose body was brought all the way from Viterbo. But Richard left his heart to the friars minor of Oxford, for whom, living in the middle of his own country, he perhaps had that sort of patronly esteem which did not necessarily go with technical patronage; and Edmund left his heart to his own foundation at Ashridge.[4]

The Bohun family similarly had scattered interests; many of the earls of Hereford were buried at Llanthony-by-Gloucester, their own west-country foundation; but when they became earls of Essex they inherited from the Mandevilles the patronage of Walden Abbey and were sometimes buried there.[5] An earlier earl of Essex, William de Mandeville who died in 1228, had his body buried at Shouldham Priory, of his patronage, but his heart at Walden *in signum*, Walden's chronicler said, *intimae dilectionis*.[6]

---

[1] *Mon.* ii. 61 (chronicle). For other Clare burials at Tewkesbury see *Ann. Mon.* i. 159, 169; iv (Worcester), p. 524; *Gervase of Cant.* ii. 215, 314.

[2] Presumably as the nearest religious house of any standing to Berkhamstead, where she died. The patrons (de Sanfords) were tenants of the Honour of Gloucester.

[3] *Ann. Mon.* i. 113–14.

[4] *Flores Hist.* ii. 474; iii. 22, 24. *Ann. Mon.* iv (Worcester), p. 549. See Midgley, *Accounts of Earldom of Cornwall*, i, pp. x–xvii.

[5] *Mon.* vi. 1. 134–5 (chronicle of Llanthony II).

[6] *Mon.* iv. 140. Amongst many other examples are the Mohuns at Newenham and Bruton: Reginald, founder of Newenham, was asked by the monks to adopt their church as his burial-place (Oliver, p. 357; cartulary, Bodl. MS. Top. Devon d. 5 f. 25*v*); Courtenays at Ford (*Mon.* v. 380: chronicle); Pecches at Barnwell

An ordinary neighbour of a monastery who wished to be buried there would make a gift of land with his body. For the patron this was almost certainly unnecessary, but it was sometimes done; Bartholomew de la Legh, leaving his body to be buried at Canons Ashby, gave half a virgate and confirmed his father's gift of a church.[1] But the patron's choice of a burialplace mattered to the convent for less simple and immediate reasons: piety, long-term gain, sentiment, and prestige. Abbot David of St. Augustine's, Bristol, wrote to ask the bishop of Exeter for permission to translate the body of one of the Berkeleys to Bristol, 'so that by constant remembrance of the deceased, the devotion of the living may increase, and there may be more plentiful almsgiving and offering of prayers for the common solace of the dead'; for 'almost all his line of consanguinity rests buried with us'.[2] To be all buried in one place was a concrete expression of family solidarity;[3] and knowing that the monastery which cared for their ancestors' souls also housed their bones, the living patron and his family would be readier to care for and endow it.[4]

A monastery that moved must take with it its old associations. Earl Henry de Lacy, giving a new site at Whalley to the Stanlaw monks, stipulated that they should take with them the bones of his ancestors and of all others buried at Stanlaw; besides calling the new abbey by the old name of Locus Benedictus, chosen by his ancestor the founder.[5]

Corresponding to his body's resting-place in the monastery, the patron would look forward to a permanent share for his soul in the convent's good works, and to being helped out of purgatory by their masses and prayers. Whether as a *confrater* or simply as a patron he would probably have his place

---

(*Liber Mem.*, pp. 48, 50); Ros at Kirkham and Rievaulx (*Mon.* v. 280–1: genealogy); Quincys at Garendon (*Mon.* v. 331); Brus of Skelton at Gisburn (*Mon.* vi. 1. 267–8: history of founders); Mortimers at Wigmore (*Mon.* vi. 1. 350–1: history of founders).

[1] Farrer, *Honours*, i. 70; Madox, *Formulare Anglicanum* (London, 1702), p. 423. Cf. David, Earl of Huntingdon, and Sawtry (*V.C.H. Hunts.* i. 391); Baldwin de Redvers and Breamore (*Abbrev. Plac.*, p. 172); William de Warenne and Lewes (*Lewes Cart.* i. 50); Robert de Courtenay and Ford (*Mon.* v. 380).

[2] Hill, *Letter-books*, p. 224.

[3] Cf. the Tewkesbury epitaph for Countess Isabel (*Ann. Mon.* i. 113–14).

[4] See p. 143; the Pecches protected Barnwell against the rebels because 'they would sooner die than let the bones of their father and kindred be burnt'.

[5] *Coucher Book of Whalley Abbey*, ed. Hulton, i. 189.

in their martyrology,[1] and his anniversary might be regularly celebrated, like that of a monk but indefinitely.[2] Sometimes a specific bargain was made, by which a particular endowment was to bear the expense of defined alms and masses. At the beginning of the century William Briwere, founding Mottisfont Priory, gave amongst other things specific lands and rents for his own and his wife's anniversaries, and a manor for hospitality and the feeding of four poor men. His son William also made a special grant for his anniversary at Mottisfont,[3] and probably also at Torre: he had a charter from the abbot and convent granting 'to William Briwere our advocate' an anniversary of masses, prayers and feeding the poor,[4] with no mention of an endowment, but this could be to avoid the appearance of simony.[5]

Sometimes the king made such arrangements with particular houses of his patronage. In 1285 the monks of Christchurch, Canterbury, promised Edward three masses a day for himself and all his family; one of the Blessed Virgin, one of St. Thomas, and one (in turn) of Dunstan, Blase, Alphegus, and All Saints. This was because they were bound to him in gratitude for exalting their church, and could not repay him with 'corruptible gold and silver'.[6] This sounds vague and general enough, but in fact the king a fortnight later pardoned them a substantial sum of corruptible gold and silver, in the form of a 3,000 marks fine that they had incurred;[7] and it seems likely that this was the temporal return for the grant of spiritual services. A more direct exchange was made by Edward in 1296 with Durham Priory; he gave £40 a year in honour of St. Cuthbert, to maintain on his feast-day and

---

[1] e.g. Tintern (*Mon.* v. 266).

[2] See Coulton, iii. 65–86.

[3] *Mon.* vi. 1. 481 (obituary).

[4] Duchy of Lanc. 25/213.

[5] See p. 134. Other examples of such endowments by the patron are Walter fitz Simon to Daventry, 1239, 1 mark p.a. from the rent of his oven, for his and his wife's anniversary (Cott. MS. Claud. D. xii, Daventry cartulary, f. 9). William de Percy (d. 1245) to Sawley; manor and forest of Gisburn for 20 marks rent and six extra monks to celebrate for his and his wife's souls (*Percy Cart.*, p. 27). John de Bellewe and his wife (Brus coheir) to Nunmonkton, 1278; 10 acres and quitclaim of a 5s. rent, for their daughter's obit (*V.C.H. Yorks.* iii. 122). Peter de Maulay to Eskdale, 1294; for two chaplains celebrating daily, and anniversaries for his father, mother, and wife (ibid., p. 193).

[6] *Mon.* i. 104 (charter).   [7] Ibid. (letter patent).

Translation large almsgiving, lights, and a pittance, as well as daily masses.[1]

But it was apparently not necessary that a specific bargain should be made. Prior Thomas of Wymondham (1224–57) assigned part of the revenues of a church to four anniversaries, including those of the third and fourth earls of Arundel, late patrons:[2] it seems that these anniversaries were already being celebrated, but that it was only now that specific revenues were assigned to them. It was right and respectable to show gratitude for liberality with or without a bargain. In the mid-thirteenth century St. Albans arranged that at the end of every hour and at grace they should pray for the repose of King Offa as their founder; that this had not been done earlier was, in the chronicler's opinion, inexcusably ungrateful.[3] And the canons of Barnwell, accused in 1275 of ingratitude to their twelfth-century patron Payn Peverel, 'that good man who gave you so many churches and lands', pointed out that he was not forgotten, for 'every day he sits at table by the prior and has his portion from cellar and kitchen'—that is, it is explained, a portion for him was daily set before whoever presided in refectory;[4] probably it was afterwards given in alms for the good of his soul.

In fact, the written and detailed stipulations were perhaps made less often by the actual patron than by other benefactors, ranging from the vassal or kinsman of the patron who gives a substantial endowment, to the peasant who gives half an acre for a place in the monks' prayers. For confraternity, or similar if less comprehensive benefits, could be enjoyed by many benefactors besides the patron. In 1285 a benefactor to Healaugh Park stipulated for fraternity, a place in the martyrology and an annual obit 'sicut pro patronis domus sue'.[5]

---

[1] Mon. i. 244. In a list of letters from various houses, promising masses and prayers for the king and queen, most do not mention recompense, but one is an indenture between Edward I and the abbot and convent of Westminster in which lands were given for an anniversary for Queen Eleanor (Ancient Kalendars and Inventories of the Exchequer, ed. Palgrave, London, 1836, i. 110–11).

[2] Mon. iii. 335 (from cartulary).

[3] Gesta Abb. i. 394. Cf. the St. Albans view of the Statute of Mortmain (see p. 39).   [4] Liber Mem., p. 134.

[5] Chartulary of Healaugh Park, ed. J. S. Purvis, Yorks. Arch. Soc. Records Series, xcii, 1935, p. 78.

The king as such had of course a claim on the prayers of all monks in the kingdom, whether of his patronage or not.[1] Or, since there was room for overlapping relationships of varying range and precision, he might make a special claim on one order. When John relaxed his demands on the Cistercians in 1200, he wished the Chapter to admit him to 'the fraternity and society of the whole order' and to let him know in writing 'what they mean to do for him in each house', while he undertook not only to found a new abbey (Beaulieu) but also 'to be patron and defender of your order'.[2] Henry III in 1249 asked the Benedictine Chapter for a daily collect for himself and the queen in all their houses,[3] 'although', Paris comments revealingly, 'he had not provided any support for this'.[4]

The assumption is that these spiritual benefits ought to be paid for somehow; either generally by founding the house or specifically by a grant for the purpose. But the latter looked remarkably like simony;[5] and in fact Archbishop Edmund Rich forbade the granting of masses or *consortium* for a price, including the customary endowment of anniversaries.[6] This was evaded, for instance by making the endowment only indirectly for the services. The Cistercian order made this same rule about simony. It also tried to limit the granting of such benefits, as if their number had been getting out of hand: no more anniversaries were to be given without licence of the General Chapter, and they were to consist simply of one mass a year privately celebrated. Nor was licence for such an anniversary even to be applied for, whether for the house's own founder or another, unless at his *maximam instantiam*.[7] Later it was laid down that anniversaries should be celebrated in groups once a month.[8]

The Cistercian order was perhaps specially concerned to limit the various claims that could be made by founders, and

---

[1] Prayers or masses might be asked for from all abbots and priors on particular occasions: e.g. 1294, for the soul of the king's friend, the duke of Brabant; 1300, for the soul of the king's cousin, the earl of Cornwall (*Cal. Chanc. Warrants*, i. 42, 115).

[2] Ralph of Coggeshall, *Chron. Anglicanum*, ed. Stevenson, p. 109. Similarly John Giffard, by founding Gloucester College, contrived a claim on all Benedictine monks of the province, and was given masses and anniversaries in all their monasteries by the General Chapter (Pantin, i. 137).

[3] Ibid. i. 31, 45.
[5] See Coulton, iii. 66–67.
[7] Ibid., pp. 28, 29, 30.

[4] *Chron. Maj.* v. 81.
[6] Fowler, p. 30 note.
[8] Ibid., p. 132.

jealous of the local and personal bonds that could attach a monastery. On the other hand, some individual Cistercian houses (such as Ford), and the Austin canons and black monks, much less coherent as orders and more comfortably entrenched in local society, seem to have accepted such relationships as natural and desirable, and to have expected also the material goods which might be given for *consortium* without scruples about simony. From the patron's point of view, any explicit bargain was really only making sure in detail of something which was due to all his line in any case.

VIII

PROTECTION

WHEN the house and the patron were on good terms, and the relationship was valued by the patron for more than its material value, he would naturally add something to his ancestor's endowment, and give besides more personal gifts: books, relics, or jewellery; or more informally, fire-wood or venison.

Timber for building and dead wood for smelting lead were frequent royal gifts, especially of Henry III with his interest in building. The close rolls contain many entries of orders to local officials to make such gifts; for instance, Henry sends twenty oaks to the nuns of Amesbury for mending their cloister, and two for their stalls;[1] he gives the sacristan of Malmesbury four oaks for the work of the church, and on the same day gives the abbot six bucks, four for himself and two for the sick monks:[2] a nice mixture of patronal interest in the convent and personal favour to the abbot.

Gifts of vestments, ornaments, and books were customary when a patron paid a formal visit.[3] There was both scandal and a touch of farce in King John's gifts at Bury of twelve pence and a cloth borrowed from the sacristan.[4] Even the hostile patron Geoffrey fitz Piers offered a silver cup on the altar at Walden, and he was expected to make some other gift when he came out of church.[5] Relics were a favourite gift on solemn occasions, much valued by the monasteries for the pilgrims that they brought and for their own sake. Countess Isabel de Clare's legacies to Tewkesbury included relics;[6] and Edmund of Cornwall gave Hailes a relic of the Holy Blood, bought by him on the continent; some years later he gave a gold cross in which to keep it.[7] Kings gave relics to their special abbey of Westminster; King Henry in 1247 gave the

---

[1] *Close R. 1227–31*, p. 486.   [2] Ibid., *1264–8*, p. 70.
[3] e.g. Henry III, visiting Merton Priory, gave a cope of cloth of gold, an image of the Virgin, and a tun of wine (A. C. Heales, *Records of Merton Priory*, London, 1898, p. 125).   [4] Brakelond, p. 116.
[5] See p. 128.   [6] *Ann. Mon.* i. 113.
[7] *Mon.* v. 686, note d (from Hailes chronicle). Denholm-Young, *Richard of Cornwall*, p. 174.

Holy Blood, which he himself carried on foot in procession from St. Paul's;[1] two years later he gave them a stone printed with Christ's footmark at the Ascension.[2] King Edward gave the same abbey a piece of the Holy Cross, found in Wales;[3] offering part of the fruits of an enterprise at the place where his fortunes were specially prayed for.

The patron might come to the rescue after some loss; when Luffield Priory was robbed in 1244, King Henry gave them three chalices, ornaments for three chaplains, and £15 in money.[4] Then he could make certain neighbourly concessions or convenient privileges. Countess Isabel of Arundel allowed Wymondham to build a lead conduit from a spring through her lands;[5] Thomas de St. Walery gave Studley a weekly cartload of firewood;[6] and Earl Hamelin de Warenne about 1185 gave Lewes Priory the right to buy the whole supply of logs in Lewes on three days a week, and leave to fish in his waters for festivals.[7]

The patron could do more for his monks than occasional presents and privileges. He might obtain indulgences which should benefit both them and himself; a series of indulgences was given in the 1280's at Henry de Lacy's request by various foreign bishops,[8] for penitents going to Stanlaw Abbey and praying for him and his ancestors as founders and as being buried there, or giving something for improving the dangerous road to the abbey or for moving to a safer place with the bones of their patrons and other nobles.[9] Thus the earl ingeniously gets prayers for himself and his ancestors, as well as winning pilgrims and gifts for his abbey to help pay for the projected move to Whalley.

[1] *Chron. Maj.* iv. 640–4.   [2] Ibid. v. 81–82.

[3] *Flores Hist.* iii. 63. Henry III gave Malmesbury the cup due to him from the late abbot to use as a reliquary (*Close R. 1242–7,* p. 399).

[4] *Ann. Mon.* iii (Dunstable), p. 165.

[5] *Mon.* iii. 332. Cf. a similar grant by Bishop Raleigh of Winchester to Titchfield (*Winchester Cath. Cart.,* pp. 43–44), and Maurice de Berkeley's promise to Kingswood to move the monks' conduit from his park to somewhere more convenient (*Kingswood Documents,* p. 224).

[6] *Mon.* iv. 253 (abstract of charters).

[7] *Lewes Cart.,* pp. 41–42.

[8] Monte Reale, Tortosa, Verceil, Parenzo, Larino, Veroli, and Bangor (dated Aberconway 1283; Whitaker suggests plausibly that the earl met the bishop there at Edward I's court).

[9] Whitaker, *History of Whalley and Clitheroe,* i. 144–6.

A more commonplace act was to make interest with a
bishop to get the monks the appropriation of a church—
either one already of their advowson, or of the patron's which
he was giving up. The monks of St. Albans in the 1250's,
wanting to have a rich church of their advowson appropriated
to them by the bishop of Durham, had letters from the king
and queen supporting their request;[1] this in spite of the fact
that the king had originally wanted the living for a chancery
clerk. This suggests another side of the question, to be
discussed later: although an appropriation might be made at
the patron's request as an influential friend, it was against his
interests and might need his perhaps grudging consent as
their lord.[2]

A bishop himself, as patron of a house, would have an
extra motive for making an appropriation; Bishop Pontissara
appropriated a church to Selborne particularly because the
priory was of his patronage.[3] And when Eynsham appealed
to Bishop Sutton about some disputed tithes, 'trusting that
he, their patron, will stand up for them against any adversary',
he appropriated to the abbey one of the churches in question.[4]

Great poverty was the only canonical justification for appropriation, and the standard reason given by a patron in asking
for one.[5] It was a form of protection against impoverishment,
with the regular motives for such protection; Henry de Bohun
asked for the appropriation to Farley Priory of Box church or
any other 'whose advowson our predecessors conferred on
them', because of their poverty and because he was bound to
help those whom his predecessors had held dear.[6] And in the
next century Henry Percy gave an advowson to Sawley Abbey,
of his patronage, hoping later to obtain the appropriation for
them; pitying the convent and not wishing his ancestors' alms
to perish.[7] So, in the accepted convention, Edward II expressed it, writing probably at Percy's request to ask the pope

---

[1] *Gesta Abb.* i. 346–9. Cf. appropriations to Beaulieu, 1232 at request of Henry
III, and 1235 at his and Earl Richard's request, as their father's foundation (*Cal.
Papal L.* i. 129, 145).   [2] See pp. 157–9.
[3] *Reg. Pontissara*, i. 141.   [4] *Eynsham Cart.* i. 335–6.
[5] One of the appropriations to Beaulieu (n. 1, above) turned out to have been
obtained by false assertions of poverty (*Cal. Papal L.* i. 155).
[6] *Charters illustrating the History of . . . Sarum*, ed. Macray, p. 185.
[7] *Cartulary of the Abbey of Sallay*, ed. McNulty, p. 47.

for the appropriation—now badly needed since Sawley was very poor, in a barren and stormy region, and lately raided by the Scots.[1] But the king for one did not always respect the canonical rule. Edward I succeeded, after much argument, in making Bishop Swinfield of Hereford allow an appropriation to Worcester Priory, not for relief of poverty but to support an extra charge: three more monks, and two candles burning at St. Wulstan's shrine.[2]

Such help by the patron might have behind it a less creditable transaction. Earl Henry de Lacy, giving the monks of Stanlaw their new site at Whalley, obtained for them the appropriation of the rich church with its dependent chapels. Later, when Nicholas IV's appropriation was annulled with other acts of his by Boniface VIII, the earl and the king wrote asking him to renew it;[3] and the earl wrote thanking the Cistercian General Chapter for allowing the move;[4] it all seems straightforward and benevolent. But in fact the earl had made conditions, getting the monks to surrender certain hunting rights of the rectors of Whalley, and one of its chapels (in Clitheroe Castle).[5] They later regarded this chapel as wrongfully held by the earls,[6] and ultimately regained it.[7] The monks of Pontefract, who themselves had a claim to Whalley church, had their own version of the affair: according to this, when the appropriation needed confirming the earl seized the church and refused to surrender it until the Whalley monks simoniacally agreed to his terms (exaggerated to 'a chapel worth 100 marks a year'). They then satisfied the bishop by money (certainly the bishop and the archdeacon were compensated for the appropriation),[8] and finally hoodwinked the pope by asking for the appropriation in the normal way without mentioning these compositions. When the earl handed over the church to the monks, the people came and shouted 'Woe on you, Simoniacs!'[9]

1 *Mon.* v. 516.
2 *Reg. Swinfield*, pp. 421, 432–7. In the appropriation the bishop mentioned, besides this charge, that the burdens of hospitality had increased beyond the monks' resources—evidently trying to make the appropriation sound canonical.
3 Whitaker, *Whalley*, i. 160–2.   4 Hill, *Letter-books*, p. 165 (No. 119).
5 Whitaker, *Whalley*, i. 174, 258. See *V.C.H. Lancs.* ii. 133.
6 Memorandum in *Whalley Coucher Bk.* i. 226.
7 Whitaker, *Whalley*, i. 259.   8 Ibid., pp. 167–8, 176 (expenses).
9 *Mon.* v. 642 (Pontefract cartulary).

This story, however distorted, shows the kind of dubious arrangements which a monastery might make with its patron by going very little beyond routine exchanges of favours; and suggests, too, how even a Cistercian house might quarrel, bargain, and be reconciled with its patron on its own, in a way which had to be concealed from authority.

The monks of Whalley found the earl useful in other ways, besides moving them to a better site and obtaining an appropriation for them. He helped them at the Papal Curia with money and advice, perhaps in this same business or their later lawsuit with Bishop Langton.[1] The abbot and convent gave their proctor a testimonial asking the earl to help and advise him, and a letter promising to pay back any money spent by the earl in prosecuting their suit; they also empowered their proctor to borrow money with the earl's counsel and assent. And some servant of Earl Henry's wrote to the abbot to say that any delay was not the fault of the abbey's proctor, who had been diligent in stirring up and soliciting 'my lord the earl' and others.[2] Evidently the earl was himself at the Curia or within reach.[3]

But in another difficulty his absence abroad was a serious setback[4]—when the abbey was being distrained by Bishop Langton for damages of 1,000 marks.[5] The abbot, however, resorted for help to the patron's servants in the neighbouring castle. He wrote to W—— de N——, evidently William de Nony, the earl's auditor and chaplain of the disputed chapel in Clitheroe Castle,[6] asking for advice on whether to write to the constable of Clitheroe to ask for a loan from the earl's money to pay off the bishop's bailiffs.[7] Probably this was done, for in 1304 the abbey owed 17 sacks of wool to the earl for £85 borrowed from the constable of Clitheroe 'in our great necessity'.[8]

---

[1] See *V.C.H. Lancs.* ii. 134.

[2] Whitaker, *Whalley*, i. 163–4. Cf. Richard de Clare's help to Tewkesbury in 1251, allowing his proctor at the Curia to act for the abbey (*Ann. Mon.* i. 147).

[3] Perhaps in October 1300 (G.E.C., *Complete Peerage*, vii. 684).

[4] See p. 142.   [5] Whitaker, *Whalley*, i. 150.

[6] *Two 'compoti'* . . . *of Henry de Lacy* . . ., ed. P. A. Lyons, p. xxiii. Here they are evidently on good terms although William was enjoying revenues to which the monks (anyhow later) thought themselves entitled.

[7] Hill, *Letter-books*, p. 161 (calendared).

[8] Whitaker, *Whalley*, i. 182. In the Lacy accounts for 1304–5, receipts include

Henry de Lacy also came to the help, perhaps to his own advantage, of Kirkstall Abbey when it was heavily in debt. In 1287 Abbot Hugh wrote to tell his monks how he went to Gascony with much hardship and at last 'found our patron, the earl of Lincoln, with other great men of the court, attending upon the king; and to him we explained fully . . . the distress of the house. He was touched with pity at the representation, and promised us all the information and assistance in his power.'[1] It was arranged that the earl should take some of the abbey's lands at a fixed rent, and advance a sum for paying pressing debts. Any movable goods left on these lands he would buy at a fair price. But apparently the abbot did not expect a fair price, for he told the monks to work hard to remove everything except standing crops, while he purposely delayed the earl's messenger.[2] Both sides were business-like and out for their own best advantage; yet underlying the transaction was the assumption that the patron should do something to help.

The patron had, in fact, a vague obligation to protect and defend his house in a general way. Certainly there are any number of cases where help from the patron might have been useful but there is no evidence that it was forthcoming; when a house was in trouble from debt or violent neighbours.[3] Yet there is much evidence that protection of a kind was expected and sometimes given. The Ford chronicler remarks in general terms that Robert and John de Courtenay would not let anyone molest the abbey;[4] and a patron of Pipewell late in the thirteenth century, William Boutevileyn of Cotesbrook, was 'a good knight . . . who always stood up like a wall for his monks in their troubles and anxieties';[5] though in both

£85 paid by the abbot and convent of Whalley, repaying a loan made to them by bond by Sir W. de Nony (*Two 'compoti'* . . ., p. 112); it is not clear whether this was the same debt, paid in money instead of wool, or another one raised through the chaplain instead of through the constable.

[1] Whitaker's translation.

[2] Whitaker, *History of Craven*, pp. 81–82. Cf. Edward I's confirmation (*Mon.* v. 537). The transaction involved the quitclaim of £4 p.a. hitherto paid by the earl to the abbey as alms (Duchy of Lanc. 27/34); and the earl's rent, 50 marks for the Lancashire lands and 30 for the Yorkshire lands, was not to begin till 1293 and 1298 respectively (Bodl., Yorks. Charters 24).

[3] See pp. 96–97 for houses not of royal foundation taken into custody by the king; but probably this was normally a royal prerogative.

[4] *Mon.* v. 379.   [5] Ibid., p. 437 (chronicle).

these cases the patrons' usefulness may have been exaggerated in contrast to their immediate successors.[1] It may have been the convention for the patron to promise counsel and help to a new prelate, as Hubert de Burgh did (as Richard de Clare's guardian) when the abbot-elect of Tewkesbury was presented to him;[2] or as the lord of Richmond's steward in 1199 ordered the bailiff of Wisset to protect and defend the new prior of Rumburgh after giving him administration.[3] The monks of St. Swithun's, writing to Henry III, said that their church, founded by the kings of England, 'has always resorted to you in its business, as to its one and only refuge';[4] and in 1300 the Durham monks asked for the king's help 'lest his monks and ministers of St. Cuthbert, founded from the alms of the lord king and his progenitors, for lack of royal defence and protection should fail unjustly in their just cause'.[5]

These were not empty phrases; the patron's absence or death might be a real misfortune. Bishop Simon de Ghent allowed an appropriation to Lacock Abbey partly because of the deaths of Lady Margaret de Lacy their patron and some other nobles, who used to help the nuns in internal and external affairs and give them counsel in adversity.[6] And Henry III granted 'simple protection' to the prior of Hinton as long as the heir of William Longspee, their patron, was a minor.[7]

Similarly when Whalley was in trouble with Bishop Langton for its 1,000 marks debt, the abbot in a complaint to the archdeacon mentioned 'the absence of our patron' as an aggravating factor. He also wrote to the patron's son-in-law and heir, Thomas of Lancaster, that 'all our refuge and hope of help on earth chiefly depends on you, sir, after our advocate and lord the earl of Lincoln'; that in spite of his, the earl's,

[1] See pp. 161–2.

[2] *Mon.* ii. 81 (account in cartulary).

[3] *Mon.* iii. 612–13. Cf. the abbot of Lonlay's request to Hugh de Nevill to accept a new prior of Stogursey and give him counsel and aid, 1265 (Duchy of Lanc. 25/171). Or such a promise might be made by a new patron, as in the later 'Forme of takyng the fownder' at Marrick (see p. 128, n. 2) Dieulacres had general charters of protection from Ranulf and John Scot, earls of Chester (*Chartulary of Dieulacres*, ed. G. Wrottesley, William Salt Soc. Collections ix, 1906, pp. 354–5).

[4] *Royal Letters . . . of Henry III*, ed. Shirley, p. 201. See pp. 8–9, 49–50 for the monks' claim to be of royal, not episcopal, patronage.

[5] *Gesta Dunelm.*, p. 15. See p. 126.

[6] *Reg. Gandavo*, i. 192–3.

[7] *Cal. Pat. R. 1247–58*, p. 607.

the king's, and other friends' requests the bishop still harried them; and that they could not fulfil their duties nor pay their debt to benefactors alive or dead. This appeals to one of the strongest motives for protection, the danger that a house's misfortunes might disable it from performing the masses, almsgiving, and other good works for which the founder hoped to be rewarded after death. The abbot asked Lancaster to obtain the king's help for them 'until the landing of our advocate'.[1]

Thus some protection really was to be expected, though its nature is vague. Actual armed protection was probably rarely required; though when in 1267 the rebels of the Isle of Ely threatened to burn Barnwell Priory, Hugh and Robert Pecche, younger brothers of the patron and amongst the rebels, opposed the project saying 'they would sooner die than let the bones of their father and kindred be burnt', and so the house was spared.[2]

Sometimes a patron might help to settle a dispute for the house. When the incumbent of one of Tewkesbury's wild Welsh benefices was deprived of it and began to plunder and threaten in revenge, Richard de Clare persuaded the monks to give him 6 marks to keep quiet, and gave the abbot a safe-conduct for going to settle the business.[3] And when the young King Henry came to Dunstable in 1229, the prior asked him to make peace between the canons and the burgesses, since he now had the rule of the whole kingdom 'and especially the patronage of that church'.[4]

The patron could help the monks in lawsuits or in dealings with the king, for the protection of their, and incidentally his, property. During the Interdict Roger de Lacy gave two palfreys to the king for the abbot of Stanlaw to hold his property in peace;[5] and he 'with all the great men of the court who were his friends' helped Kirkstall to recover a grange from the

---

[1] Whitaker, *Whalley*, i. 150.

[2] *Liber Mem.*, p. 123. Posting a porter at the gates in a vacancy was partly for protection against robbery: see p. 82.

[3] *Ann. Mon.* i. 125–6.

[4] Ibid. iii. 118. Cf. Henry's peacemaking between the abbot and convent of Westminster, on which Paris comments that he was 'known to be a special lover of that church' (*Chron. Maj.* v. 83).

[5] Cheney, in *Trans. R. Hist. Soc.* 4th Ser. xxxi. 135; *P.R. 12 John*, p. 65.

king.[1] Abbot David of St. Augustine's, Bristol, wrote to the patron Robert de Berkeley asking him to put his seal to some letters to the papal judges in a case about a mill, 'for our protection and the conservation of your right'; later, Robert wrote to the judges on the abbot's behalf, pointing out the canons' rights in this mill: 'They have held it hitherto by our predecessors' bounty and our grant.'[2] When in 1285 the earl of Gloucester was suing Peterborough for a manor, the abbot sent to the king for help, pleading 'that the house of Burgh was his house, and founded by his ancestors, and that the abbot could lose nothing without his losing it too'. The king gave them a writ dated earlier than one given previously to the earl.[3]

But in 1202, in a protracted lawsuit between Croyland and Spalding, the king gave little help to the royal abbey of Croyland, apparently because the abbot was brother to William de Longchamp, then out of favour; while Earl Ranulf of Chester, according to the Croyland chronicler, 'diligently fostered the side of Spalding as their patron and advocate . . . for he asserted that what was done to them was done to him', which had the effect of making the *curiales* favourable to Spalding.[4]

One kind of protection in the courts, standing to warranty, was of course the normal duty and interest of any landlord to any tenant.[5] A variant on this, however, is found in 1227, when the prior of Lewes and Earl William de Warenne together sued Adam de Novo Mercato for the advowson of a

---

[1] *Mon.* v. 531–2 (chronicle). Cf. Hubert Walter's debt of two palfreys for confirmations (i.e. of property) for the prioresses of Ickleton and Campsey (in the patronage of his family, de Valognes): *P.R. 5 John*, p. 27. (See *V.C.H. Suffolk*, ii. 112: Campsey had a confirmation charter that year). They were not confirmations *of* the prioresses, as stated in *V.C.H. Cambridge*, ii. 223.

[2] Hill, *Letter-books*, pp. 218, 219 (between 1215 and 1219). Cf. King John's intervention (by appeal to the pope) in a case before judge-delegates between Osney and St. Frideswide's about St. Mary Magdalen church, because the church was his gift to Osney which he was bound to warrant (*Oseney Cart.* ii. 227).

[3] *Hist. Burgensis*, Whytesley, pp. 148–9.

[4] *Hist. Croyland Continuatio*, in *Rerum Anglicarum scriptores veteres*, ed. W. Fulman (Oxford, 1684), i. 457, 467. Spalding had also been supported by its earlier patron Earl William de Roumara.

[5] As expressed by Henry III forbidding Peter fitz Herbert to sue Amesbury Priory about lands given by Henry II: 'the king ought to defend and warrant the deed and grant of his grandfather King Henry' (*Close R. 1227–31*, p. 591).

church, on the grounds that the earl's ancestor had been seised
of it and had given it to a prior of Lewes. The defendant
claimed that as the earl's ancestor had given away any right
in the advowson, he need not answer the earl. Earl William
said that his only claim in the advowson was 'as the advocate
of the prior for that advowson'.[1] There is no mention in this
of the prior vouching the earl to warranty, though it is the
same sort of obligation to maintain an ancestor's grant; his
interest in the matter is as patron of the house and particularly
as grantor, overlord, and protector of that particular piece of
property. There is no need to give to 'advocate' more meaning
than this, though it may here have had a flavour of the old
Frankish meaning, real advocacy in the courts. Generally
speaking this was not necessary, for monks could normally
quite well defend their own rights in the courts. For exceptions such as the Carthusians, however, the patron had an
extra responsibility, which Henry III expressed in appointing
a commission to inquire about encroachments on Witham
Priory's common, contrary to Henry II's foundation: 'The
king is bound to provide for their tranquillity, the more so as
by the statutes of their order they cannot and will not plead to
recover their rights in any secular courts.'[2] In 1261 he appointed Bracton (who had interests in the south-west) for the
special protection of Witham.[3]

Besides protection against rival claims there was protection
against impoverishment. Help in obtaining an appropriation
was one form of this.[4] The king's action in taking custody in
debt was another. Often this was done at the request of abbot
or convent or both: and although the king often took custody
of houses not of his own patronage,[5] royal patronage was a
strong point to urge in asking for it. The monks of Bardney
in 1278 petitioned for themselves and their goods to be taken
into the king's protection, while they lived quietly without
too many guests, till they could pay off their debts; this
petition was addressed to the king in the name of the abbot

---

[1] Bracton, *Note Book*, ed. Maitland, ii. 201–2.
[2] *Cal. Pat. R. 1247–58*, p. 511.
[3] *Close R. 1259–61*, p. 458 (order to sheriff to help him). Cf. the grant of protection to Hinton, also Carthusian (p. 142).
[4] See pp. 138–9.
[5] See p. 97.

and convent *dont il est avouz*.[1] And the monks of Bordesley, in asking for help about a debt, mentioned that they were of royal foundation.[2]

When the king took custody he might make the bishop take action; the bishop of Coventry and Lichfield wrote to the abbot of Burton, in the hands of a royal custodian, that he had been ordered by the king, in letters not only *monitorias et exhortatorias* but even *munittorias et praeceptorias*, to do something about their ruinous state.[3] Or king and bishop might work independently to the same end, as with Reading, which the king after various slighter measures took into his custody,[4] while the archbishop and the bishop of Salisbury imposed economies.[5]

A milder protective measure than taking custody was to forbid the entertainment of royal or other officers, or the removal of goods for the king or anyone else.[6] Or the house might be forbidden to increase its numbers, as was Acornbury in 1267, when in debt and burdened by too many nuns.[7] The nuns of Burnham claimed to have had such an order from their patron the earl of Cornwall.[8] In 1256 the king as patron forbade the citizens and merchants of Winchester to lend money to the monks or the deposed prior of St. Swithun's, deeply in debt through extravagance.[9] While a house was in custody, vacant or otherwise, the king could order a tallage on the tenants for the benefit of the house, to relieve its poverty; this was done for Selby in 1253–4, 'as has been done in other vacancies, and as the king can'; further, the escheator was to be all the more kind and favourable to the monks and their tenants because of their poverty.[10]

The prioress and convent of the poor and obscure Yorkshire house of Foukeholm, in the later thirteenth century, took the extreme step of committing themselves and all their temporal goods to the management and disposal of their patron William Colville and his heirs, to end the contentions that had arisen between them and their former patron, William's father Philip. He alone was to appoint a *magister* or

[1] *Rot. Parl.* i. 6.
[2] Ibid., p. 1.
[3] *Mon.* iii. 46.
[4] *Cal. Pat. R. 1281–92*, p. 242.
[5] *Reg. Swinfield*, pp. 165–9.
[6] Wood-Legh, p. 25.
[7] *Cal. Pat. R. 1266–72*, p. 109.
[8] See p. 111.
[9] Prynne, ii. 833.
[10] *Close R. 1253–4*, p. 97.

custos, and his consent was to be asked for the reception of new nuns or other inmates.[1] This was probably the kind of transaction forbidden by the Second Council of Lyons.[2]

The motive of protection against impoverishment might lead the patron to urge the deposition of a bad head; Prior Durand of Montacute was deposed by the bishop at King John's instance, ordering him to turn the prior out if the monks' accusations of maladministration were true.[3] Next year, however, the monks had to give 60 marks so that John should not interfere to restore Durand, but should help them to acquire a useful prior, 'to the honour of God and advantage of the king, whose special alms they are'.[4] So the monks appeal to his interest and duty for help against a wasteful prior.

After John's reign any such active part in a deposition might have been frowned on as encroachment on spiritualities; the patron should not be allowed to interfere with discipline even for the house's good. He might, however, be consulted by ecclesiastical authority: in 1303 Archbishop Corbridge refused to accept the prioress's resignation at the Cistercian nunnery of Esholt until he had visited them or discussed their condition with the patron, Simon le Ward.[5] And the patron could urge action on the authorities, as Archbishop Romeyn urged the Cistercian visitors and the abbot of Clairvaux to amend the bad temporal state of Fountains, and to keep those responsible away from the abbot's election; he was deeply concerned with the deplorable condition of the abbey, *ratione fundationis et patronatus*.[6] Direct action as patron would have been unwarrantable, and of course he had no powers there as diocesan. Henry III, however, was less discreet in supporting one party against another at Bardney, apparently for what seemed to him the good of the house; he was severely rebuked by Grosseteste, who said that even if he acted so out of devotion he was overstepping his powers.[7] But the king could insist that custody in such circumstances was his alone; in

---

[1] *V.C.H. Yorks.* iii. 116, and (for the text) *Yorks. Archaeol. Journal*, ix. 335.
[2] c. 22; Hefele-Leclerq, vi. 199–200.
[3] *Rot. Lit. Pat.*, p. 78.
[4] *Rot. de Oblatis*, p. 420; *P.R. 10 John*, p. 110.
[5] *V.C.H. Yorks.* iii. 161.
[6] *Fountains Memorials*, i. 179–81.
[7] See pp. 95–96.

1258, when the prior of Lenton was in conflict with his monks and finally deposed, Henry took custody and ordered the removal of the prior of Prittlewell to whom the Cluniac visitor had given custody: this was 'manifestly against our crown and dignity'. He wished the visitor to enforce discipline, but required a report from him, and that there should be no alienation of goods through the visitation.[1]

In fact, although complaints of interference with discipline are uncommon, it was in this sphere of relations with a mother-house, and especially over visitation, that it was most likely to arise;[2] not normally with the motive of interfering in spiritualities, but either as a move to secure his own temporal rights[3] or else to preserve the temporalities. For one of the most important forms of protection by patrons was protection against exaction or exploitation by mother-houses. In 1275 the king took steps to prevent the abbot of Ghent selling the woods of Lewisham Priory, and to examine any default or withdrawals in almsgiving, since it pertained to him to see that the alms of his and his predecessors' patronage were preserved from waste and that the almsgivings established by them were observed.[4] (He had, however, only two months earlier licensed the abbey to sell Lewisham 'manor' to the bishop of Rochester;[5] this was never done and he turned to protecting the priory.)

Similarly Peter de Maulay in 1294, confirming a mill to the English brothers of Eskdale Priory, undertook not to let visitors from Grandmont or any overseas brothers have any claim on the mill or ruin the temporalities in his fee, as had been done in his ancestors' time.[6] And it was probably exploitation by Grandmont which provoked Crasswall Priory's patron, in or before 1315, to expel the corrector (or prior) and all but one brother.[7] According to the prior of Grandmont

---

[1] *Close R.* 1256–9, pp. 346, 459.

[2] In an agreement 1218–22 between the abbot of Lessay and William de St. John, about the dependency Boxgrave, one clause was that the patron should not meddle with discipline (*Chartulary of the High Church of Chichester*, ed. Peckham, pp. 76–77).

[3] e.g. assent to elections (pp. 57, 60–61). And Robert de Tateshall, patron of Wymondham, twice shut the gates against the abbot of St. Albans on visitation, to extract a livery he claimed (*Gesta Abb.* ii. 23).

[4] *Cal. Close R.* 1272–9, p. 242.

[5] *Reg. Roffense*, p. 471.

[6] Graham, *Eng. Eccl. Studies*, p. 232.

[7] Ibid., pp. 230, 231–2.

(who does not seem at all scandalized by this show of lay force) the patron declared that he would admit none but men capable of restoring the priory, almost ruined by the others, and reviving the good repute of the order.[1] In 1210 Robert fitz Walter sued the abbot of St. Albans for oppression of Binham Priory—staying there with too many horses and followers, tallaging the priory's men, putting in too many monks, and exacting more than the 1 mark a year which was due; but especially for removing a prior put in by Robert,[2] so that here it is primarily his own right that he defends (though concern about the prior's appointment could itself be provoked by the mother-house's exploitation).[3]

Many founders of Cluniac houses stipulated that the mother-house was only to take some such sum as 1 mark a year for all temporal service;[4] in 1240 William de Warenne complained, successfully, that an agreement to this effect made by his parents for Lewes, because of inroads on the priory's property made by the abbot of Cluny, was being broken by the exaction of a Tenth for Cluny.[5] But even apart from such stipulations the patron's objection might be a useful argument for the house: Bermondsey Priory tried to avoid paying this Tenth partly on the grounds that they would incur the king's 'inestimable rancour' if they had to reduce their numbers or withdraw hospitality.[6] In 1289 Edward I forbade English Cluniacs to make any payments to Cluny till further order;[7] and the Statute of Carlisle shows that payments to mother-houses abroad were still specially resented. But about the same time an argument used at St. Albans against granting a heavy pension was that expense might fall on the cells, whose patrons would then object *tuitorie et acriter*.[8]

[1] All Souls College Archives, Alberbury No. 120 (a letter from the new prior, dated 9 March 1315/16, to the corrector of Alberbury, committing to him certain business in England).

[2] *Cur. Reg. R.* vi. 55.   [3] See pp. 54–55.

[4] Either in the foundation charter or in some later settlement: e.g. Lewes (Duckett, i. 92. See p. 58), Pontefract (Duchy of Lanc. 25/46. See p. 55), Lenton, Farley, Prittlewell, Monks Horton, Mendham, Horkesley (*Mon.* v. 111, 27, 22–23, 34, 58, 157). A non-Cluniac example is Boxgrave, 3 m. to Lessay, under a composition with William de St. John (*Mon.* iv. 646).

[5] *Cal. Papal L.* i. 186.   [6] Bernard et Bruel, vi. 4746.

[7] Graham, *Eng. Eccl. Studies*, p. 106.

[8] *Gesta Abb.* ii. 91. Cf. Edward II's objection to a tax by the archbishop on the religious of Canterbury diocese (*Reg. Roffense*, pp. 106–7).

Far more important was the same attitude to the pope's taxes. Patrons might try to protect their houses against these, if only in their own interests as overlords. On the pope's request for a subsidy in 1226, the king forbade prelates holding baronies of him 'to bind their lay fees for the Roman church, whence he might be deprived of the service due to him',[1] while in 1229 Earl Ranulf of Chester 'would not let the religious men or clerks of his fief pay these Tenths'.[2] And these objections might be used by the churches as a welcome excuse for resistance. The prelates in 1226 told the pope that they could not reply without the king and all patrons;[3] and one of the bishops' objections to the demand for a Fifth in 1240 was that 'it is to the prejudice of the patrons of churches'.[4] The abbots complained of this levy to the king as 'patron of their churches': 'We hold baronies of you, and cannot impoverish them without your prejudice; nor can we both answer to you for them as we ought, and satisfy the pope incessantly extorting from us. . . . We come to the shelter of your counsel and the asylum of your patronage.' But in this case the king refused his help and turned them over to the legate.[5] In 1244–5, however, he renewed his resistance, got an aid for himself, and repeated his prohibition of 1226[6] (though he gave in eventually);[7] while Paris attributes to the abbots, weighing the nuncio's demands against the king's, the consideration that 'the king our lord and patron, and founder and enricher of many of our churches . . . asks for our help for the defence . . . of the realm, that is, the republic'.[8] Here the idea of keeping the property intact to perform the services to the patron is sublimated in the idea of duty to the kingdom; but it exists for patrons other than the king. In this same year the answers of the lower clergy to the pope's demand for money against the emperor,[9] repeating the answers attributed

[1] Wendover, in *Chron. Maj.* iii. 103; Lunt, *Financial Relations*, p. 185.
[2] Wendover, in *Chron. Maj.* iii. 189.
[3] Ibid., p. 103; *Ann. Mon.* iii (Dunstable), p. 99; Lunt, p. 185.
[4] *Chron. Maj.* iv. 38; Lunt, pp. 200–1.
[5] *Chron. Maj.* iv. 36; Lunt, p. 202.
[6] *Chron. Maj.* iv. 375.
[7] Lunt, pp. 210, 218.
[8] *Chron. Maj.* iv. 370. (This suggests that calling the aid of that year an aid *pur fille marier* was acknowledged as a fiction.)
[9] *Ann. Mon.* i (Burton), p. 266.

to the Berkshire rectors in 1240,[1] include the statement that
they cannot agree to such a contribution without consulting
their patrons, who had endowed the churches with lands and
rents for special purposes, such as hospitality, which would
have to be stopped if such exactions were made; the patrons
might then take the line that they had been 'cheated of their
right and of their purpose in giving', and could therefore take
back what they had given.[2] This refers directly only to parish
churches, but the same argument would apply to religious
houses, and was so applied in the case of provisions.

For papal provisions were subject to the same objections as
taxation. Although it was early made clear that provisions
were not to be made to livings in a layman's advowson,[3] they
still hit laymen indirectly as patrons of religious houses to
whose livings provisions were made; and this was a major
reason for the lay magnates' concern in the matter.

The English barons complained to the cardinals at Lyons
in 1245 that they were gravely injured when monasteries were
thus defrauded of their advowsons, since their ancestors, as
God-fearing men concerned for their souls, had founded
monasteries and endowed them with demesne land and with
the patronage of churches, so that the religious could live
there and worship in peace, supported by those demesnes,
and served and defended in external matters by their clerks
in those churches[4]—in other words, the religious could use
these advowsons for the payment of their agents and lawyers.
Next year, the English clergy's letter to Innocent IV on his
demands included this statement: 'The nobles and magnates
assert that if churches conferred by them on monasteries are
conferred on Italian clerks, they can justly recall those churches
and other benefices to their own property; because the fruits
coming from them ought by right to be put to the use of the
poor and of pilgrims, since this was the intention of the givers

---

[1] *Chron. Maj.* iv. 41; see Lunt, p. 201.

[2] Cf. the reaction to the 1246–7 subsidy, according to Paris: 'they greatly feared
lest princes and magnates . . . who or whose predecessors founded, endowed and
enriched churches, and largely cut into their own possessions for this . . . might
take back the churches' goods and possessions, taught by the pope's example, *non
obstante* the tenor of such-and-such a charter' (*Chron. Maj.* iv. 619; see Lunt,
p. 223).

[3] *Chron. Maj.* iii. 610–14 (1239 correspondence).

[4] *Chron. Maj.* iv. 441–2, and Cole, *Documents*, p. 352.

and the cause of their giving'.[1] In the barons' letter to
Alexander IV in 1258, which can be partly reconstructed
from the pope's reply, they made the further point that they
and their ancestors had given advowsons to religious men in
the belief that good appointments would result—that they
would present rectors who would attend to the salvation of
souls and the support of the poor; that this intention was frus-
trated by papal provisions and also by appropriations; and
that they ought therefore to recall these advowsons to their
own lordship.[2]

But besides these motives, of respecting his ancestors' intentions, protecting the monastery against loss of his ancestors'
alms, and so safeguarding the spiritual services due from those
alms, the patron had a more material interest in resisting provisions. This was expressed in the plan drawn up for action
at the Second Council of Lyons. The clauses about provisions
were to be resisted, because the king and the barons thereby
lost their custodies: 'for although such churches are ... of the
advowson of religious men, nevertheless the king or the barons
are patrons and founders of those religious, and in many cases
can present to such parish churches ...';[3] when, in fact, the
house was vacant and in the patron's custody. And apart from
vacancies, the patron might often ask to have his own relative
or clerk presented;[4] provisions would interfere with this. In
this same plan the general point was made that benefices
ought to be available for noble and lettered clerks, and especially younger sons;[5] while the Statute of Carlisle said that 'the
poor nobles and learned men' were being excluded from pre-
ferment.[6]

The patron's resistance to a provision in a particular case
is shown in 1241, when the monks of Peterborough refused
the pope's demand because the king forbade it, as their
'defender, patron and governor'.[7] Three years later Henry

---

[1] *Ann. Mon.* i (Burton), pp. 278–9, and *Chron. Maj.* iv. 531–2. The same claim,
to reclaim what had been given if it were turned from its intended use, was made
later by the Norman patrons—presumably a group of benefactors' descendants—
when Clement V gave Ogbourne Priory (an English cell of Bec) in commendation
to his nephew (Morgan, pp. 31–32).

[2] *Ann. Mon.* i (Burton), pp. 487–8.

[3] Cole, p. 358.   [4] See pp. 112–13.

[5] Cole, pp. 359–60.   [6] *Rot. Parl.* i. 207, 220.

[7] *Chron. Maj.* iv. 101–2.

required the papal collector Martin not to interfere with Peterborough for presenting 'our familiar clerks' to churches, and asserted his own duty to protect 'bishops and abbots who hold baronies ... as we would protect laymen';[1] and in 1245 the abbot was summoned to Lyons for giving a church at the king's command, against the pope's provision.[2] Perhaps the same benefice was at issue all the time; anyhow the king's interest in protecting the abbey is clear, though it is interest bound up with a duty.

Similarly in 1243 the abbot of Abingdon, in a dilemma between a papal provision and the king's request for Aymer de Valence, was advised by his monks: 'If the king will protect you from papal attack, we consider it more tolerable to confer the church on the brother of the king, your prince and patron, than on the Roman.' But in this case Henry let them down in the end, giving no help when the abbot was sentenced to compensate the Roman.[3] And a provision in favour of a royal clerk could, of course, detach the king from the cause of patrons in general.[4]

Thus the position of many lay barons as patrons of monasteries, with an obligation and an interest to protect them, has considerable bearing on the lay attitude to papal provisions and taxation, and on Henry III's suspect position as chief of the lay patrons and yet the intermittent ally and favourite of the pope.[5] Sir Maurice Powicke has pointed out how the sense of patronage was aroused by papal demands;[6] it was a constant concern, recurring even in the demands of the Disinherited.[7] The religious and the clergy generally looked to the king and the nobles for help, quoting the laymen's claims for their own justification in resisting the head of the Church; just as on a smaller scale the Burnham nuns welcomed, if they did not invent, their patron's interference with the admission of new nuns, as helping them to resist Archbishop Pecham's request

[1] *Close R. 1242–7*, p. 259; Powicke, i. 348, 354.
[2] *Hist. Burgensis*, Swaffham, p. 117.
[3] *Chron. Maj.* v. 38–39. Cf. Henry's order to the sheriff of Lincoln, 1249, to turn out or exclude any provisors from any benefice to which Thorney Abbey might present Aymer (*Close R. 1247–51*, p. 348).
[4] e.g. John Mansel's provision to Thame prebend in 1241 (*Chron. Maj.* iv. 152).
[5] See Paris on the king's defection in 1246 (*Chron. Maj.* iv. 560–1, 577).
[6] Powicke, i. 354–7 and ii. 718.
[7] *Ibid.* ii. 540.

for a place.[1] This was the kind of strain within the Church, between various corporations and authorities, combined with the coherence of the kingdom as a common society of clergy and laity, which prevented canon law having its full effect against lay influence.

But this is not to say that the English churches always or usually welcomed such influence. It was just as desirable to guard themselves against lay exploitation. One set of lay claims might be used against another;[2] or the claims of the spiritual power might be invoked, as in 1283 (years before *Clericis laicos* made it for a few months a clear issue of obedience) the clergy resisted royal taxation on the grounds of the pope's needs and the duty of consulting him.[3] For if to outsiders' demands clergy and laity presented a fairly united front on grounds of tradition or national need, between themselves they disputed on more general principles.[4] Through the patron's attitude runs the feudal feeling that property is given conditionally, that the giver and his heirs retain a hold on it and can take it back if it is alienated or misapplied—if the services or alms are not performed. When all this was embodied in the Second Statute of Westminster, the clergy protested; it was contrary to the Church's ideas of the permanence and freedom of its property, and protection on these terms might seem plain self-interested interference.

Indeed the objection to claims by mother-house or pope is closely linked with the general concern to prevent alienation of property, which might involve opposing the monks' own plans for a sale that was good business or necessary to pay off debts. The patrons' attitude, implied in the legislation already discussed,[5] was partly a straightforward concern to protect monasteries against irresponsible or short-sighted prelates anxious to shuffle the burden of debt on to the future; partly an interest complementary to that behind the Statute of Mort-

---

[1] See p. 111.

[2] e.g. the prior of Hurley excused himself from paying 'tallage' (apparently the 1200 carucage: see R. S. Hoyt, *Royal Demesne in English Constitutional History*, New York, 1950, p. 111) because the priory was a cell and Geoffrey fitz Piers was its advocate (ibid., p. 118, n. 105); while, on a different level, the Cistercian abbots refused aid to John partly because of their spiritual obligations to others (see p. 117).

[3] *Chron. Petroburgense*, ed. Stapleton, p. 63.

[4] See pp. 33–35, 37–39.

[5] See pp. 36–37.

main, unwillingness that the house should alienate land except back to the grantor; partly a sense that if their gift were lost their spiritual rewards were endangered.

It is not clear what right the patron had to be consulted in an alienation before the Second Statute of Westminster, though his hold may have been tighter than that of a lord on any ordinary tenant (apart from the special control on tenants-in-chief).[1] The patron's consent was certainly often sought, as when, early in the thirteenth century, Burscough Priory gave a canon's lands to his son with the consent of the patron, the lord of Latham,[2] or as Merton Priory and St. Mary du Val gave up cells to each other 'by the will of the patrons of both places'.[3] But in the similar case of Bruton Priory giving up lands and rights in France to Troarn Abbey, there is no mention of the Mohuns, who were patrons of Bruton and had given the French property now being alienated.[4] This may be because since the loss of Normandy the family had no interest in these lands;[5] but there are other cases, not explicable in this way, where there is no mention of the patron's consent.[6] This does not of course prove that he was not consulted; but it suggests that his consent was not essential enough to be recorded as part of the transaction.

Control might be secured to the patron by a special arrangement, as in a composition between William de St. John and

---

[1] On alienation by lay tenants see Plucknett, pp. 9, 104.

[2] Duchy of Lanc. 25/270.

[3] *Reg. Bronscombe*, p. 275. Cf. 1209, a composition about land between Chester and Stanlaw, made before and sealed by their respective patrons, Earl Ranulf and his constable Roger de Lacy (*Whalley Coucher Bk.*, ii. 534). Another, provisional till the majority of Edmund de Lacy (ibid., pp. 545–7). 1269, prior of Lewes demised at farm and for ever certain tithes to a rector, with consent of John de Warenne (*Lewes Cartulary, Norfolk portion*, ed. J. H. Bullock, Norfolk Rec. Soc. xii, 1939, p. 43). 1272–1300, Rewley gave a rent to Thame with assent of Edmund of Cornwall (*Mon.* v. 405). 1287, Buildwas gave a grange by exchange to Croxden, confirmed by Henry de Lacy (not patron of Buildwas, but overlord for that grange) provided that Croxden did the same service as Buildwas used to do (*Mon.* v. 360). 1311, grant of Kennington church by Colne Priory to its mother-house Abingdon with 'will and consent' of the earl of Oxford, patron of Colne (*Mon.* iv. 103).

[4] Royal confirmation was sought and granted, reserving certain royal rights in Bruton's cell Horsley (*Cal. Charter R.* ii. 36).

[5] But see the converse case of Ogbourne, p. 152, n. 1.

[6] e.g. several agreements between Chester and Stanlaw besides those mentioned above, n. 3, none of which has any mention of their lords and patrons (*Whalley Coucher Bk.*, ii. 536–41).

the abbot of Lessay made 'when the goods of Boxgrave Priory
were being spent otherwise than was fit', by which the prior
could alienate nothing without the consent of chapter, bishop,
and patron.[1] But in the common law the patron's control was
probably not defined until the Edwardian legislation, like the
wider question of alienation by any tenant. Bracton, discus-
sing the acquiring and granting of property, had said that
some could not give without the consent of others, as abbots
without their chapters 'or the chapter itself without the consent of the king or other patron, for the consent of all those
whom the matter touches will be necessary'.[2] But in the context this need not be a general rule, and he does not discuss its
application. The tendency of legislation was to tighten control, and by the fourteenth century the king's control as
patron was strict, his confirmation being often required for
corrodies, leases, or even the manumission of a villein.[3] Yet as
early as 1236 Henry III confirmed the abbot of St. Albans'
grant of a pension to a clerk,[4] and in 1259 he objected to the
bishop's allocation of a Barking Abbey manor to support a
resigned abbess.[5]

A bishop who was also patron could use spiritual weapons
to prevent alienation. In 1304 Bishop Gainsborough of Worcester wrote to the monks of Little Malvern, reminding them
that the priory was of his patronage, and forbidding them
under pain of excommunication to alienate anything immov-
able without special leave; he hears that by such alienations
by various religious in the diocese, 'their established condition
is enormously reduced'.[6] Here the interests of the diocesan
for discipline and stability coincide with those of the patron
for the property; he addresses a particular house of his own
advowson, but mentions the whole diocese.[7]

Just as patrons, or any lords of any tenants, might object to
property being granted away by the holder, so they might
object to its being as it were completely swallowed by the
holder; in either case it slipped farther out of the lord's reach.
A transfer of property from abbot to convent was in a way an

---

[1] *Chichester Cart.*, pp. 76–77.   [2] *De Legibus*, ii. 52.
[3] Wood-Legh, p. 29.   [4] *Cal. Charter R.* i. 219.
[5] *Close R. 1256–9*, p. 400.   [6] *Mon.* iv. 450 (from register).
[7] A bishop who was not patron might forbid alienations as diocesan: e.g. Thomas
of Cantilupe's injunctions to Chirbury, of royal patronage (*Reg. Cantilupe*, pp. 147–8).

alienation; for the patron lost his custody in vacancies. It seems that such a transfer needed the patron's consent, at least in royal houses: when the abbot of St. Albans assigned certain revenues to the monks' bread and ale, his charter was confirmed by King Henry 'because we have found by inquest ... that this provision and ordinance falls to our and our heirs' exoneration and utility in times of vacancy of the said abbey'.[1] This probably means that the saving in the custodian's expenses would compensate for the loss in revenue. On the other hand the Ramsey cartulary includes various assignations by thirteenth-century abbots to obediences, or to a cell, with no mention of royal assent.[2]

The same considerations applied to appropriations of churches; though the patron could still ask the house to present a clerk of his, it would be only to a poor vicarage instead of to the rectory; and more important, he lost the presentation he would have had in time of vacancy. That this was a considerable loss is shown by the breaches of the rule complained of by the clergy in 1300,[3] though it is not clear whether patrons had been trying to ignore the appropriation and present to the whole rectory, or simply to present to the vicarage—the patronage of which, as a spirituality, should not have been in their custody.[4] There was, in fact, controversy at this time about whether a rector's presentation to a vicarage came under the lay or church courts, involving controversy whether it was a spirituality or not.[5] In the previous year, when Archbishop

---

[1] *Chron. Maj.* v. 668–72. Cf. Bury (*Cal. Charter R.* ii. 259). In 1320 a composition between the abbot and convent of Abingdon, dividing either property or revenues (this was controversial), was annulled by king and parliament on the grounds that it was made without the consent of the king's ancestors and to the diminution of their alms—it is not clear how. (*Mon.* i. 523–5, from the close rolls; *Cal. Pat. R. 1317–21*, pp. 526–7; see Reich, p. 299.)

[2] *Ramsey Cart.* ii. 217–25, 228, 230, 233, 236, 240, 280–1. Abbots sometimes bequeathed their movable goods to one of the community; this needed royal consent (Reich, pp. 304–5).

[3] See p. 95.

[4] In 1323 Edward II presented to a vicarage as in his gift because of the vacancy of the bishopric of Winchester, to which the church was presumably appropriated (*Reg. of John de Sandale and Rigaud de Asserio*, ed. F. J. Baigent, Hants. Rec. Soc. 1897, pp. 612–13).

[5] 1300 grievances (*Reg. Winchelsey*, p. 1026). The claim for the lay court was said to be a new usurpation, but it was implied in 1285 in Westminster II (c. v, providing for litigation about vicarages along with other benefices), and the clergy had complained of this (*Concilia*, ii. 119).

Winchelsey complained of Edward I's action in taking custody of Ely Priory while it was not vacant, one of the king's injustices had been to present clerks to appropriated churches, two of which were badly needed, being assigned to the monks' food and to the poor;[1] here the king's presentees were evidently claiming the rectorial tithes.

It followed that for an appropriation, as for a transfer from abbot to convent, the patron's assent might be required; Edward's answer to the 1300 complaint was that he would respect appropriations which had royal consent.[2] For example, he allowed St. Mary's, York, for a fine, to appropriate a church, finding by inquest that it would not be to his prejudice except that in a vacancy he would not be able to present to it.[3] In 1313 Edward II sued the abbot of St. James's, Northampton, for the presentation to a church appropriated without his licence: apparently partly on the grounds that appropriation was a kind of grant in mortmain,[4] but chiefly (since the appropriation antedated the Statute of Mortmain) on the king's loss of the presentation in a vacancy.[5]

The patron's natural interest against appropriations is shown in the agreement between Walden Abbey and Geoffrey fitz Piers after a lawsuit for the abbey's advowsons,[6] by which the monks promised to present the earl's and his eldest son's presentees to nine named churches, but the earl undertook not to impede their attempts to get these churches appropriated.[7] In this case he would, perhaps, continue to present clerks as vicars; there is an example of an arrangement to that effect in 1312, when Isabel of Panton sued a provisor for a vicarage on the grounds that 'she is entitled to name a clerk to the prior of Langwell and he presents this clerk to the ordinary';[8] but this was probably rare, and in any case the disposal of the much richer rectory was lost.

[1] Reg. Winchelsey, pp. 253-4, 258; see p. 78.
[2] Ibid., p. 1019. [3] Mon. iii. 568.
[4] Year Bk. Ser. xiii. 75.
[5] Ibid., pp. 75-78, 81. An argument for the defence was that the advowson concerned was not held in chief, but this was countered by the point that the abbey was held in chief and therefore the king would have the presentation in the abbey's vacancy (probably by his prerogative wardship of all lands of a tenant-in-chief: see p. 87, n. 2). [6] See pp. 113, 168.
[7] Harl. MS. 3697 (cartulary), f. 20.
[8] Year Bk. Ser. xii. 170-1. 'Langwell' might be Langworth or Langwade hospitals.

So here for once the patron's interest in the property splits off from his duty of protection, and he must choose between helping his monks to gain an appropriation and opposing it in his own interests. But this strain may well have been eased by a growing tendency amongst laymen (as Alexander IV's letter to the barons shows) to disapprove of appropriations altogether, to lump them with provisions as contrary to their ancestors' intentions, and to contemplate restoring the monasteries' benefices to lay patronage.[1]

The assignation of revenues to an anniversary might similarly need or be strengthened by the patron's consent. The Ramsey cartulary, again, contains such settlements without mention of royal consent;[2] but Abbot Crokesley of Westminster, who died in 1258, had his anniversary paid for by two entire manors and other rents, and this had the king's consent as founder and patron. After nine years, however, it was abolished by papal delegates as unnecessarily pompous and expensive.[3] Here it is the authority of the Church which checks extravagance which the patron for once had condoned.

All this shows how sometimes lay and church powers united for discipline and economy, while at other times each tried to protect and monopolize a source of wealth or power; as the rulers of the Church resisted the king's exactions or other patrons' oppressions, while kings and nobles protected their churches against the demands of their ecclesiastical superiors.

The patron's protection of his house, then, was largely for the preservation of his property, and might be spoken of as a right rather than a duty; a donor to Buildwas Abbey made his gift free of all secular exactions, but retained 'the defence and protection against the incursions of others'; and they were not to assart or sell without his leave[4]—a check on alienation, part of the same self-interested protection.

And yet there was more to it than this.[5] The Church

---

[1] *Ann. Mon.* i (Burton), pp. 487–90.

[2] *Ramsey Cart.* ii. 226–7, 232.

[3] *Mon.* i. 272 (editors' notes, from cartulary). 10 marks a year were assigned instead, for a simpler celebration.

[4] *Mon.* v. 359.

[5] A founder's descendant who was no longer landlord might retain a duty of protection; in the twelfth century, Roger de Berkeley, allowing Kingswood Abbey to leave his fief and hold of a new lord (Bernard de St. Walery, at Tetbury), promised: 'et manutenebo eos pro posse meo sicut fundator' (*Mon.* v. 426).

expected a special protection, beyond that owed to any tenant;
Winchelsey told the king over his dealings with Ely Priory
that patrons ought to help and protect their churches, 'and as
they ought to enjoy an abundant peace, bound for ever to the
Divine service and living in decent religion outside the noise
of the world, so ought the patron to drive off from them all
trouble and expense'.[1] The patron, too, could feel this duty as
something special, a matter of affection, pride, and family
tradition—of concern for the souls of his ancestors, combined
with the ordinary anxieties of a landlord for the prosperity of
the lands held of him; interest merged with piety in the preservation of spiritual gains. A whole gamut of interest, sentiment, and convention is suggested by Henry de Lacy's letter
to the king in 1295, about the seizure of Spalding Priory as
alien; explaining that it was quite English and independent,
complaining that alms would be withdrawn 'to the damage of
the souls of my ancestors' who founded the house, and asking
him 'as dearly as I know how' to give back their possessions
to the prior and convent: 'and be sure, sir, that no possession
that my ancestors have left me do I more wish to save and
guard than those which they gave in alms, and especially to
the priory of Spalding. Therefore I pray you dearly that in
this matter you will do me such grace that they may feel that
my prayer is of some use to them.'[2]

1 Reg. Winchelsey, pp. 253-4.
2 Mon. iii. 225-6.

IX

QUARRELS

IN canon law the patron or advocate was looked upon as one who, though he should protect, would probably oppress his monastery; who, besides exercising unlawful power in the appointment of a prelate, would keep a hold on the property and make unlawful profits from it. In England by the thirteenth century the patron's position had, on the whole, been regularized. The young Robert de Ferrars's unexplained destruction of Tutbury Priory[1] lies isolated at the extreme of violence. But there was plenty of room for dispute. The patron might interfere too much, or try to raise his profits; the house might deny him his customary rights. The sense of confraternity might be absent; the patron might regard the house simply as a piece of property which some rash ancestor had disposed of unprofitably; the house might see him simply as a hard landlord and unwelcome guest.

The Ford chronicle stresses the fact that Robert and John de Courtenay, in the first half of the century, did them no harm, as if this were remarkable. Its account of Hugh de Courtenay I, who followed John, is a vivid account of what for the monks constituted a bad patron. In him all virtues were 'chilled and dulled'; he was *infestus et molestus*, and used for horses and dogs what his forefathers had intended for pious uses. In other words, he exacted from land given as frankalmoin a 'fixed, dire and hard service'—providing a horse, cart, and harness for war, and keeping two horses, their grooms, and a dog for him. He seized their oxen in distraint for this service; there was much litigation, and a *pax talis qualis*. In 1290 he was seizing their cattle again, though he was beaten off with arrows from one manor by the abbey's servants. This Courtenay and his wife, unlike most of them, were buried not at Ford but at their much less important foundation, Cowick Priory.

Hugh de Courtenay II made the same feudal claims; he also, according to the monks' account, adding two evils to his

---

[1] *Ann. Mon.* i (Burton), p. 491.

father's one, claimed suit of court for a certain manor, forcing them by threats to give up their charter of immunity; and upheld a rector against them in a tithes dispute.[1]

Another Cistercian abbey, Pipewell, had similar trouble at the end of the century with its patron Robert Boutevileyn, lord of Cotesbrook. Unlike his father, who protected and helped the monks, Robert 'in many ways vexed and persecuted them'; claiming, amongst other things,[2] stabling for one horse in the abbot's stable and accommodation for his hounds at the monks' expense. Furthermore he denied that they had ever had a foundation charter; presumably he would have liked to impugn their right to hold the land at all, and in any case would not let them hold it free of secular service.

The Pipewell chronicle describes in delightfully concrete detail how he tried to enforce his claim to stabling.[3] A boy brought the horse to the abbot's stable and tethered it in an empty stall, not asking the abbot. He, clearly a cautious man, consulted lawyers; on whose advice he waited till the boy took the horse to water, and then shut them out. At this the boy left the horse at the stable gate, took a horn and went out to raise the hue and cry against the monks. The abbot, still consulting experts at every step, now sent two monks and some laymen to return the horse to Cotesbrook; where they found the yard deserted, and left the horse tethered in his master's stable. But, just as they were leaving, Boutevileyn's men came in from the fields, caught one of the laymen, and kept him prisoner for a few days until Boutevileyn's arrival. When he came he threatened personal violence 'like another Herod'; but a concord was finally made, by which for £40 he confirmed their foundation, and with it, presumably, the frankalmoin tenure which was normal for Cistercians.[4] Incidentally these cases of Ford and Pipewell show that in some respects a Cistercian house could have as close and acrimonious relations with its patron as any other.

Although these quarrels show bad feeling and a gap in interest, they are largely concerned with ordinary feudal matters, over which any landlord and tenant might fall out. From the

---

[1] *Mon.* v. 380.   [2] See p. 116.
[3] This passage is translated in Coulton, iii. 490–1.
[4] *Mon.* iv. 437.

patron's point of view his violent actions were doubtless often
no more than legitimate assertion of feudal rights by distraint,
and not such 'horrible enormities' as the monks tried to make
out. For they were inclined to have the best of both worlds—
to compete as men of business in secular affairs, and to be
indignant as men of religion if treated in too business-like a
manner.

Of such an ordinary feudal kind was the habitual friction
between Tewkesbury Abbey and Richard de Clare, about
feudal dues, suit of court, advowsons, liberties, and rights of
pasture.[1] In 1250–1 they had a long dispute about the abbot's
right of hanging thieves at Wimborne in Dorset; throughout
the abbot was clamorous and pertinacious, the earl grudging
but patient, and the whole affair sounds not very bitter. It
began when a thief caught on the abbot's land was allowed to
be hanged at the earl's court at Cranborne, 'by the stupidity
of the abbot's bailiffs'. The next to be caught was haggled
over as a test case for the remainder of his life. The earl's
bailiff would not allow him to be tried in the abbot's court,
whereupon the abbot hurried to the earl. The earl ordered an
inquiry, but this was put off until the abbot worried him about
it again. Then during the inquiry the abbot went once more
to complain to the earl; who was just going abroad, and told
the abbot he could keep his thief in prison until his, the
earl's, return, when the inquiry would begin again. The abbot
pointed out that he had no prison; so the earl allowed him his
claim for the meanwhile, and the thief was hanged.[2] In spite
of this kind of trouble the earl was on reasonably good terms
with the abbey in the intervals.[3]

A more bitter dispute was that between Quarr Abbey and
Isabel de Forz, though it was equally of a kind which might
happen between any landlord and tenant, with the added com-
plication of violence to religious men. By the abbot's account
when he sued the countess, she had oppressed the abbey even
after the king had taken it under his protection because of
disputes with her; her men had assaulted and imprisoned
monks, lay brothers, and servants, stolen three horses, and

[1] *Ann. Mon.* i. 137, 146, 155.
[2] Ibid. i. 140–4; *Mon.* ii. 82 (account in cartulary).
[3] See pp. 118, 119–20, 121, 127, 140 n. 2, 143.

trampled their corn; she had prevented the abbot from collecting his salt, distrained him for suit of court, and torn up a charter of exemption from this[1] (which the king had then renewed).

The countess's defence was that the arrests had been made for the defence of the island, by the legal method of hue and cry, when monks and lay brothers were found armed. The jurors agreed with this: Quarr men had been found by Carisbrooke men armed in defence of some disputed tithes; the men arrested had been released; and nothing of any account had been stolen. The rights of the suit of court question were worried out, and the countess won her case.[2] Here again the 'oppressions and extortions' seem much exaggerated; but the countess's dealings with Breamore Priory suggest that she was a somewhat hard patron.[3]

Near neighbourhood of a monastery and its patrons' *caput* may have increased the chances of friction. Walter fitz Simon of Daventry and his son Robert fitz Walter both had disputes about property with Daventry Priory,[4] which at least once led to violence: in 1239 Walter undertook to maintain a lamp at the high altar 'in part satisfaction for the attack made on the priory by me and my men'.[5]

Trouble might arise over matters less purely feudal, more particularly concerned with patronage; such as denial by the house, or usurpation by the patron, of rights in elections or in custody. Some of these disputes have already been described. Some patrons were notoriously exacting, like William and Ida de Beauchamp in their two quarrels with Newnham Priory about the election and installation of the priors.[6] Paris says they were known enemies of religious houses, and that William was hard and stony, *petrinus* rather than *patronus*.[7] Two cases in the diocese of Exeter are also of some interest. Bishop

---

[1] Actually her steward Adam de Stratton had done so, according to the royal reconfirmation (*Cal. Charter R.* ii. 211–12; *Rot. Parl. hactenus inediti*, p. 3).

[2] *Sel. Cases in the King's Bench*, i. 120–8.

[3] See p. 167.

[4] Cott. MS. Claud. D. xii (Daventry cartulary), ff. 7–10.

[5] Ibid., ff. 8–9.

[6] See pp. 73–74.

[7] *Chron. Maj.* v. 356. Cf. their dispute (not as patrons) about a warren with Wardon Abbey (Oxenedes, p. 192; *Ann. Mon.* iii, Dunstable, p. 192). But see Fowler and Chambers in *Beds. Hist. Rec. Soc.* i. 10–14.

Bronscombe had trouble in 1263 with Plympton Priory, of his patronage, which evidently denied him both custody and rights in the election. In their final submission the canons recognized the bishop's rights, and the prior-elect resigned and was re-elected with licence and consent. Further, they promised the bishop, while he was staying with them, 100 marks for his injuries and expenses; this he pardoned them two years later, when they were evidently on good terms again.[1]

The same bishop laid claim to the patronage of Hartland Abbey against the Dinhams, and accused Oliver de Dinham, in 1275, of seizing custody in a vacancy against the canons' opposition.[2] This dispute may have underlain Oliver de Dinham's unexplained quarrel with the canons in 1272, which culminated in bloodshed in their church.[3] Similar trouble may have caused another display of violence, when Thomas of Multon was accused in 1261 of *laicalis insolentia* in holding Lanercost by force against the prior and the bishop;[4] he may well have been holding on to custody, for its own sake or from objection to a new prior. Another unexplained dispute was between Earl Henry de Bohun and Prior Martin of Llanthony-by-Gloucester, in 1204. According to the earl's record, the prior came to him with a party of supporters, the abbot and two canons of Cirencester as well as canons of Llanthony, to beg his mercy in some unspecified grievances that he had against the prior; the earl proposed to take the case before the king and justiciar, being unwilling to accept the prior's submission on the spot because he had found him 'unstable and unfaithful in word and deed'.[5]

As the converse of the patron's special protection the monks might incur his special anger, for disloyalty or ingratitude. It was said that when the banner of Peterborough Abbey was hung with the rebel barons' banners on the battlements of Northampton, King Henry swore to destroy the abbey

---

1 *Reg. Bronscombe*, pp. 225, 226, 228.
2 Oliver, p. 208.
3 *Reg. Bronscombe*, p. 101. Cf. Pearse Chope, in *Trans. Devon. Assoc.* lviii. 77–78.
4 *V.C.H. Cumberland*, ii. 156.
5 *Select Cases of Procedure without Writ*, ed. Richardson and Sayles, Selden Soc. lx (1941), pp. clxxx–clxxxi. The editors point out that Prior Martin was in office less than two years, and suggest that the earl's displeasure made him resign.

'because it was of his and his ancestors' foundation, and the abbot and monks, like degenerate servants, had rebelled against him, their founder and foster-son'.[1] And Archbishop Pecham, writing to the abbot of Cluny about the appointment of a prior of Lewes and stressing the Earl Warenne's position as patron, said 'you are bound by the laws of gratitude to comply with him as far as you are able without offence to God; and do not believe that the monastery can prosper in spiritualities or temporalities if he is offended'.[2]

Even those disputes which seem purely feudal often have a special quality, partly because of the generous treatment expected of a good patron, so that a merely business-like and just lord might seem a mean or hard patron; partly because of the potential contradictions between the feudal view of the lord's permanent hold on the tenant's land, and the ecclesiastical view of the permanence, sacrosanctity, and if possible freedom from service, of gifts to the Church.

The fact underlying the Statute of Mortmain—that land given to religious houses was unlikely to yield much profit, and could never escheat—led to quarrels between houses and patrons not only about rights and services but about the possession of the land itself.[3] Robert de Beauchamp, some years after his father's foundation of Frithelstock Priory, tried to recover some of the foundation;[4] and Alice de Nerford feared her impoverished heirs might attack her foundation, Creake Abbey, for which reason she gave the advowson to the king.[5] The Bolebec coheiresses disputed the whole foundation of Medmenham Abbey, suing Woburn, the mother-house, by a plea *quare fundavit abbaciam*.[6]

Deathbed grants may have been specially liable to dispute. John the Scot sued Sawtry Abbey for 8 virgates given by his father Earl David with his body;[7] the daughter of Bartholomew de la Legh sued Canons Ashby for an advowson that he had

---

[1] *alumpnus* (perhaps he had been admitted to confraternity). *Hist. Burgensis*, Whytesley, p. 134.

[2] *Reg. Peckham* (R.S.), iii. 904; see p. 64.

[3] See p. 36; and Coulton, iii. 29–33.

[4] Oliver, p. 220. Cf. Belvoir Priory and the Ros family, who claimed a church given by their ancestor William d'Albini (*V.C.H. Lincs.* ii. 124).

[5] *Mon.* vi. i. 487 (account in cartulary).

[6] *Cur. Reg. R.* iii. 103–4.

[7] *V.C.H. Hunts.* i. 391.

confirmed to them in the same way.[1] In 1267 Isabel de Forz
sued Breamore Priory for her brother Earl Baldwin's gift of
Lymington manor with his body, and repudiated her own
charter of confirmation on the grounds that it was granted
during the disturbed times between Lewes and Evesham,
when the prior was a partisan of the younger Simon de Montfort, by whom she was being harassed.[2] After her death the
priory had a church appropriated to it by Bishop Pontissara
on the ground of poverty due to lawsuits and the oppressions
of the powerful, especially the late countess who 'spoiled them
of 40 librates of land or more',[3] presumably by this suit. Yet
she had just been buried at Breamore, with a patron's conventional piety.[4]

The grant of some or all[5] of the family advowsons to a
monastery might be a special grievance to a later generation;
late in the twelfth century Earl William de Mandeville,
patron of Walden, complained that he had no advowsons left
for his own clerks because the abbey had them all.[6]

This objection to a predecessor's liberality underlay a great
quarrel between Walden and a later patron, Geoffrey fitz
Piers, which is worth describing at some length since it shows
some typical causes and gambits of such a quarrel; and because
there exists a long, able, and vivid account of it in the abbey's
chronicle.

Geoffrey fitz Piers acquired the Mandeville lands when
Geoffrey de Say failed to pay King Richard's price for them;
including the lordship of Walden Abbey, to which was later
explicitly added the advowson. He was on almost consistently
bad terms with the monastery; the shorter chronicle states
briefly and tartly that he 'took several properties away from

---

[1] Farrer, *Honours*, i. 70. Cf. the charge against the Pecches of suppressing their
mother's will, but eventually admitting a legacy of £10 to Barnwell (*Liber Mem.*,
p. 176).

[2] *Abbrev. Plac.*, p. 172; see Powicke, ii. 708. The suit ended with a concord by
which the prior gave up the manor and the reversion of two other manors given by
Countess Amice, in return for 20 librates of land.

[3] *Reg. Pontissara*, i. 123.

[4] *Complete Peerage*, i. 356.

[5] See Colvin, p. 83.

[6] *Mon.* iv. 143 (chronicle). Cf. Ixworth Priory, which had not just the advowsons
but the appropriations of 'all churches of the barony' of William de Blund, according to his inquisition post mortem (*Cal. Inqu. P.M.* i, p. 185).

us and gave them to his own men to hold, and we do not know of any good work to ascribe to him'.[1] The longer chronicle describes how at his succession he travelled round his new lands, coming to Walden manor on the way, 'that is, to that vill which he had bought with the rest, since he needed to see it'; evidently he was viewing his property, not visiting the monks. But the abbot was clearly determined to set up the proper patronal relationship with the new lord, who after all had married the founder's great-niece; he rode out with two monks to meet him, 'as it were to congratulate the new advocate'; they met him respectfully and asked him to come and see his monks, but Geoffrey received them rudely and silently. He just kept his temper, however, went to the abbey, entered the church and stared round it curiously; 'he did not stay long, and said little or nothing'. He had probably been assessing the abbey's wealth, for he went next to the cloister, stood in the chapter door, and there burst out at the abbot: 'You, lord abbot, and your monks have disinherited me and mine; getting my priory turned into an abbey, and gaining control of everything while I was kept down by the power of the king.'[2]

This outburst must refer to the time before he obtained the Mandeville lands, while Geoffrey de Say still held them provisionally. When Geoffrey de Say first acquired the barony, he was accompanied at court by the prior and two monks of Walden;[3] later at the prior's request he and his mother, Beatrice de Say, carried out the very liberal terms of the deathbed charter of the last earl, William de Mandeville, who had given the priory half his demesne at Walden.[4] Later events show that it was this grant to which Geoffrey fitz Piers chiefly objected; he may also have resented the monks' assistance at court to his brother-in-law and rival; and Richard I's promotion of the house to an abbey had been accompanied by his retention of the patronage. There was also trouble about the advowsons given to the abbey,[5] which William de Mandeville himself had felt as a loss. In any case Geoffrey was jealous of the absorption of part of his acquisitions by a prosperous

---

[1] *Mon.* iv. 140.
[2] Ibid., pp. 145–6.
[3] Ibid., p. 145.
[4] Ibid., pp. 145, 149–50 (chronicle and charters).
[5] Settlement after lawsuit, Harl. 3697 (cartulary), f. 20; see pp. 113, 158.

religious foundation in which he had no close family or personal interest.

He went away from this first interview in a threatening mood, despite the abbot's attempts to conciliate and reason with him. Next day he forbade them to occupy the lands given them by Earl William, seized these lands and started to plough them, and ordered his own men of Walden manor to harass and boycott the abbey. The bishop of London at first excommunicated the offenders, but later was induced by Geoffrey to withdraw his protection of the monks, like 'a dumb dog that would not bark'. Next the monks applied to the justiciar, the king being abroad, but Geoffrey scorned his authority; as he did the pope's letters.[1]

Then the monks appealed to the king; Geoffrey denied having disseised them, and made the counter-claim that the lands concerned were wrongfully occupied by them, since Earl William's charter was either forged or invalid. It was proved both genuine and valid, but the king, persuaded by Geoffrey, allowed the disseisin; though he later urged Geoffrey to recompense Walden by giving it lands he had intended for Shouldham Priory.[2] Shouldham was a Gilbertine house founded by Geoffrey fitz Piers himself about 1190; a foundation which naturally diverted his favour and piety from Walden,[3] and which was regarded at Walden as evidencing a frivolous pursuit of 'vain and new things'.[4]

Geoffrey fitz Piers in fact offered some land and rents to Walden, and a kind of peace was made; but he delayed the final settlement. Then he was made earl of Essex by King John; he tried to get the king to make the abbey once more a priory; failing in this, he got from the king the right to institute the abbot so far as a layman could,[5] which King Richard had kept for himself.[6] Now, after trying to

[1] *Mon.* iv. 146.   [2] Ibid., p. 147.
[3] He was buried at Shouldham (*Mon.* iv. 140).
[4] Ibid., p. 146.   [5] Ibid., pp. 147–8.
[6] Duchy of Lanc. 25/8, 27/5: charters of Archbishop Hubert Walter and of William, bishop of London, confirming John's restoration of the advowson to Geoffrey fitz Piers, relating that Richard 'ad quorundam suggestionem et persuasionem prioratum de Waledene que ad donationem Comitis Willelmi et antecessorum suorum tanquam ad donationem patronorum pertinebat, in abbaciam convertisset et donationem eiusdem abbacie sibi retinuisset' (archbishop's charter; the bishop's is to the same effect). See pp. 98–99.

induce the monks to hand over Earl William's charter as
the price of his friendship, he paid his second visit, which has
already been described.[1] The chronicler insists on the hollow-
ness of the spectacular welcome accorded to the earl, and
grumbles at his meanness, his arrogance in proclaiming his
new powers, and his secret discussion with the old abbot on
a suitable successor; but it seems that better relations were
none the less established, and not long afterwards the earl restored at least part of their property.[2]

The whole story illustrates the kind of quite ordinary feudal
dispute about property which might arise between the house
and its lord, together with the bitter overtones due to the
expectation of a religious and more than feudal relationship;
overtones of righteous indignation in the monks' attitude,
and of a peculiar resentment in the patron's.

But open and violent quarrels are not common. The normal
relationship is an unspectacular one of give and take, making
part of the basic function as well as of the social entangle-
ments of the monks; part of the outlook and interests of
barons and country knights; and an aspect of the complicated relations of church and lay powers.

[1] pp. 127–8.
[2] His son William restored more (Harl. 3697, ff. 20–20v).

BIBLIOGRAPHY

Works or sources referred to once only are generally omitted here.

MANUSCRIPT SOURCES (except isolated charters)

Duchy of Lancaster records (Public Record Office):
 Deeds   (25)
 Deeds with seals   (27)
 Ancient correspondence (34)
Cartularies:
 British Museum, Cottonian MSS., Claudius D xii (Daventry); Harleian
  MSS. 3650 (Kenilworth), 3656 (Newnham, Beds.), 3697 (Walden).
 Public Record Office, Exchequer, King's Remembrancer Miscellaneous
  Books 20 (Godstow), 29 (Langdon).
 Bodleian Library, MS. Top. Devon d. 5 (Newenham).

PRINTED SOURCES

 Chronicles (unless in *Annales Monastici* or commonly known by the writer's
name) and cartularies, &c. will be found under the name of the monastery.
Abbreviatio Placitorum, Record Commission (London, 1811).
Acta Stephani Langton Cantuariensis archiepiscopi, A.D. 1207–28, ed. Kathleen
 Major, C. and Y. Soc. l (London, 1950).
ADAM OF DOMERHAM, *Historia de rebus gestis Glastoniensibus*, ed. T. Hearne
 (London, 1727).
Annales Monastici, vols. i (Margan, Tewkesbury, Burton), ii (Winchester,
 Waverley), iii (Dunstable, Bermondsey), iv (Osney, Worcester); ed. H. R.
 Luard, R.S. xxxvi (London, 1864–9).
ATHELNEY, *see* MUCHELNEY.
Barnwell chronicle, in *Walteri de Coventria Memoriale*, vol. ii, ed. W. Stubbs,
 R.S. lviii (London, 1873).
—— *Liber memorandorum ecclesie de Bernewell*, ed. J. W. Clark (Cambridge,
 1907).
BERNARD, A., et BRUEL, A., *Recueil des chartes de l'abbaye de Cluni*, 5 vols.
 (Paris, 1876–1903).
BILSINGTON, *The Cartulary and Terrier of the Priory of Bilsington*, ed. N.
 Neilson, British Academy Records of Social and Economic History, vii
 (London, 1928).
BRACTON, *De Legibus Anglie*, ed. G. E. Woodbine, 4 vols. (New Haven,
 1932–42).
Bracton's Note Book, ed. F. W. Maitland, 3 vols. (London, 1887).
BRUTON, *Two Cartularies of Bruton and Montacute*, Somerset Rec. Soc. viii
 (London, 1894).
BURY, *Memorials of St. Edmund's Abbey*, ed. T. Arnold, R.S. xcvi, 3 vols.
 (London, 1890–6).
Calendar of Chancery Warrants, vol. i, Record Publications (London, 1927).
Calendar of the Charter Rolls, vols. i–iii, Record Publications (London,
 1903–8).

Calendar of the Close Rolls, Record Publications (London, 1892–).

Calendar of Documents preserved in France, Record Publications (London, 1899).

Calendar of Documents relating to Ireland, Record Publications (London, 1875–81).

Calendar of Fine Rolls, vols. i and ii, Record Publications (London, 1911–12).

Calendar of Inquisitions, Miscellaneous, vols. i and ii, Record Publications (London, 1916).

Calendar of Inquisitions post mortem, Record Publications (London, 1904–).

Calendar of Liberate Rolls, vols. i–iii, Record Publications (London, 1917–37).

Calendar of Papal Registers: Papal Letters, vol. i, Record Publications (London, 1894).

Calendar of the Patent Rolls, Record Publications (London, 1891–).

Canterbury and Dover chronicles, in *Gervase of Canterbury*, vol. ii, ed. W. Stubbs, R.S. lxxiii (London, 1880).

—— St. Augustine's, *see* THORNE.

Catalogue of Ancient Deeds, vol. i, Record Publications (London, 1890).

Charters and Documents illustrating the History of the Cathedral and City of Sarum, ed. W. D. Macray, R.S. xcvii (London, 1891).

CHESTER, *Annales Cestrienses*, ed. R. C. Christie, Lancs. and Chesh. Rec. Soc. (London, 1887).

CHICHESTER, *The Chartulary of the High Church of Chichester*, ed. W. D. Peckham, Sussex Rec. Soc. xlvi (Lewes, 1946).

Close Rolls, Henry III, Record Publications (London, 1902–38).

COLE, H., *Documents illustrative of English History in the 13th and 14th Centuries*, Record Commission (London, 1844).

CUMBWELL, 'Charters of Cumbwell Abbey', in *Archaeologia Cantiana*, v (London, 1863).

Curia Regis Rolls, Record Publications (London, 1923–).

DALE, 'The Chronicle of Thomas de Musca', ed. W. H. St. J. Hope, in *Derbyshire Archaeol. Journal*, vol. v (London, 1883).

Dover chronicle, *see* Canterbury.

DUCKETT, G. F., *Charters and Records of Cluny* ..., 2 vols. (Lewes, 1888).

DUGDALE, W., and others, *Monasticon Anglicanum*, ed. Caley, &c., 6 vols. in 8 (London, 1817–30).

DURHAM, *Annales Dunelmenses*, ed. F. Barlow, Surtees Soc. clv (Durham, 1945).

—— *Feodarium Prioratus Dunelmensis*, ed. W. Greenwell, Surtees Soc. lviii (Durham, 1872).

—— *Gesta Dunelmensia*, ed. R. K. Richardson, in Camden Miscellany, xxi, Camden Series III, xxxiv (London, 1924).

—— *Historiae Dunelmensis Scriptores Tres*: Robert de Graystanes, ed. J. Raine, Surtees Soc. ix (Durham, 1839).

EVESHAM, *Chronicon abbatiae de Evesham*, ed. W. D. Macray, R.S. xxxix (London, 1863).

EYNSHAM, *Cartulary of Eynsham Abbey*, ed. H. E. Salter, Oxford Hist. Soc. xlix, li (Oxford, 1906–8).

FARRER, W., and CLAY, C. T., *Early Yorkshire Charters* (Edinburgh, 1914–).

FOUNTAINS, *Memorials of the Abbey of Fountains*, ed. J. R. Walbran, Surtees Soc. xlii, lxvii (Durham, 1863–78).

FOWLER, J. T., *Cistercian Statutes 1256–88* (London, 1890).

FRIEDBERG, A., *Corpus Iuris Canonici*, 2 vols. (Leipzig, 1878–81).

Furness and Stanley chronicles, in *Continuation of William de Newburgh*; *Chronicles of the reigns of Stephen, Henry II and Richard I*, vol. ii, ed. R. Howlett, R.S. lxxxii (London, 1884).

GISBURN, *Cartularius prioratus de Gyseburne*, ed. W. Brown, Surtees Soc. lxxxvi, lxxxix (Durham, 1889–94).

GLASTONBURY, *The Great Chartulary of Glastonbury Abbey*, ed. A. Watkin, Somerset Rec. Soc. lix, lxiii (Frome, 1947–52).

GLOUCESTER, *Historia et Cartularium monasterii S. Petri Gloucestrie*, ed. W. Hart, R.S. xxxiii, 3 vols. (London, 1863–7).

HARROLD, *Records of Harrold Priory*, ed. G. H. Fowler, Beds. Hist. Rec. Soc. xvii (Aspley Guise, 1935).

VON HEFELE, K. J., ed. Leclerq, *Histoire des conciles d'après les documents inédits*, t. v and vi (Paris, 1912–15).

HILL, ROSALIND, *Ecclesiastical Letter-books of the 13th Century* (privately printed).

The Honour of Dunster, ed. H. C. Maxwell-Lyte, Somerset Rec. Soc. xxxiii (London, 1917–18).

HOSTIENSIS, *In I–VI Decretalium Libros Commentaria* (Venice, 1581).

INNOCENTII IV, *In Quinque Libros Decretalium Commentaria* (Venice, 1578).

JOCELYN OF BRAKELOND, *Chronicle*, ed. H. E. Butler (London, 1949).

JOHANNES DE OXENEDES, *Chronica*, ed. H. Ellis, R.S. xiii (London, 1859).

KINGSWOOD, 'Documents relating to the Monastery of Kingswood', ed. V. R. Perkins, in *Trans. of the Bristol and Gloucester Archaeol. Soc.* xxii (Bristol, 1899).

LEFÈVRE, P. F., *Les Statuts de Prémontré* (Louvain, 1946).

LEWES, *The Chartulary of Lewes Priory*, ed. L. F. Salzman, Sussex Rec. Soc. xxxviii (Lewes, 1933).

Magna Vita Sancti Hugonis episcopi Lincolniensis, ed. J. F. Dimock, R.S. xxxvii (London, 1864).

MATTHEW PARIS, *see* PARIS.

MIDGLEY, L. M., *Ministers' Accounts of the Earldom of Cornwall*, Camden Series III, lxvi, lxviii (London, 1942–5).

MISSENDEN, *The Cartulary of Missenden Abbey*, ed. J. G. Jenkins, Bucks. Archaeol. Soc. ii (London and Aylesbury, 1938).

MONTACUTE, *see* BRUTON.

MUCHELNEY, *Two Cartularies of Muchelney and Athelney*, ed. E. H. Bates, Somerset Rec. Soc. xiv (London, 1899).

OLIVER, J., *Monasticon Diocesis Exoniensis* (Exeter, 1846).

OSNEY, *The Cartulary of Oseney Abbey*, ed. H. E. Salter, Oxford Hist. Soc. lxxxix–xc, xcvii, xcviii, ci (Oxford, 1929–36).

PANTIN, W. A., *Chapters of the English Black Monks*, Camden Series III, xlv, xlvii, liv (London, 1931–7).

PARIS, MATTHEW, *Chronica Majora*, ed. H. R. Luard, R.S. lvii, 6 vols. (London, 1872–83).

Patent Rolls, Henry III, 1216–32, Record Publications (London, 1901–3).

The Percy Chartulary, ed. M. T. Martin, Surtees Soc. cxvii (Durham, 1911).

PETERBOROUGH, 'Chronicon Johannis abbatis . . .' and 'Historiae coenobii Burgensis scriptores varii' (Robert Swaffham, Walter de Whytesley), ed. J. Sparke, in *Historiae Anglicanae Scriptores Varii* (London, 1723).

—— *Chronicon Petroburgense,* ed. T. Stapleton, Camden Soc. xlvii (London, 1849).

The Pipe Rolls, Henry II, Richard I and John, Pipe Roll Soc. (London, 1884–).

PRYNNE, W., *An Exact Chronological Vindication . . . of our . . . King's Supreme Ecclesiastical Jurisdiction,* vol. ii (London, 1665).

RALPH DE COGGESHALL, *Chronicon Anglicanum,* ed. J. Stevenson, R.S. lxvi (London, 1875).

RAMSEY, *Cartularium monasterii de Ramseia,* ed. W. H. Hart and P. A. Lyons, R.S. lxxix, 3 vols. (London, 1884–93).

—— *Chronicon abbatiae Rameseiensis,* ed. W. D. Macray, R.S. lxxxiii (London, 1886).

Register of Godfrey Giffard, Bishop of Worcester, ed. J. W. Willis-Bund, Worcester Hist. Soc. (Oxford, 1899–1902).

Register of John le Romeyn, Archbishop of York, ed. W. Brown, Surtees Soc. cxxiii, cxxxiii (Durham, 1913–16).

Register of Oliver Sutton, Bishop of Lincoln, ed. Rosalind Hill, Lincoln Rec. Soc. xxxix, xliii (Hereford, 1948–50).

Registers of Walter Bronscombe and Peter Quivil, ed. F. C. Hingeston-Randolph (London, 1889).

Register of Walter Giffard, Archbishop of York, ed. W. Brown, Surtees Soc. cix (Durham, 1904).

Register of Walter Gray, Archbishop of York, ed. J. Raine, Surtees Soc. lvi (Durham, 1872).

Register of William Wickwane, Archbishop of York, ed. W. Brown, Surtees Soc. cxiv (Durham, 1913).

Registrum Collegii Exoniensis, ed. C. W. Boase, Oxford Hist. Soc. xxvii (Oxford, 1894).

Registrum epistolarum Johannis Peckham, ed. C. T. Martin, R.S. lxxvii, 3 vols. (London, 1882–5).

Registrum Johannis de Pontissara episcopi Wintoniensis, ed. C. Deedes, C. and Y. Soc. xix, xxx (London, 1915–24).

Registrum Ricardi de Swinfield episcopi Herefordensis, ed. W. W. Capes, C. and Y. Soc. vi (London, 1909).

Registrum Roberti Winchelsey Cantuariensis archiepiscopi, ed. Rose Graham, C. and Y. Soc. (London, 1917–).

Registrum Roffense, ed. J. Thorpe (London, 1769).

Registrum Simonis de Gandavo episcopi Saresbiriensis, ed. C. T. Flower and M. C. B. Dawes, C. and Y. Soc. xl, xli (London, 1914–33).

Registrum Thome de Cantilupo episcopi Herefordensis, ed. R. G. Griffiths, C. and Y. Soc. ii (London, 1907).

Report on the MSS. of the Dean and Chapter of Wells, Historical MSS. Commission (London, 1907).

Roberti Grosseteste episcopi Lincolniensis Epistolae, ed. H. R. Luard, R.S. xxv (London, 1861).

Roger of Wendover, with Paris, *Chronica Majora*, q.v.

Rotuli de Oblatis et Finibus, ed. T. D. Hardy, Record Commission (London, 1835).

Rotuli Hugonis de Welles episcopi Lincolniensis, ed. W. P. W. Phillimore and F. N. Davis, C. and Y. Soc. i, iii, iv (London, 1907–9).

Rotuli Litterarum Clausarum, 1204–27, ed. T. D. Hardy, Record Commission, 2 vols. (London, 1833–44).

Rotuli Litterarum Patentium, 1201–16, ed. T. D. Hardy, Record Commission (London, 1835).

Rotuli Parliamentorum, vol. i (London, 1783).

Rotuli Parliamentorum hactenus inediti, ed. H. G. Richardson and G. A. Sayles, Camden Series III, li (London, 1935).

Rotuli Roberti Grosseteste, ed. F. N. Davis, C. and Y. Soc. (London, 1913).

Royal and other Historical Letters illustrative of the Reign of Henry III, ed. W. W. Shirley, R.S. xxvii, 2 vols. (London, 1862–6).

RYMER, *Foedera*, vols. i and ii, Record Commission (London, 1816).

St. ALBANS, *Gesta Abbatum monasterii Sancti Albani*, ed. H. T. Riley, R.S. xxviii, 3 vols. (London, 1867–9).

—— *Willelmi Rishanger Chronica et Annales*, ed. H. T. Riley, R.S. xxviii (London, 1865).

ST. FRIDESWIDE'S, *Cartulary of the Monastery of St. Frideswide*, ed. S. R. Wigram, Oxford Hist. Soc. xxviii, xxxi (Oxford, 1895–6).

SAWLEY, *The Chartulary of the Abbey of Sallay*, ed. J. McNulty, Yorks. Archaeol. Soc. Record Series, lxxxvii, xc (Wakefield, 1933–4).

SELBY, *The Coucher Book of Selby*, ed. J. T. Fowler, Yorks. Archaeol. and Top. Assoc. x, xiii (Durham, 1891–3).

SELE, *The Chartulary of the Priory of Sele*, ed. L. F. Salzman (Cambridge, 1923).

Select Cases in the King's Bench, ed. G. O. Sayles, Selden Soc. lv, lvii, lviii (London, 1936–9).

Select Cases before the King's Council, 1243–1482, ed. I. S. Leadam and J. F. Baldwin, Selden Soc. xxxv (Cambridge, Mass., 1918).

Stanley chronicle, *see* Furness.

Statutes of the Realm, vol. i, Record Commission (London, 1810).

STENTON, F. M., *Documents illustrative of the Social and Economic History of the Danelaw* (London, 1920).

STUBBS, W., *Select Charters*, ed. H. W. C. Davis (Oxford, 9th ed., 1913).

THORNE, WILLIAM, *De rebus abbatum Cantuarie* . . . , ed. R. Twysden, in *Historiae Anglicanae Scriptores Decem* (London, 1652).

Two 'compoti' of the Lancashire and Cheshire manors of Henry de Lacy Earl of Lincoln, ed. P. A. Lyons, Chetham Soc. cxii (Manchester, 1884).

Westminster chronicle, in *Flores Historiarum*, ed. H. R. Luard, R.S. xcv (London, 1890).

WETHERAL, *The Register of the Priory of Wetheral*, ed. J. E. Prescott (London, 1897).

WHALLEY, *The Coucher Book of Whalley Abbey*, ed. W. A. Hutton, Chetham Soc. x, xi, xvi, xx, 4 vols. (Manchester, 1847–9).

WHITBY, *Cartularium abbathiae de Whiteby*, ed. J. C. Atkinson, Surtees Soc. lxix, lxxii (Durham, 1878–9).

WILKINS, D., *Concilia Magnae Britanniae et Hiberniae*, vols. i and ii (London, 1737).

WINCHCOMBE, *Landboc sive registrum monasterii de Winchelcumba*, ed. D. Royce, 2 vols. (Exeter, 1892–1903).

Winchester Cathedral Cartulary, ed. A. W. Goodman (Winchester, 1928).

WORCESTER, *Registrum prioratus beatae Mariae Wigorniensis*, ed. W. H. Hale, Camden Soc. I. xci (London, 1865).

Year Books, 20–22, 30–35 Edward I, ed. A. J. Horwood, R.S. xxxi, 5 vols. (London, 1863–83).

Year Books of Edward II, Year Books Series, Selden Soc. (London, 1903–   ).

SECONDARY WORKS

BENTHAM, J., *History and Antiquities of the Church of Ely* (Cambridge, 1771).

BISHOP, E., *Liturgica Historica* (Oxford, 1918).

CHENEY, C. R., 'King John's Reaction to the Interdict', in *Transactions of the Royal Historical Society* 4th Ser. xxxi (London, 1949).

CHEW, HELENA, *The English Ecclesiastical Tenants-in-chief* (Oxford, 1932).

COCKAYNE, G. E., *The Complete Peerage*, ed. Vicary Gibbs, &c. (London, 1910–   ).

COLVIN, H. M., *The White Canons in England* (Oxford, 1951).

COULTON, C. G., *Five Centuries of Religion*, vol. iii (Cambridge, 1936).

DENHOLM-YOUNG, N., *Seigneurial Administration in England* (Oxford, 1937).

—— *Richard of Cornwall* (Oxford, 1947).

EYTON, R. W., *Antiquities of Shropshire*, 12 vols. (London, 1854–60).

FARRER, W., *Honours and Knights' Fees*, 3 vols. (London and Cambridge, 1923–5).

FLAHIFF, G. B., 'The Use of Prohibitions by Clerics against Ecclesiastical Courts', in *Mediaeval Studies*, iii; 'The Writ of Prohibition to Court Christian in the 13th Century', in *Mediaeval Studies*, vi and vii (Toronto, 1941, 1944, 1945).

FLOWER, C. T., *Introduction to the Curia Regis Rolls*, Selden Soc. lxii (London, 1928).

GIBBS, MARION, and LANG, JANE, *Bishops and Reform 1215–72* (Oxford, 1934).

GRAHAM, ROSE, *English Ecclesiastical Studies* (London, 1929).

—— *St. Gilbert of Sempringham and the Gilbertines* (London, 1901).

—— 'The Cluniac Priory of St. Martin des Champs and its Dependent Priories in England and Wales', in *Journal of the British Archaeological Association*, Series III, xi (London, 1948).

HAINES, C. R., *Dover Priory* (Cambridge, 1930).

HILL, ROSALIND, 'Bishop Sutton and the Institution of Heads of Religious Houses in the Diocese of Lincoln', in *E.H.R.* lviii (London, 1943).

KIMBALL, E. G., 'Tenure in Frankalmoin and Freedom from Secular Services', in *E.H.R.* xliii; 'Judicial Aspects of Frankalmoin Tenure, in *E.H.R.* xlvii (London, 1928, 1932).

KNOWLES, D., *The Monastic Order in England* (Cambridge, 1940).

—— *The Religious Orders in England* (Cambridge, 1948).

—— 'Abbatial Elections', in *Downside Review*, xlix (Exeter, 1931).

—— *The Religious Houses of Medieval England* (London, 1940); used for this book, but now superseded by:

KNOWLES D., and HADCOCK, R. N., *Medieval Religious Houses, England and Wales* (London, 1953).

LAPRAT, R., 'Avoué, avouerie', in *Dictionnaire d'histoire et de géographie ecclésiastiques*, t. v (Paris, 1931).

LESNE, E., *Histoire de la propriété ecclésiastique en France*, t. i, ii (Paris, 1910–28).

LUNT, W. E., *Financial Relations of the Papacy with England to 1327* (Cambridge, Mass., 1939).

MCKECHNIE, W. S., *Magna Carta* (Glasgow, 2nd ed., 1914).

MORGAN, MARJORIE, *English Lands of the Abbey of Bec* (Oxford, 1946).

MYRES, J. N. L., 'Notes on the History of Butley Priory, Suffolk', in *Oxford Essays in Medieval History presented to H. E. Salter* (Oxford, 1934).

PEARSE CHOPE, R., 'Hartland Abbey and the Dinhams', in *Transactions of the Devonshire Association*, lviii (Plymouth, 1926).

PLUCKNETT, T. F. T., *Legislation of Edward I* (Oxford, 1949).

POLLOCK F., and MAITLAND, F. W., *History of English Law before the time of Edward I*, 2 vols. (Cambridge, 2nd ed., 1911).

POWER, EILEEN, *Medieval English Nunneries* (Cambridge, 1922).

POWICKE, F. M., *King Henry III and the Lord Edward*, 2 vols. (Oxford, 1947).

REICH, ALOYSE M., *The Parliamentary Abbots to 1470*, in University of California Publications in History, Vol. XVII (Berkeley, &c., 1941).

SENN, F., *L'institution des avoueries ecclésiastique en France* (Paris, 1903).

SHAW, S., *History and Antiquities of Staffordshire*, 2 vols. (London, 1798–1801).

THOMAS, P., *Droit de propriété des laïques sur les églises* (Paris, 1906).

The Victoria County Histories (London, 1900–   ).

WHITAKER, T. D., *History and Antiquities of the Deanery of Craven* (London, 1812).

—— *History of the Original Parish of Whalley and Honour of Clitheroe*, 2 vols. (London, 4th ed., 1872–6).

WOOD-LEGH, KATHLEEN, *Church Life in England under Edward III* (Cambridge, 1934).

INDEX

abbeys (as distinct from priories), 26, 98–99, 168, 169.

Abbotsbury, abbey of, 72 n. 5, 108.

Abingdon, abbey of, 18, 84 n. 4, 86, 92 n. 7, 93–94, 107, 153, 155 n. 3, 157 n. 1.

— abbot of, 153.

Acornbury, priory of, 26–27, 111 n. 5, 122 n. 1, 146.

advocate, 2, 8, 14, 16–21, 103, 145.

aids, 116–17, 154, 154 n. 2.

Alban, St., 30, 126.

Albemarle, earls of, 88 n. 4, 124 n. 6.

Alberbury, priory of, 21 n. 3.

— corrector of, 149 n. 1.

Albini family, 124 n. 6.

— Hugh de, earl of Arundel, 22.

— Isabel de, countess of Arundel, 61, 64, 137.

— William de, earl of Arundel (d. 1221), 63, 133.

— — — (d. 1224), 63–64, 133.

— of Belvoir, William de, 166 n. 4.

Alcester, abbey of, 12 n. 5, 44 n. 7, 82 n. 6, 92 n. 5, 99 nn. 6 and 7.

Alexander IV, Pope, and the English baronage, 152, 159.

alien priories, 5, 6, 58–59, 97–98.

alienation of patronage, 8, 9, 11–12, 21–25.

— of property, patron's control over, 4, 36–38, 154–7.

almsgiving, 37, 117, 132, 133, 143, 148, 151–2, 158, 160.

Alnwick, abbey of, 124 n. 6.

Amesbury, priory of, 122, 136, 144 n. 5.

Anemere, William de, 31 n. 4.

Angers, abbey of St. Nicholas of, 62, 98.

Anglesey, priory of, 118.

Angoulême, abbot of, 92.

anniversaries, 13, 132–4, 159.

appointment of prelate by the patron, 31, 40–42, 45, 60, 62, 65, 149.

appropriations, 88 n. 1, 95, 126 n. 6, 138–9, 152, 157–9, 167, 167 n. 6.

Arcy, de, see d'Arcy.

Argentein, Giles de, 71.

Arundel, earls of, see Albini.

Ashridge, house of Bonshommes of, 130.

Aske family, 128 n. 2.

assize *utrum*, 33–34.

Athelney, abbey of, 17 n. 5.

Aubervil, William de, 15, 110 n. 6.

Augustinian canons, 3, 41, 135.

— canonesses, 26–27.

Axholm, priory of, 10 n. 4.

Badelee, Robert de, 31 n. 2.

Badlesmere, priory of, 10 n. 4.

Balliol family, 7 n. 2.

Bamburgh, priory of, 6 n. 2.

Bangor, bishop of, 137 n. 8.

Bardney, abbey of, 84 n. 4, 90 and n. 4, 95–96, 109 n. 2, 145–6, 147.

— Walter, abbot of, 95–96.

Bardolf, Robert, 18 n. 7.

— William, 29 n. 3.

Barking, abbey of, 42–43, 64–65, 91, 108 n. 3, 156.

— Maud, abbess of, 122–3.

Barlings, abbey of, 18 n. 7.

Barlynch, priory of, 117 n. 4.

Barnstaple, priory of, 56, 59 n. 1, 77 n. 4.

Barnwell, priory of, 24, 25, 46–47, 75 n. 2, 82, 123, 130 n. 6, 133, 143, 167 n. 1.

— prior of, 123.

baronage, 6–7, 41, 64, 68, 75, 98, 102, 151–2, 153, 159.

Barons' Petition of 1258, 98.

— Wars, 121, 123–4, 143, 153, 165–6, 167.

Basset, Gilbert, 112.

Bath and Wells, bishop of, 8, 24, 30, 32–33, 42 n. 2, 45 n. 7, 70, 77, 80. *See* Jocelyn; Roger; Savary.

— cathedral priory of, 51 n. 4.

— city of, 23–24.

Battle, abbey of, 42, 76 nn. 1 and 7, 82 n. 7, 84 n. 6.

Bayeux, Ranulf de, 19.

Beauchamp, Isabel de, countess of Warwick, 129 n. 3.

— of Bedford, William and Ida de, 73–74, 164.

— of Hatch, Robert de (c. 1150), 17 n. 5.

— — — (d. 1251), 166.

Beaulieu, abbey of, 130, 134, 138 nn. 1 and 5. *See* Hugh.

PRINTED IN
GREAT BRITAIN
AT THE
UNIVERSITY PRESS
OXFORD
BY
CHARLES BATEY
PRINTER
TO THE
UNIVERSITY